Butterflies in Origami

NICK ROBINSON

DOVER PUBLICATIONS, INC.
Mineola, New York

To access the video tutorials;
type the following link:
www.nuinui.ch/video/it/m19/farfalle

Butterflies in Origami, first published by Dover Publications, Inc., in 2018, is an unabridged English translation of the work originally published by NuiNui, Switzerland, in 2018.

Library of Congress Cataloging-in-Publication Data

Names: Robinson, Nick, 1957– author.
Title: Butterflies in origami / Nick Robinson.
Description: Mineola, New York : Dover Publications, Inc., [2018] | "Butterflies in Origami, first published by Dover Publications, Inc., in 2018, is an unabridged English translation of the work originally published by NuiNui, Switzerland, in 2018."
Identifiers: LCCN 2018027661| ISBN 9780486828770 | ISBN 0486828778
Subjects: LCSH: Origami. | Butterflies in art.
Classification: LCC TT872.5 .R6258 2018 | DDC 736/.982—dc23
LC record available at https://lccn.loc.gov/2018027661

Manufactured in the United States by LSC Communications
82877801 2018
www.doverpublications.com

Text and diagrams
Nick Robinson

Photographs and videos
Nick Robinson

Contents

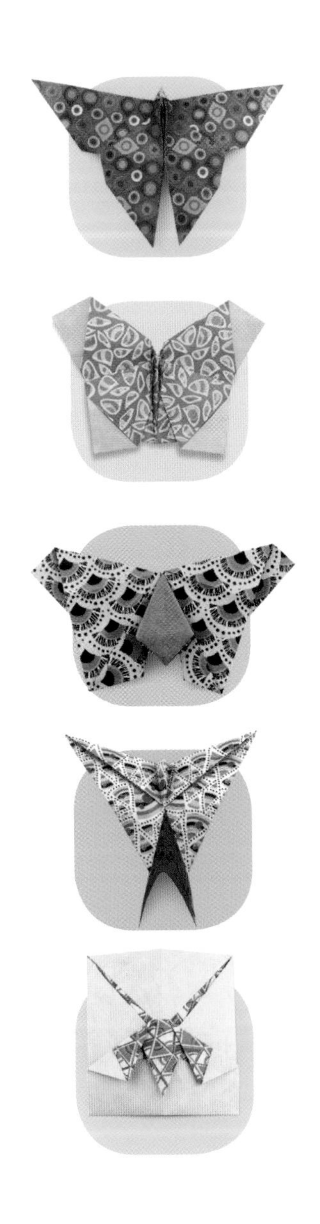

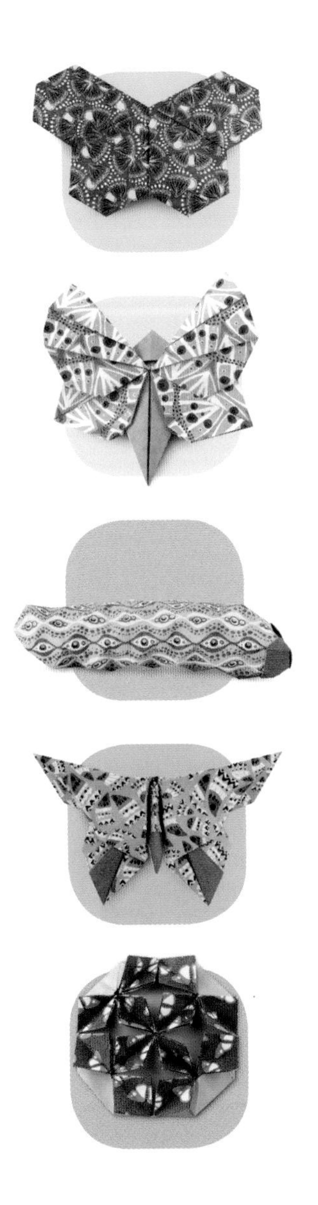

Introduction

Butterflies are insects that have been on the planet for the last 56 million years. Well-known for their large, colored wings and erratic flight, they are enchanting creatures that fill your heart with delight. They have a four-stage life cycle, starting as an egg, which hatches into a caterpillar. This in turn pupates into a chrysalis, a process known as metamorphosis. When this is complete, the pupa splits and the adult insect emerges. Butterflies are closely related to moths but generally have thin antennae with small clubs at the end. Moth antennae can be quite varied in appearance, but in general do not have a club at the end.

It is important that we don't take these beautiful creatures for granted. Very few butterflies are as common as they once were and their habitat is under constant threat from development and industrialization. Hedges are torn out, along with all the wildflowers that grow beneath them. Open woodland is replaced by conifers, beneath which little can survive. Wetlands are drained and used for agriculture. The plants that provide food for the butterfly larva are often classed as "weeds" and sprayed with poisons that destroy both plant and butterfly.

Origami models of butterflies and moths vary from very simple to relatively complex. In this book we focus mainly on the simpler end of the spectrum, although there are some designs that will prove a challenge to master. Unless you are an experienced folder, you should try the projects in the general order they are presented in. Beautiful results won't happen without practice, and you should fold each design several times in order to understand how each fold works and to fold the model sensitively so it is attractive to look at.

Remember that origami is a creative process and that designs can often be adapted to develop different types and patterns of butterflies. Look at the folding sequences carefully to see how you can change angles and distances to vary the results. Don't be afraid to experiment!

Foreword

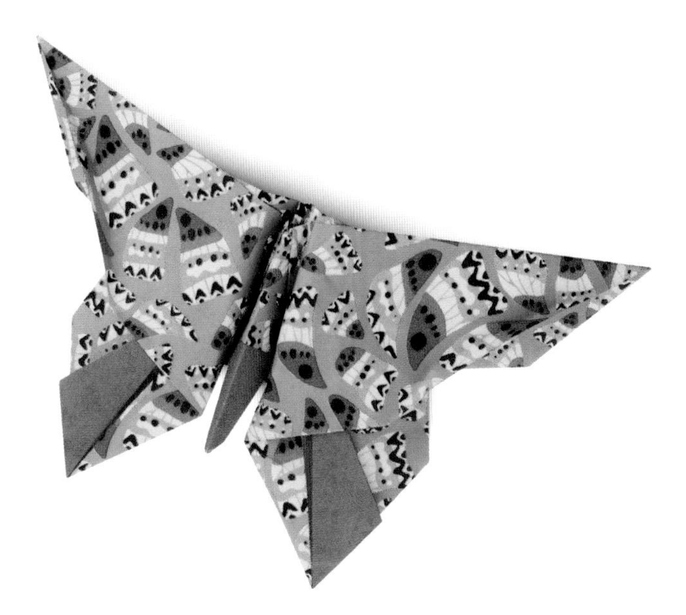

The butterfly is perfectly suited to represent the metamorphic art of origami. The designs are elegant and can often be folded in just a few minutes, the wings display beautiful papers well, and the magic of origami conjures up their remarkable, metamorphic lifecycle. The best folds seem to make tangible the rhythm and rhyme of a concert of geometric principles.

A piece of paper is transformed through origami by folding—nothing is added, nor removed—it is a truly metamorphic art, the square sometimes morphing so far beyond its simple geometry it may yield something that can scarcely be imagined as a product of folding. This transformation seems as miraculous to me as the changes within a chrysalis. These, and other beloved origami transformations (such as the traditional Japanese origami crane), are often impromptu, cherished gifts. Indeed, even a discarded piece of paper can become "trash to treasure" when rescued by an origami lover sharing the gift of a magical folding sequence. For these reasons, I like to think of such paper-folding marvels as "poems for the fingers."

Back in the 1960s when I first began to fold paper, learning the basic models from books and friends, origami was not widely appreciated. There may have been a few dozen projects in print. A new book of designs was a rare publishing event. There were few origami butterflies, and of these, I felt that only Akira Yoshizawa's was truly elegant. The tens of thousands of origami models we have today simply didn't exist.

Richard Alexander and I have published instructional video collections of our origami butterfly designs since 1992, spurred on by the innovative patterns displayed by Russell Cashdollar. We have authored several DVDs and four print titles on the subject, and we are delighted that our work has in turn inspired creators around the world. The idea of compiling an international collection of origami butterfly designs simply could not have happened until recently.

We are delighted to see Nick Robinson tackling this topic with his clear and uniquely styled diagrams, sure to make learning these wonderful models a most enjoyable, lasting love.

Michael LaFosse & Richard Alexander, Origamido Studio

How to fold

Folding paper neatly and accurately isn't always easy for newcomers to origami. However, there's no good reason why you can't progress in the subject, no matter how little confidence you have. Here are a few simple tips.

- Fold slowly–it's not a race. You will get much better results.
- It's generally better to fold the paper away from you rather than towards you (where your hands can get in the way).
- Set aside plenty of time to fold; it's not good for your concentration if you have distractions.
- Fold at a well-lit table, with enough space to rest your elbows and to follow the instructions in the book.
- Make all creases sharp to begin with, making sure the paper is perfectly positioned before flattening.
- Make each model at least 3 times using cheaper paper before using your best paper.
- If you make your own squares from a larger sheet, cut the paper as accurately as possible. A rotary trimmer is a good investment.
- Folding in a small group is fun and will also teach you a lot in a short time.
- Teaching the model to other people will really help your understanding of the folding sequence.

Choosing paper

Origami usually requires paper that is perfectly square. There are lots of options for "proper" origami paper (which can be bought cheaply on the internet), but you can also choose from many other types of paper, especially if you want to fold a large version of a model. The paper should be crisp and capable of "remembering" a crease (so it doesn't try to unfold itself). Craft and art shops have a huge range of beautiful papers–try to choose a pattern that really suits the final design. It will be better value to buy a large sheet and then cut it down to make several smaller squares. Here is a simple method for creating a square from a rectangle.

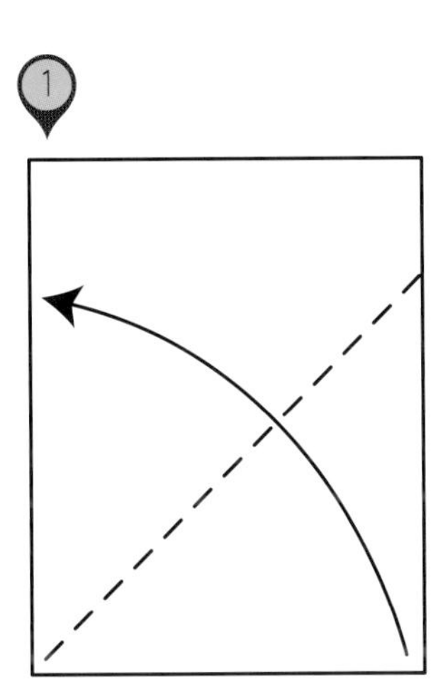

Fold a short edge to a long edge.

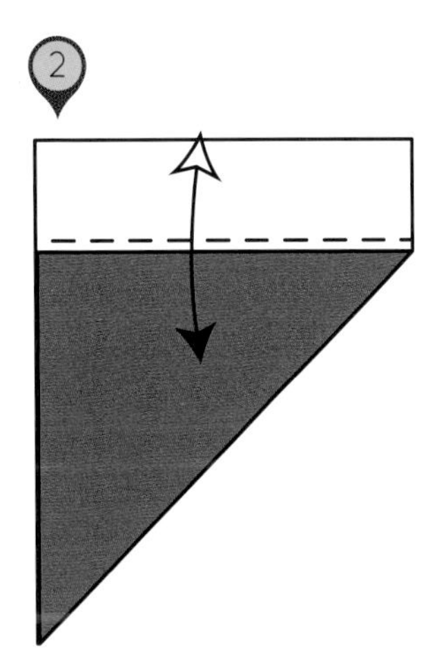

Fold the surplus paper over the edge, crease and unfold.

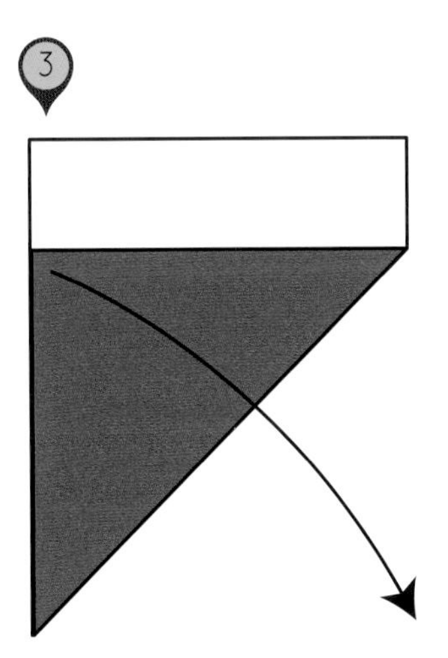

Unfold the paper fully.

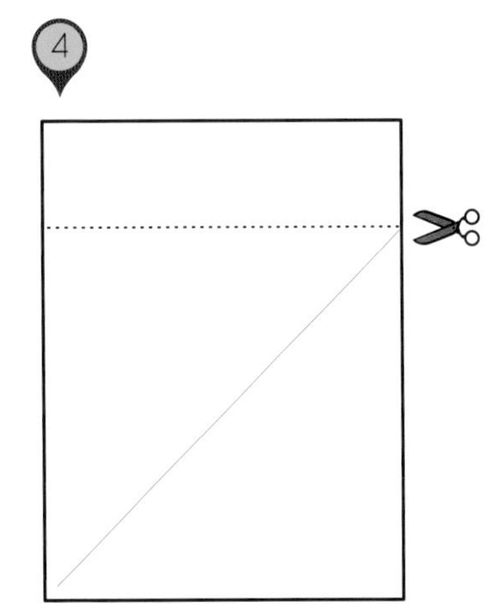

Cut off the surplus paper to leave a square.

Techniques

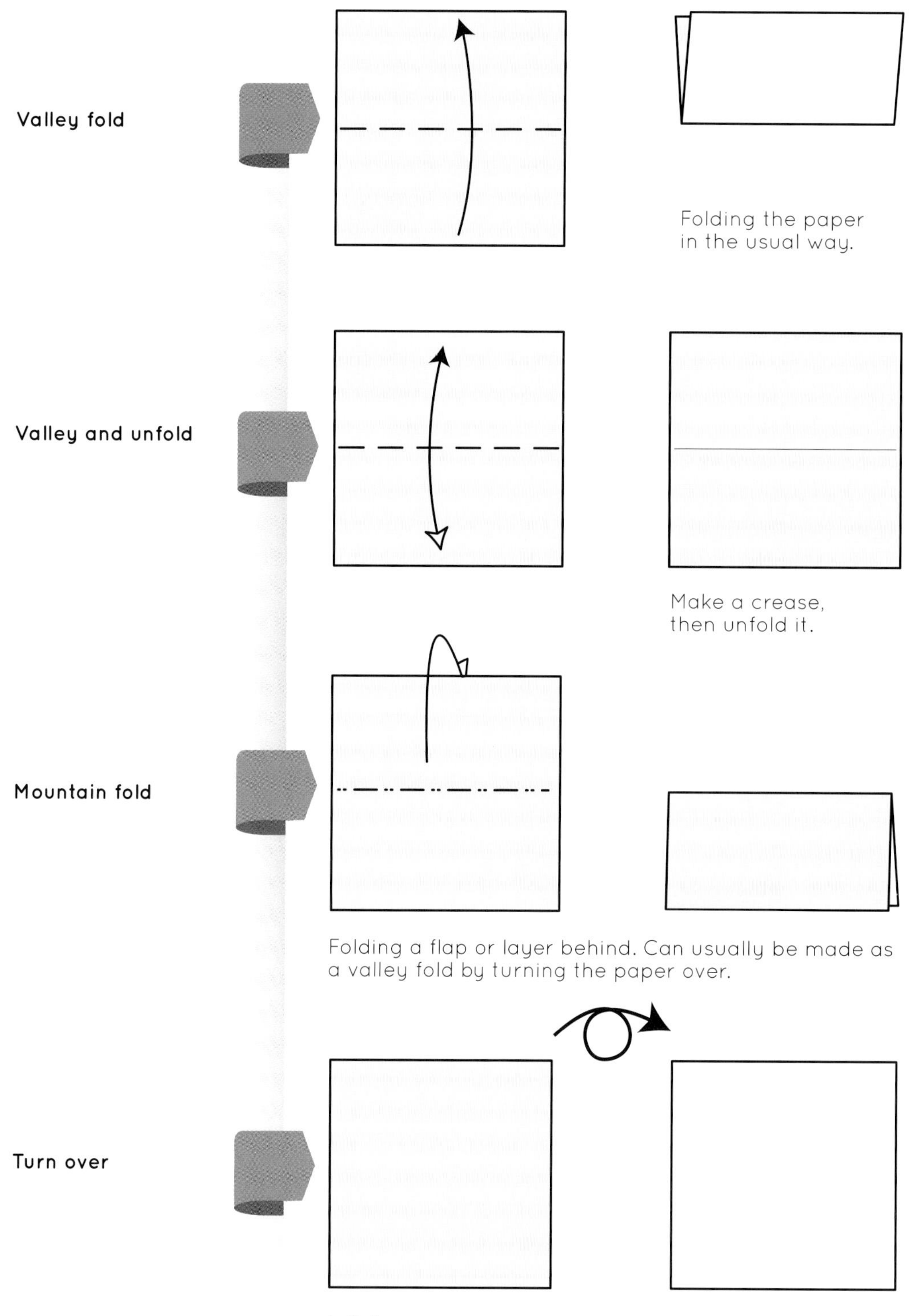

Lift the paper up and turn it upside down, like flipping a pancake.

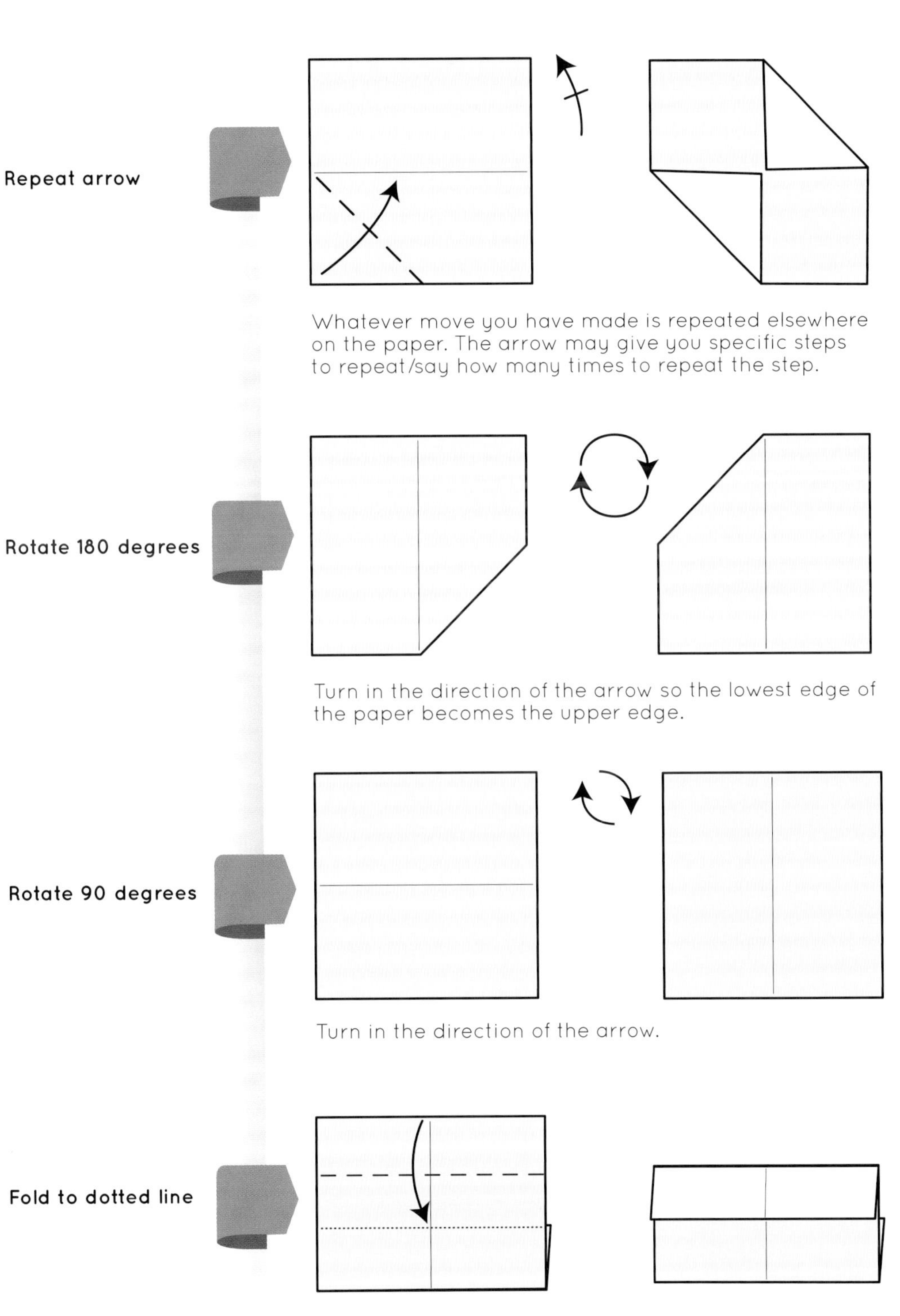

Repeat arrow

Whatever move you have made is repeated elsewhere on the paper. The arrow may give you specific steps to repeat/say how many times to repeat the step.

Rotate 180 degrees

Turn in the direction of the arrow so the lowest edge of the paper becomes the upper edge.

Rotate 90 degrees

Turn in the direction of the arrow.

Fold to dotted line

A dotted line shows an imaginary crease or edge as guidance for a fold.

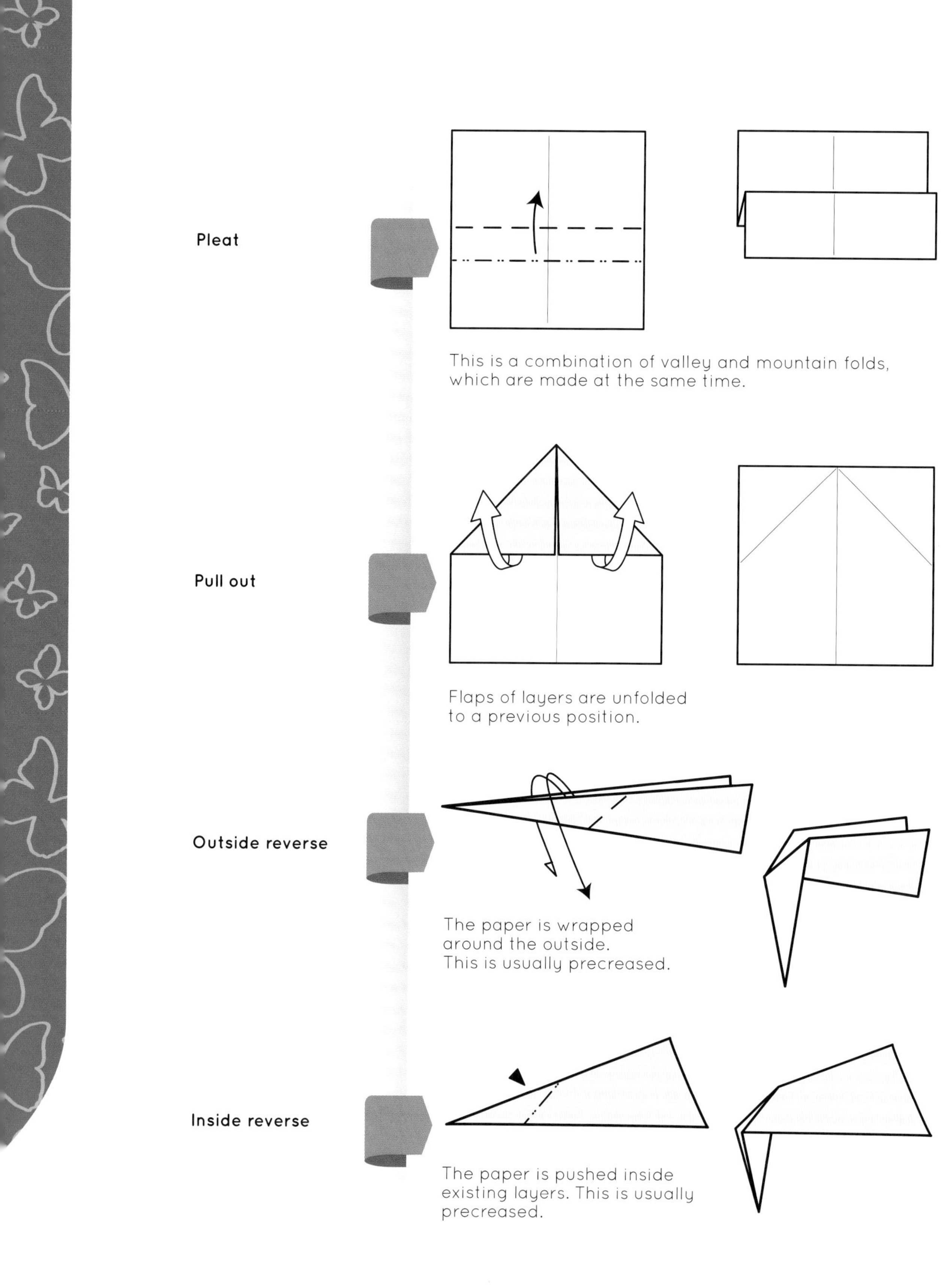

Pleat

This is a combination of valley and mountain folds, which are made at the same time.

Pull out

Flaps of layers are unfolded to a previous position.

Outside reverse

The paper is wrapped around the outside. This is usually precreased.

Inside reverse

The paper is pushed inside existing layers. This is usually precreased.

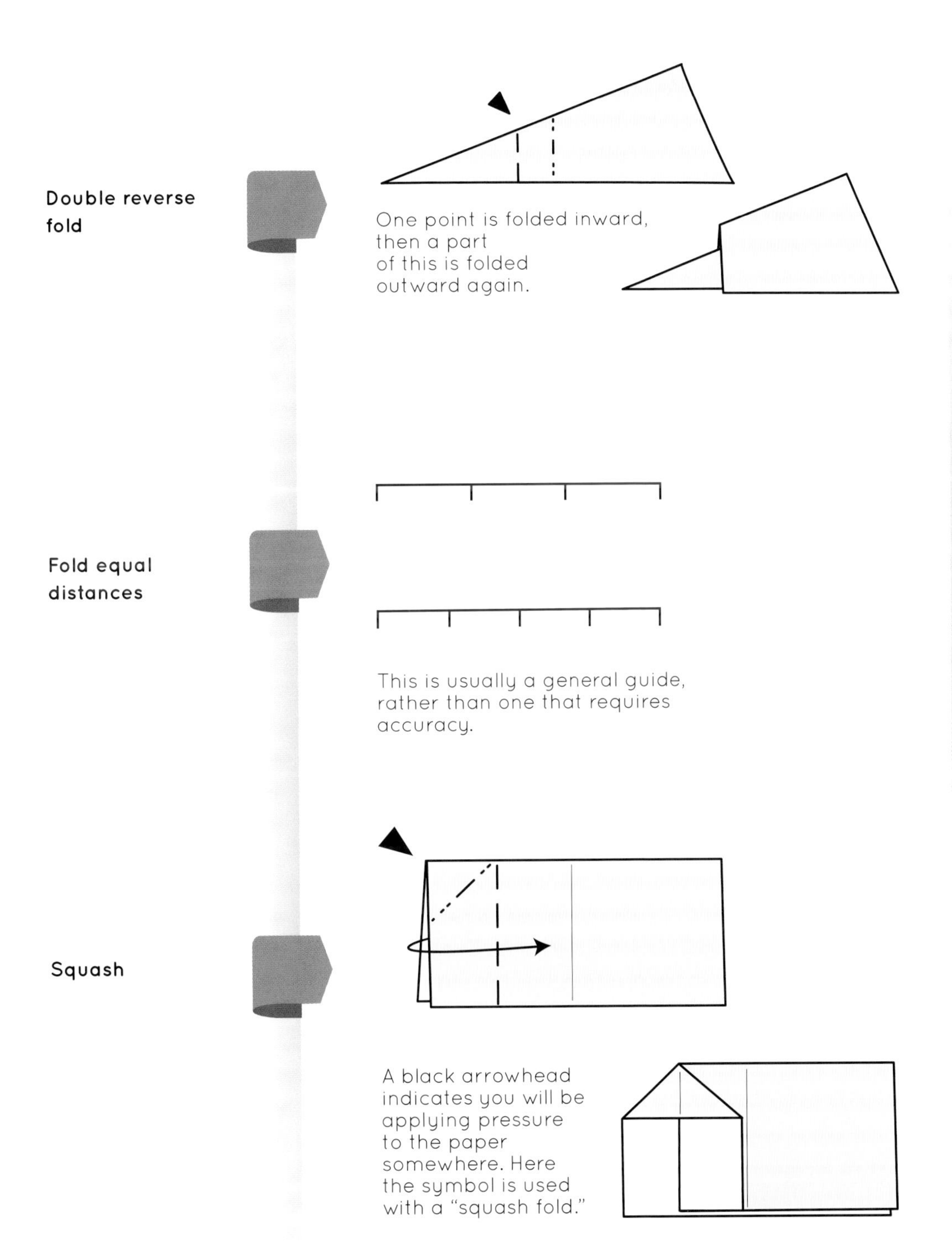

Double reverse fold

One point is folded inward, then a part of this is folded outward again.

Fold equal distances

This is usually a general guide, rather than one that requires accuracy.

Squash

A black arrowhead indicates you will be applying pressure to the paper somewhere. Here the symbol is used with a "squash fold."

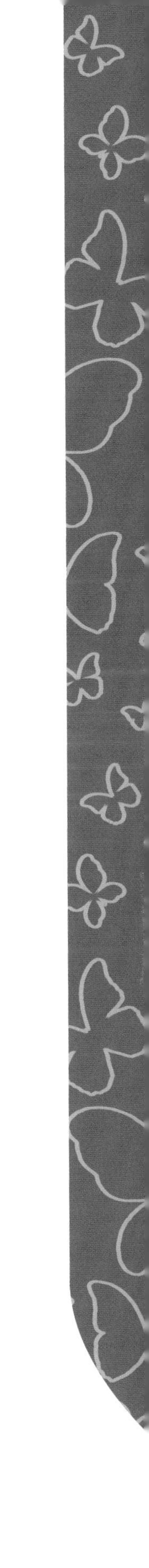

VIDEO

www.nuinui.ch/video/it/m19/farfalle/p16

9-Fold Butterfly

Lee Armstrong

Lee developed this design to illustrate how, in step 1, there are an infinite number of ways to divide a square equally in half. If you are happy with a 2D result, leave out the last two steps for a 7-fold butterfly!

Size of the sheet: 7 x 7 in

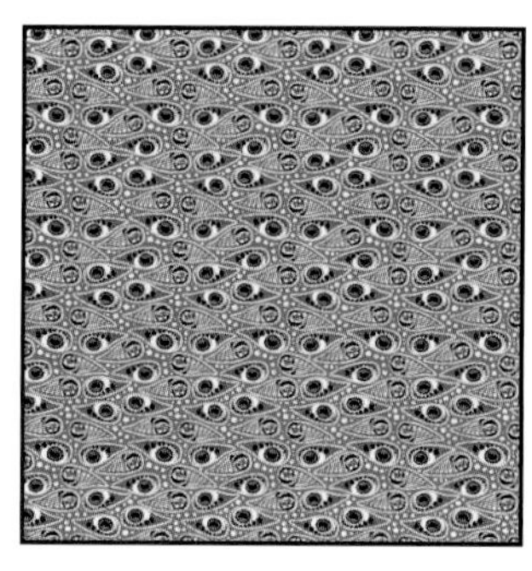

Paper

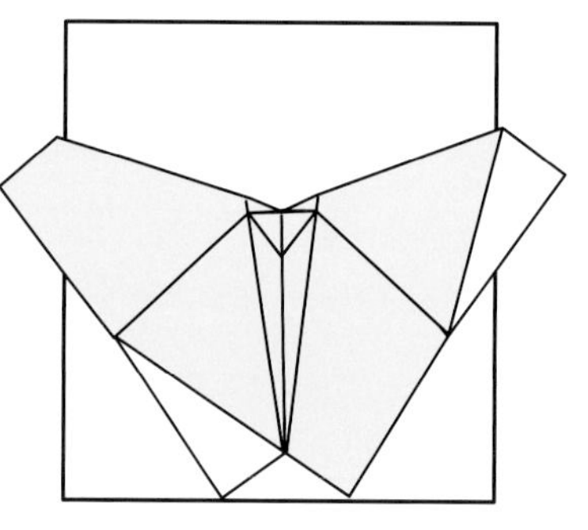

Relationship between the paper and the origami

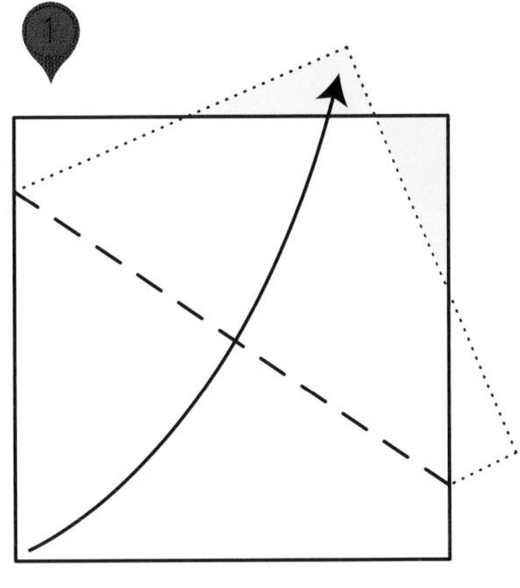

1) White side up, fold the lower left corner to match the dotted line. The idea is to make the two shaded areas identical. Rotate the paper slightly.

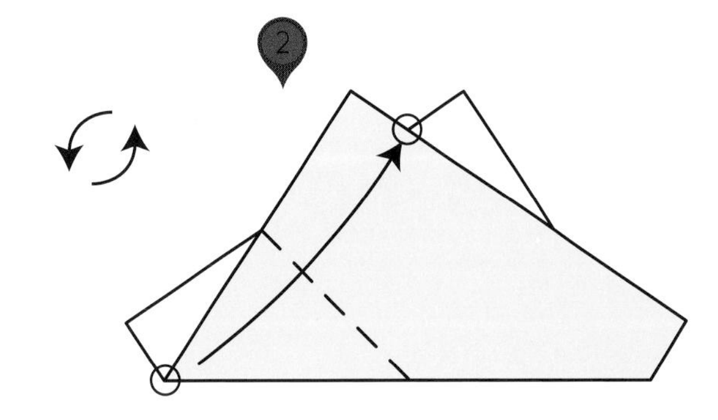

2) Fold so the circled corners meet.

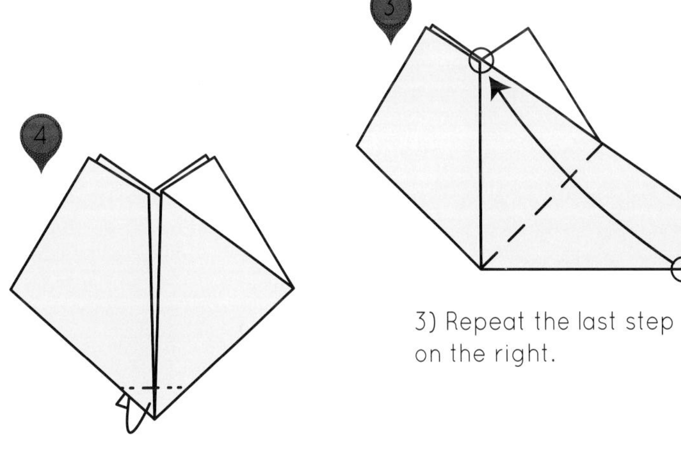

3) Repeat the last step on the right.

4) Fold the lower corner behind.

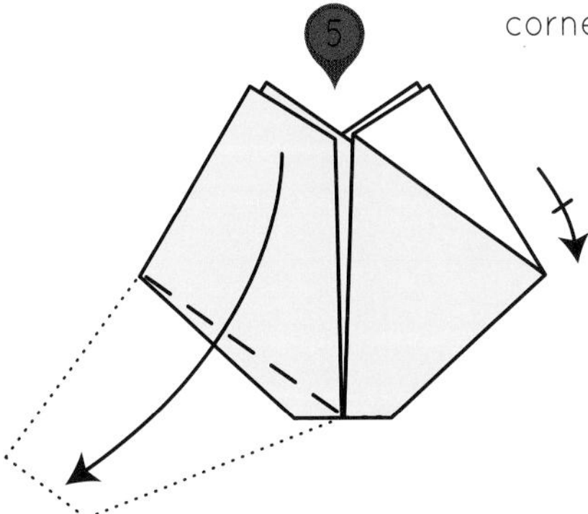

5) Fold a flap to meet the dotted line. Repeat on the right.

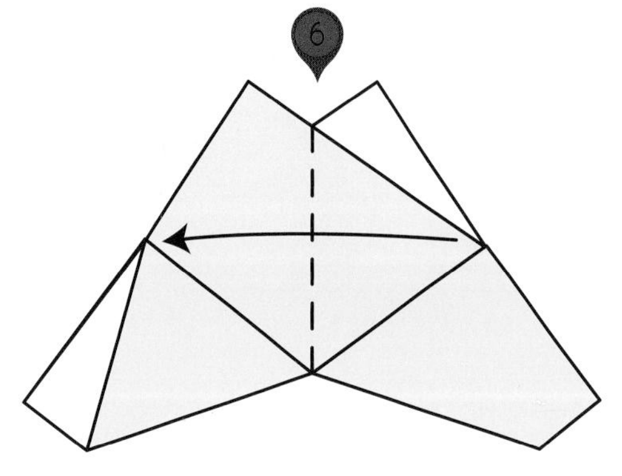

6) Fold in half from right to left.

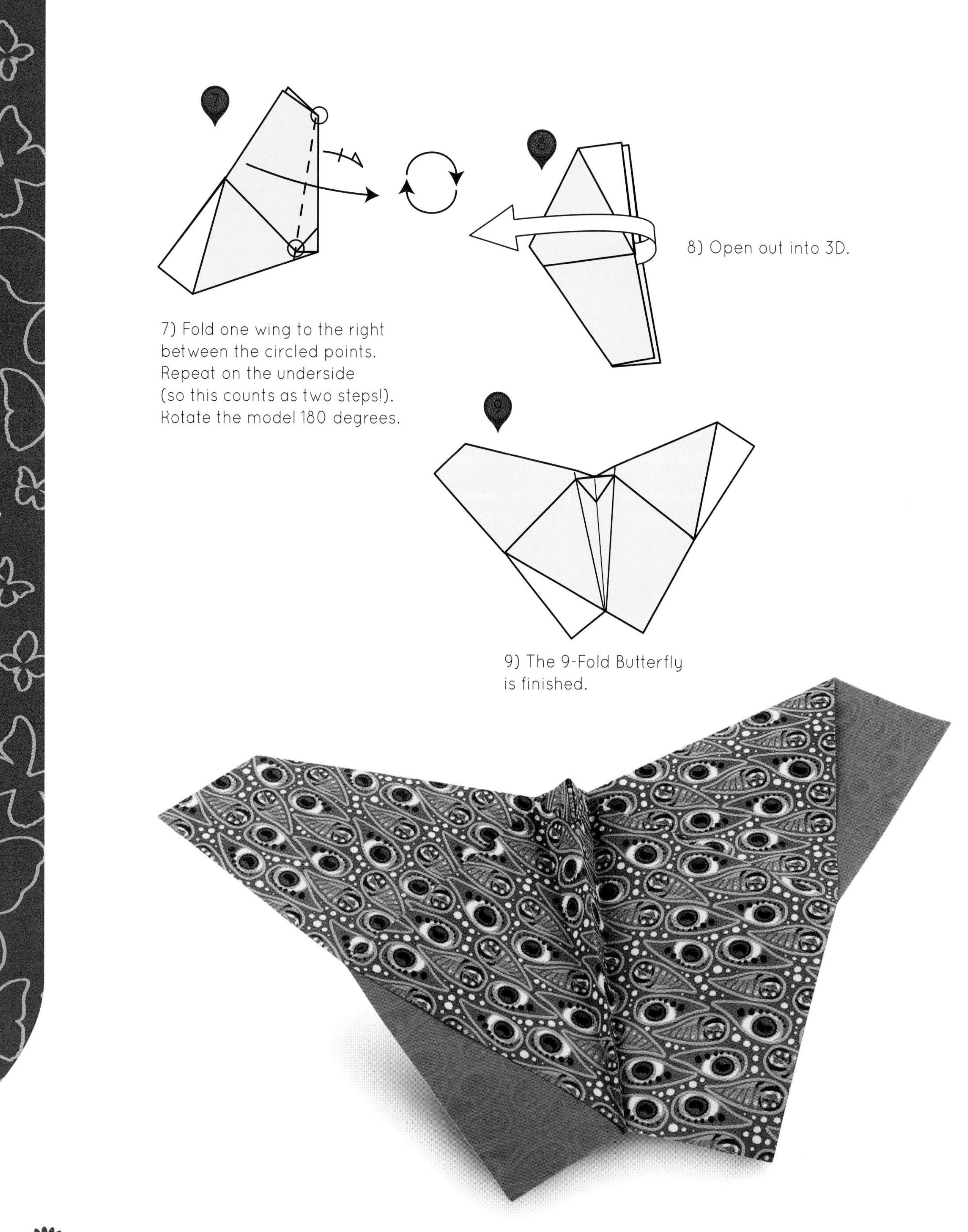

7) Fold one wing to the right between the circled points. Repeat on the underside (so this counts as two steps!). Rotate the model 180 degrees.

8) Open out into 3D.

9) The 9-Fold Butterfly is finished.

VIDEO

www.nuinui.ch/video/it/m19/farfalle/p20

Pinwheel Butterfly

Traditional

This is a design made from an origami form called the "pinwheel" base.

Size of the sheet: 7 x 7 in

Paper

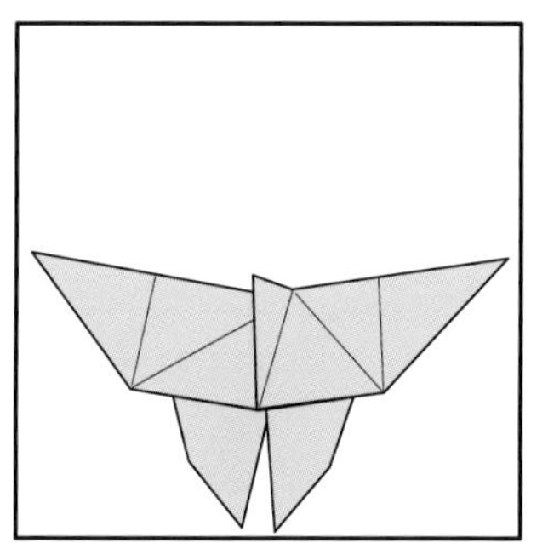

Relationship between the paper and the origami

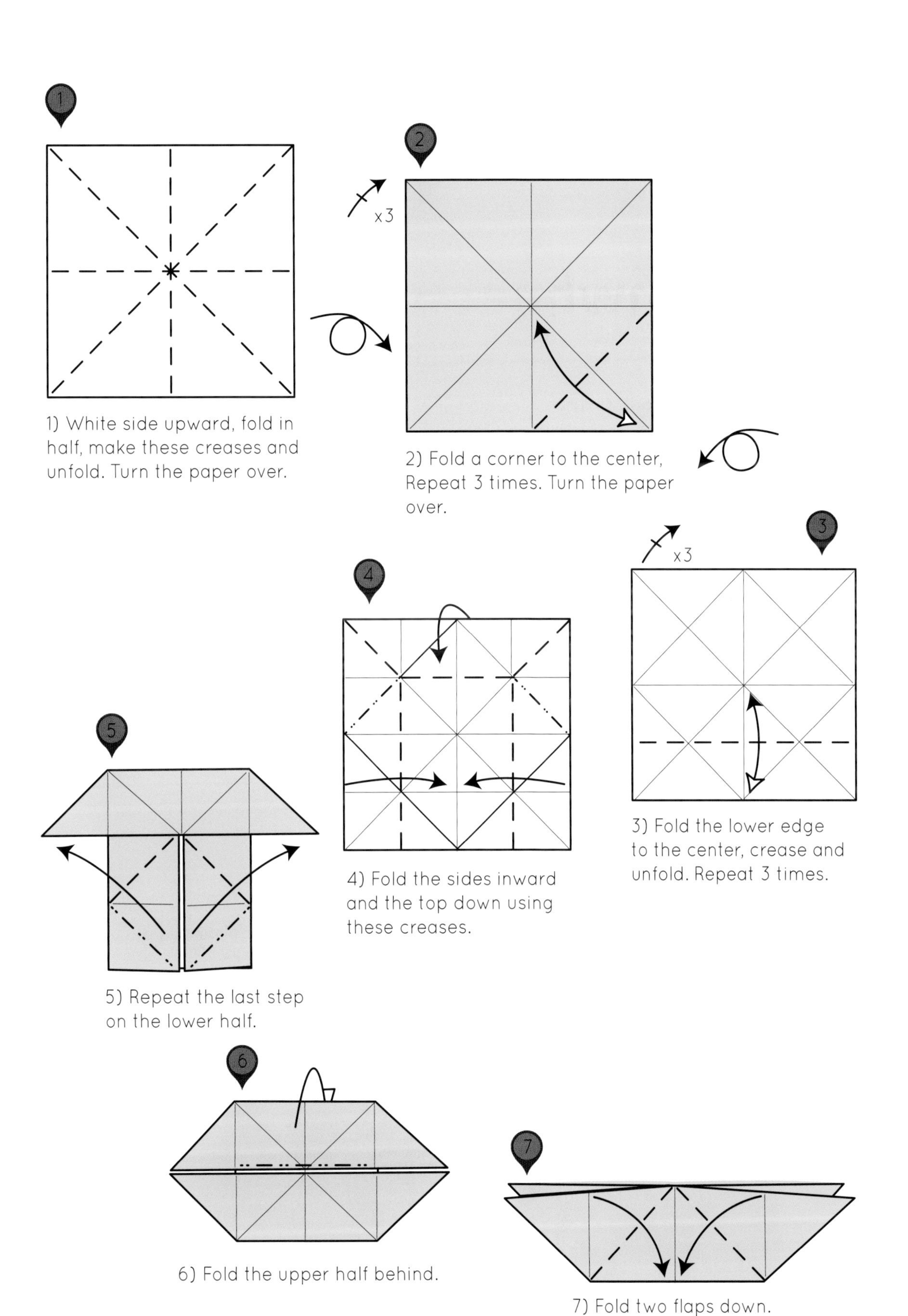

1) White side upward, fold in half, make these creases and unfold. Turn the paper over.

2) Fold a corner to the center, Repeat 3 times. Turn the paper over.

3) Fold the lower edge to the center, crease and unfold. Repeat 3 times.

4) Fold the sides inward and the top down using these creases.

5) Repeat the last step on the lower half.

6) Fold the upper half behind.

7) Fold two flaps down.

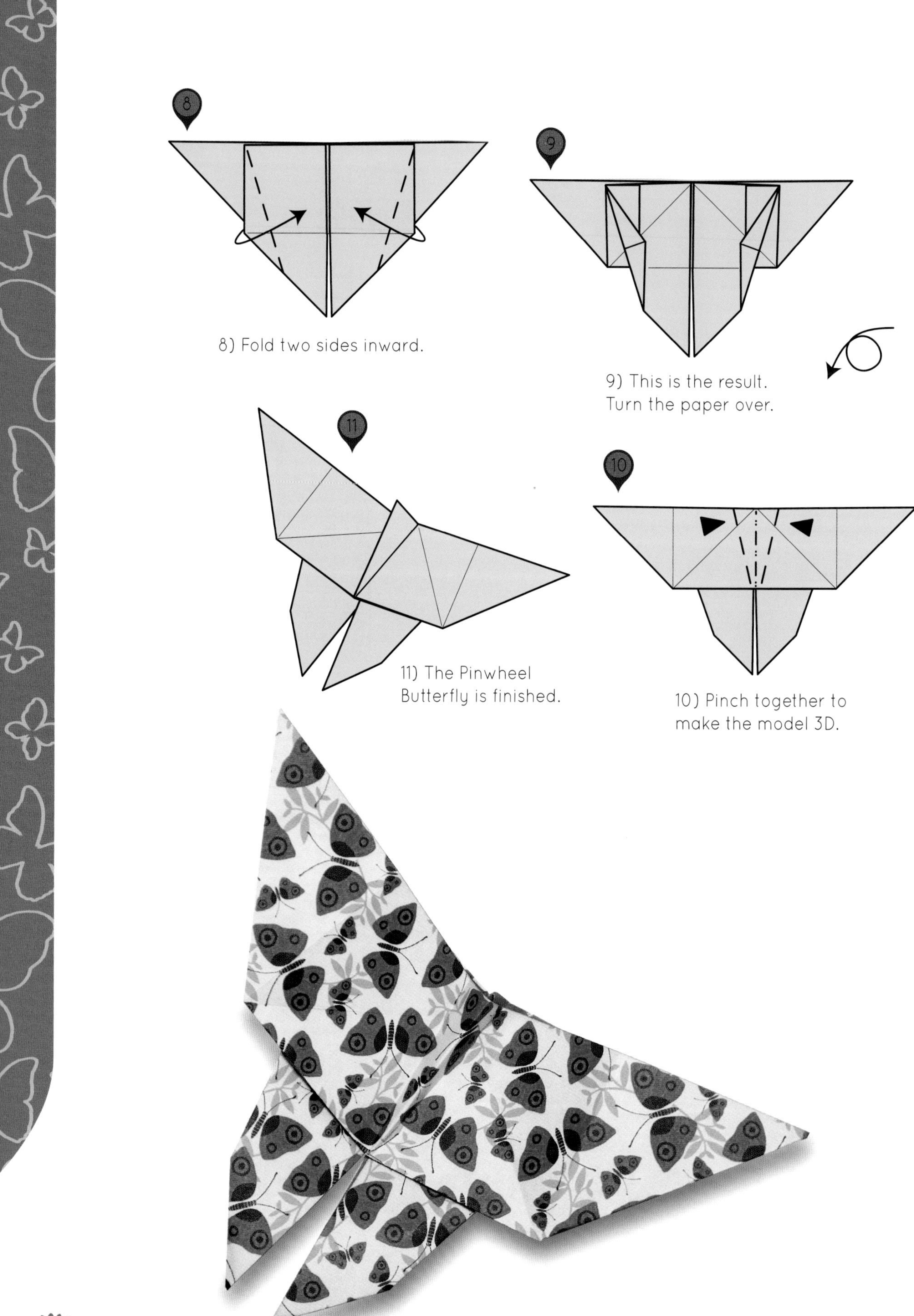

8) Fold two sides inward.

9) This is the result.
Turn the paper over.

10) Pinch together to make the model 3D.

11) The Pinwheel Butterfly is finished.

Emerging Butterfly

Nick Robinson

The birth of a butterfly is a truly moving event. The beauty that emerges from the cocoon is one of nature's miracles. Here we use two sheets (one dull, one colorful) to achieve an elegant result.

Size of the sheet: 7 x 7 in

Paper

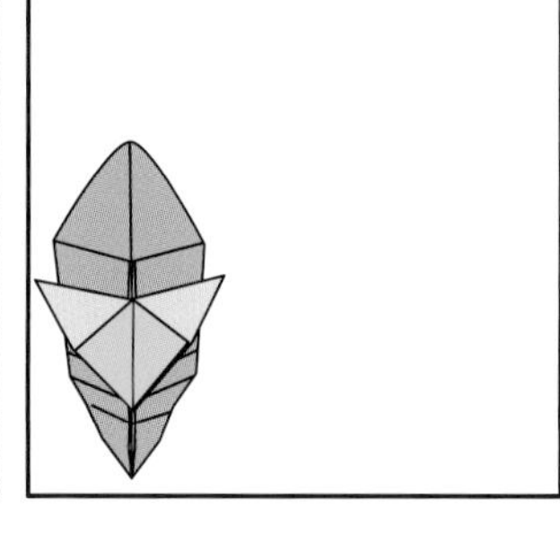

Relationship between the paper and the origami

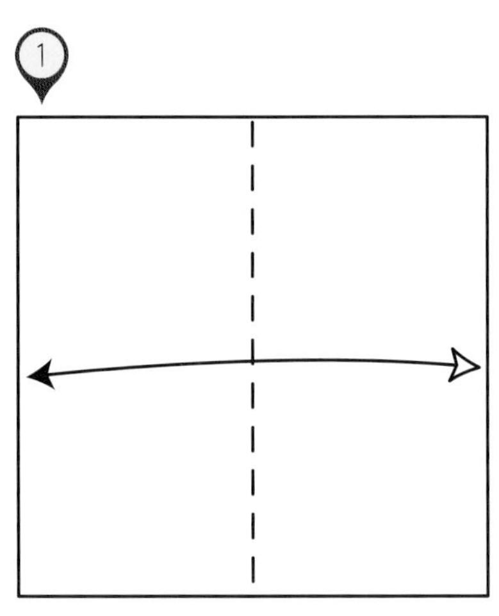

1) White side up, crease and unfold the center crease.

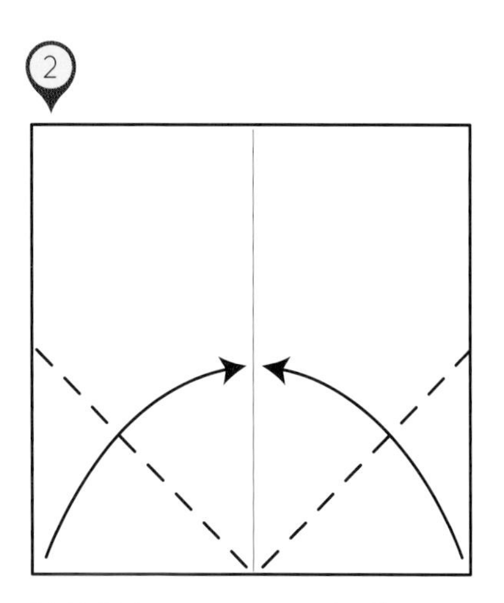

2) Fold lower corners to the center crease.

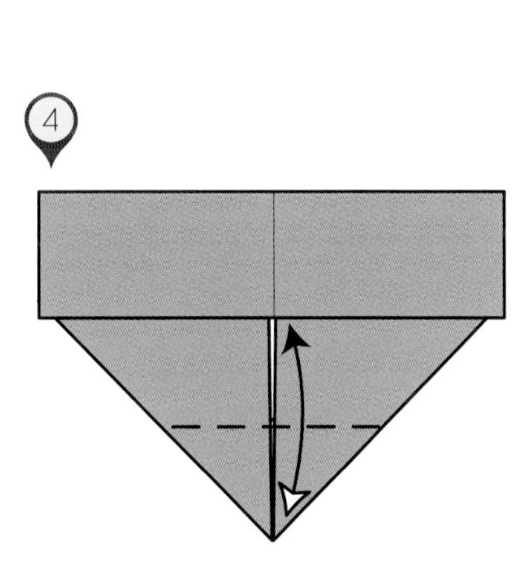

4) Fold the lower corner to the horizontal edge, crease and unfold.

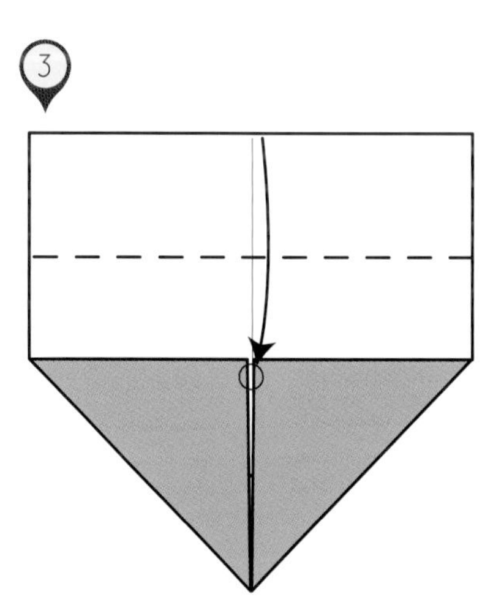

3) Fold the upper edge to just below the inner corners.

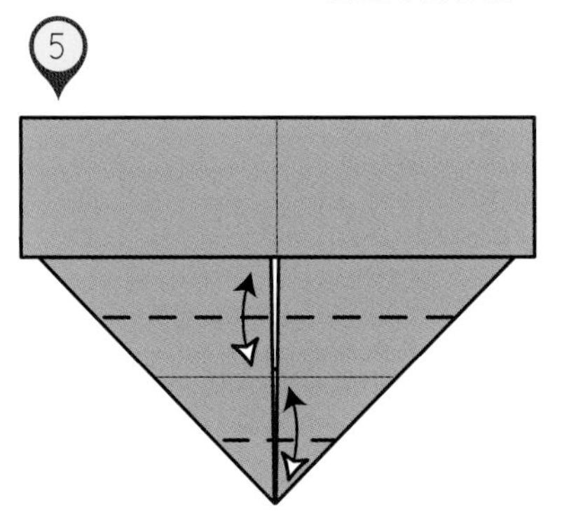

5) Add quarter creases and turn the paper over.

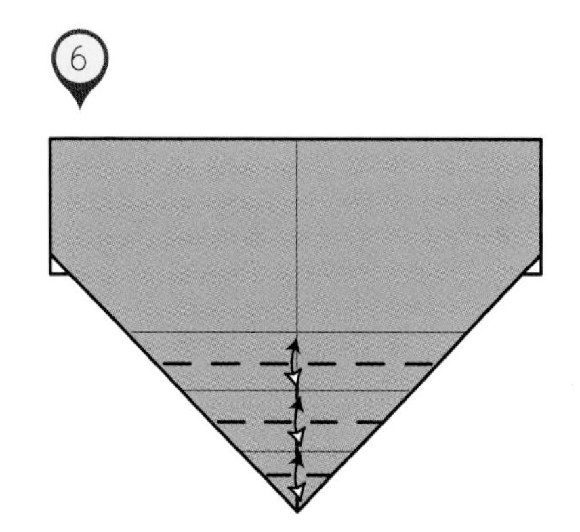

6) Add eighth creases.

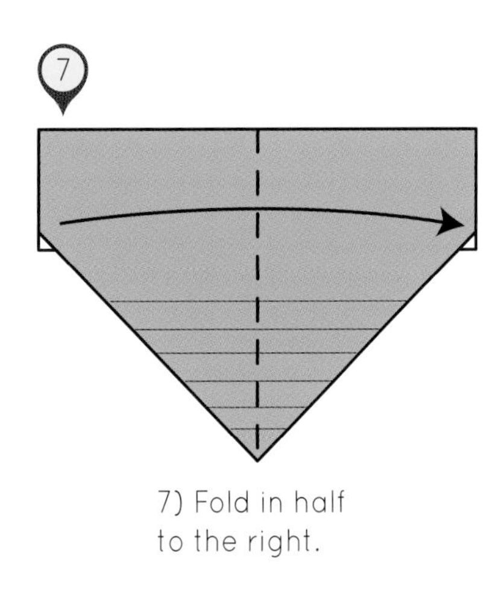

7) Fold in half
to the right.

8) Fold the corner to
meet an edge, crease
and unfold.

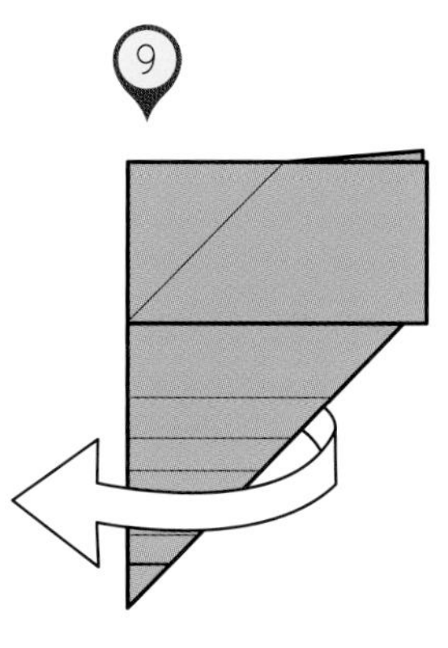

9) Unfold back to step 7.

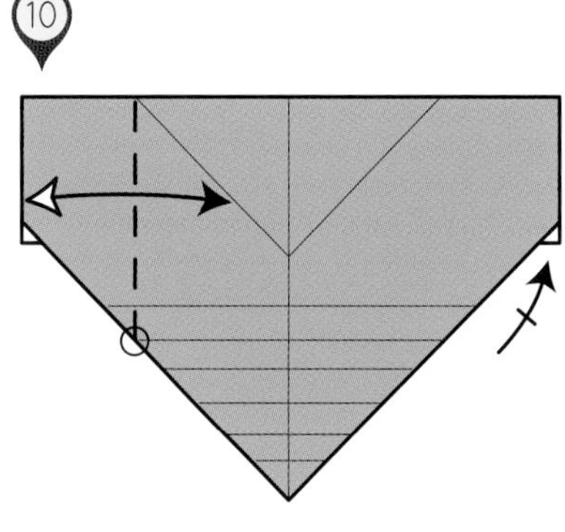

10) Crease and unfold on
both sides.

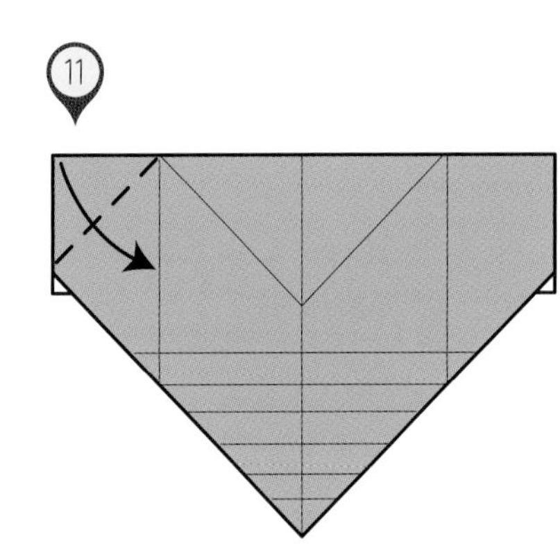

11) Fold the top right
corner to the crease.

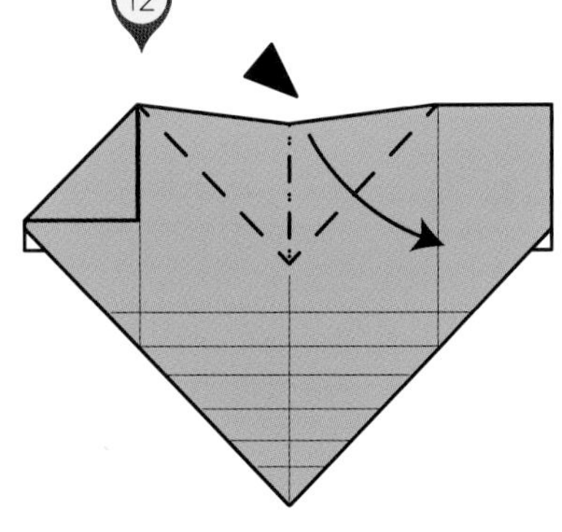

12) Partially fold in half to the
right, pushing in the corner.

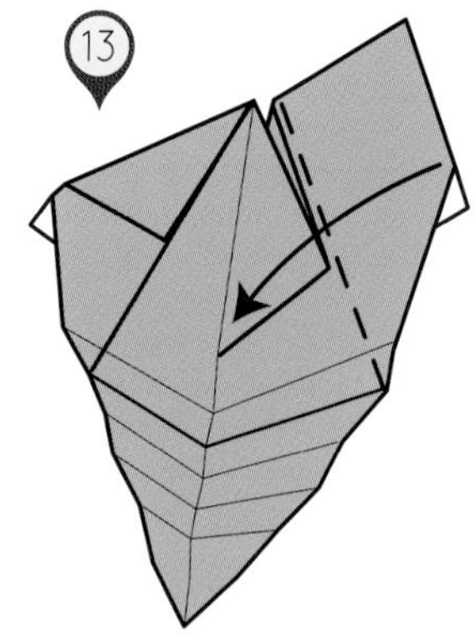

13) The paper is 3D.
Fold a flap inward.

14) Fold a matching
flap inward.

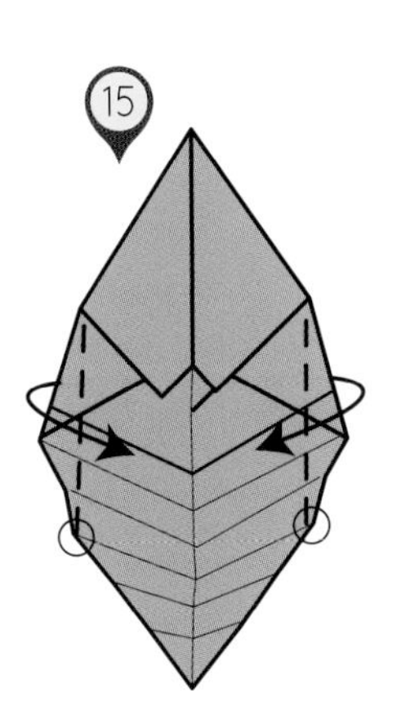

15) Fold two corners
in where shown.

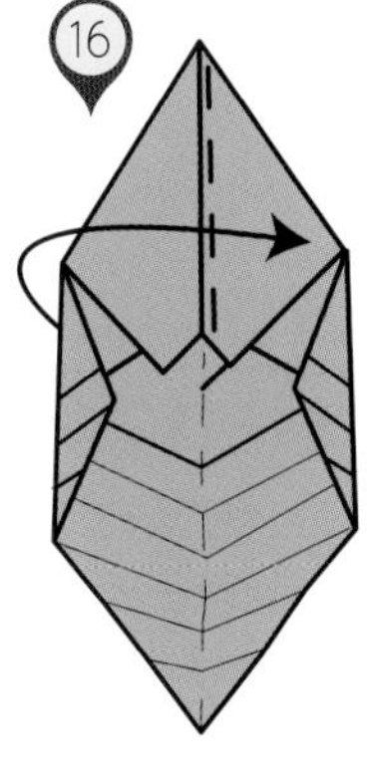

16) Fold the model
in half to the right.

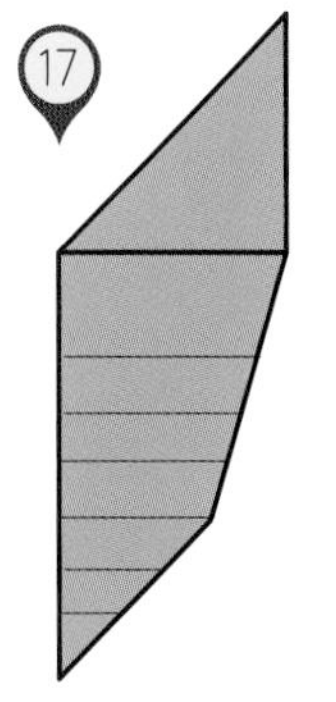

17) The cocoon
is complete.

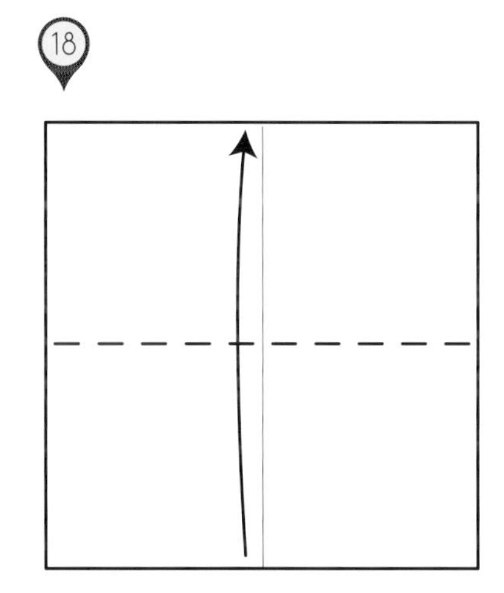

18) Start at step 2 of the cocoon,
using a square 1/4 of the size.
Fold in half upward.

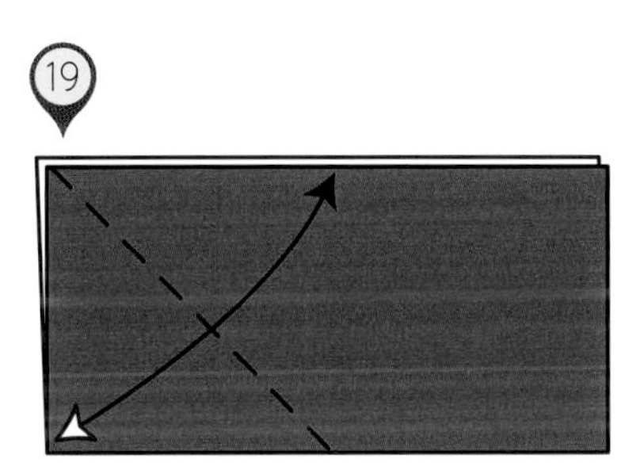

19) Fold the left edge to the
upper edge, crease and unfold.

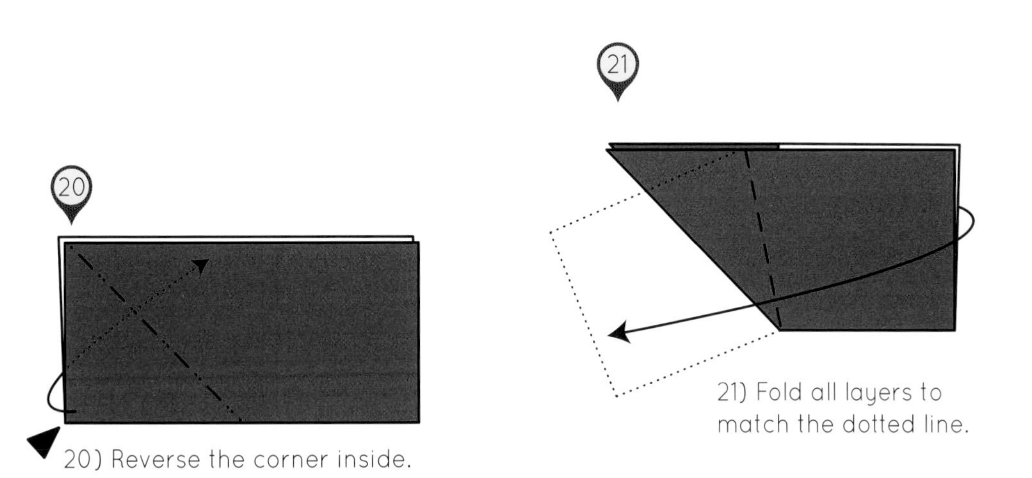

20) Reverse the corner inside.

21) Fold all layers to
match the dotted line.

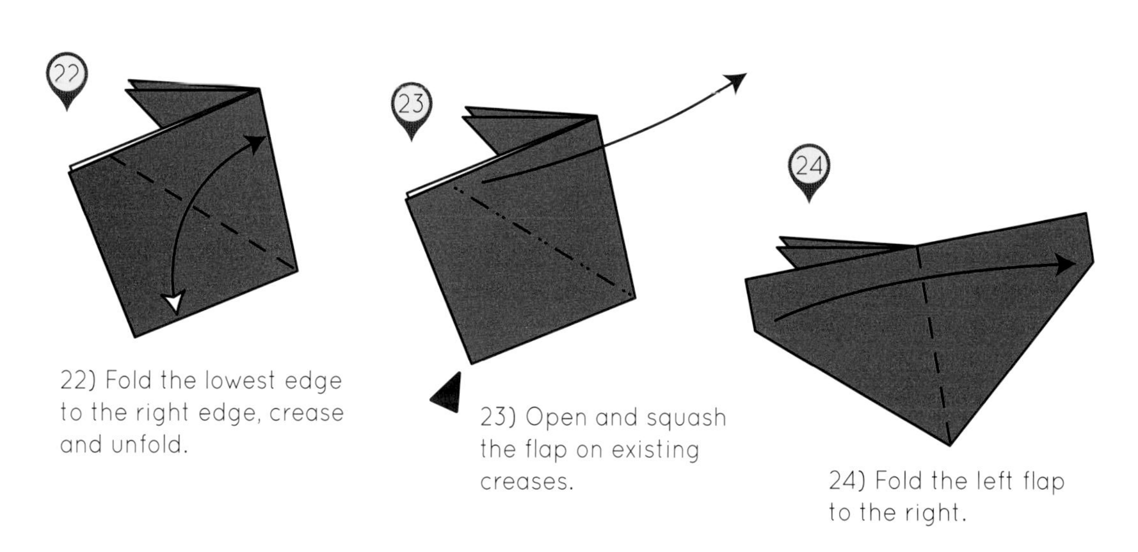

22) Fold the lowest edge to the right edge, crease and unfold.

23) Open and squash the flap on existing creases.

24) Fold the left flap to the right.

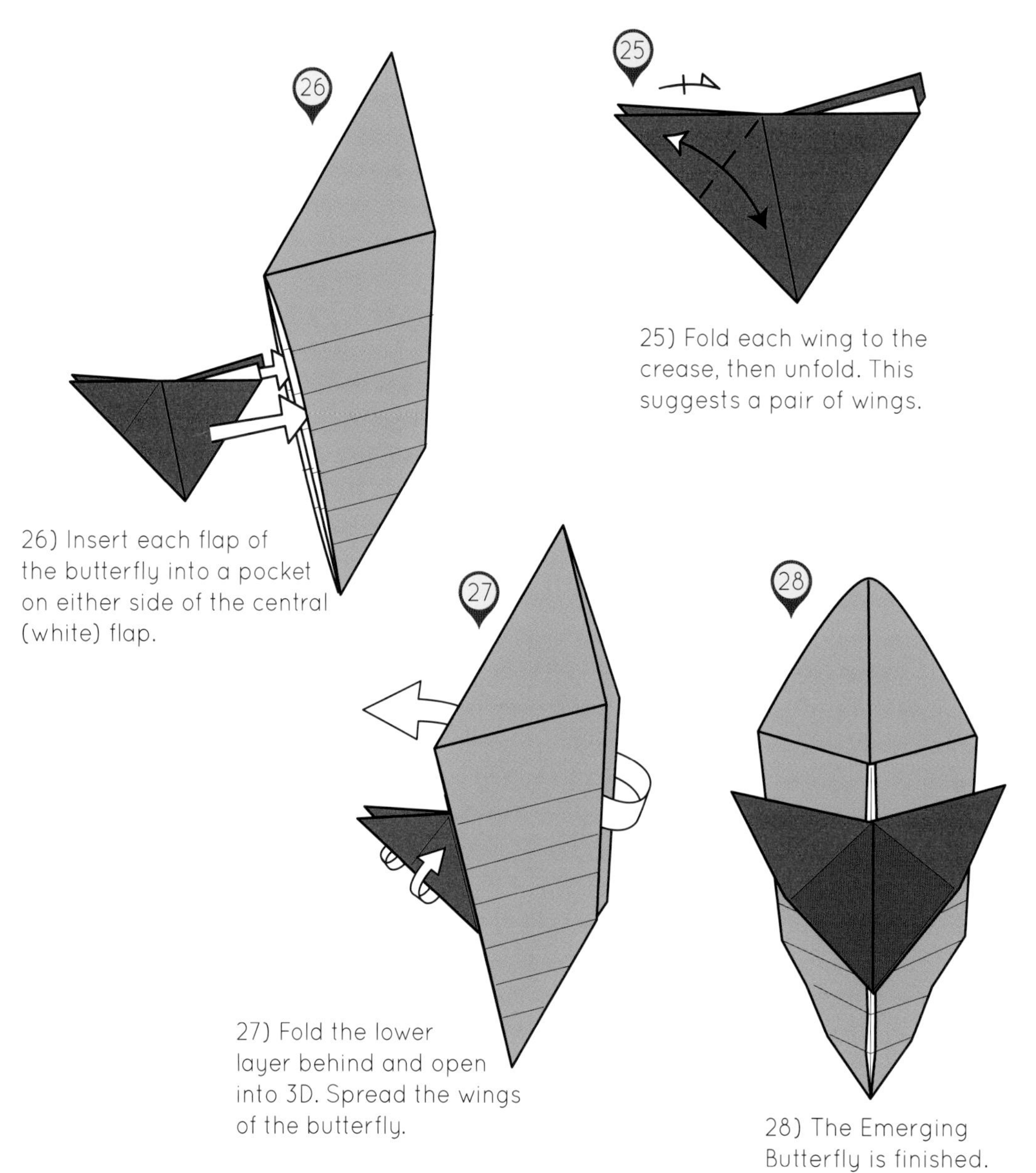

25) Fold each wing to the crease, then unfold. This suggests a pair of wings.

26) Insert each flap of the butterfly into a pocket on either side of the central (white) flap.

27) Fold the lower layer behind and open into 3D. Spread the wings of the butterfly.

28) The Emerging Butterfly is finished.

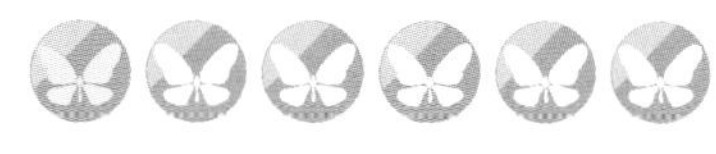

VIDEO
www.nuinui.ch/video/it/m19/farfalle/p30

Butterfly Envelope

Evi Binzinger

Here is a practical design with a lovely butterfly motif on the front. You can make a pleat in the body before step 14, so the body becomes smaller.

Size of the sheet: 7 x 7 in

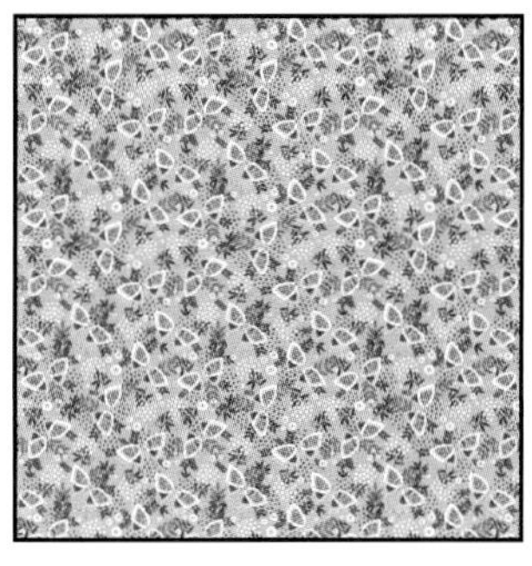

Paper

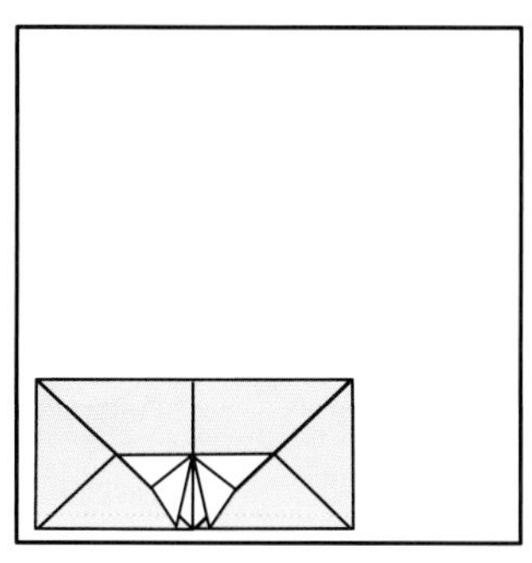

Relationship between the paper and the origami

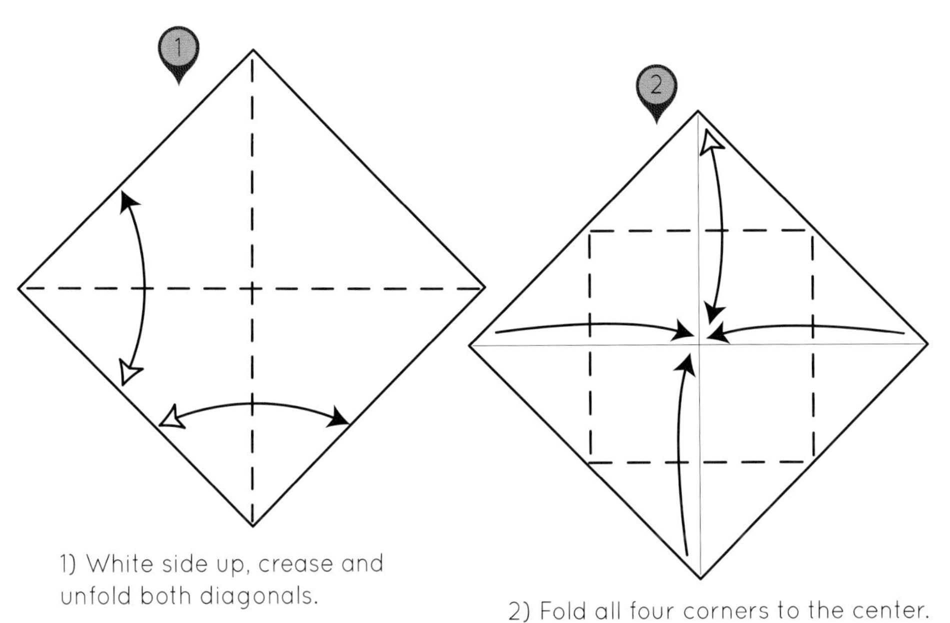

1) White side up, crease and unfold both diagonals.

2) Fold all four corners to the center.

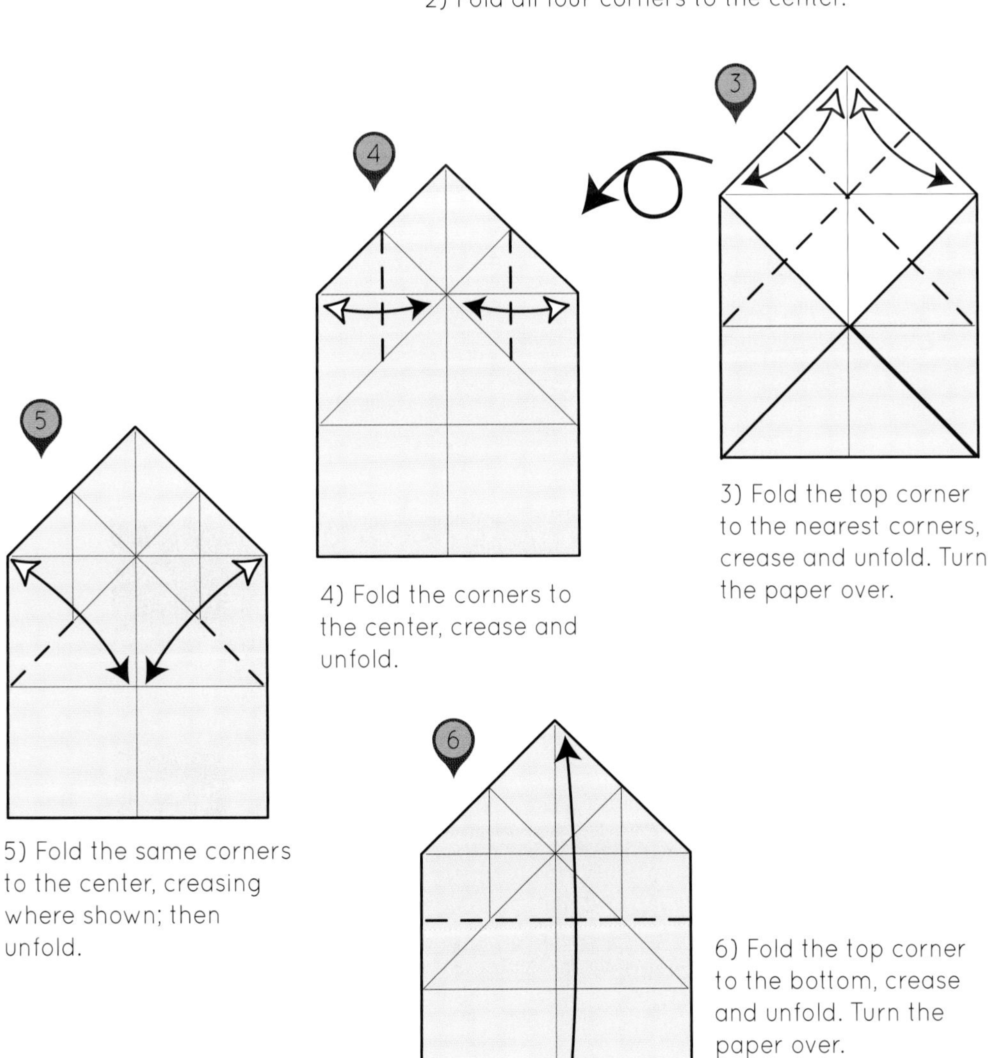

3) Fold the top corner to the nearest corners, crease and unfold. Turn the paper over.

4) Fold the corners to the center, crease and unfold.

5) Fold the same corners to the center, creasing where shown; then unfold.

6) Fold the top corner to the bottom, crease and unfold. Turn the paper over.

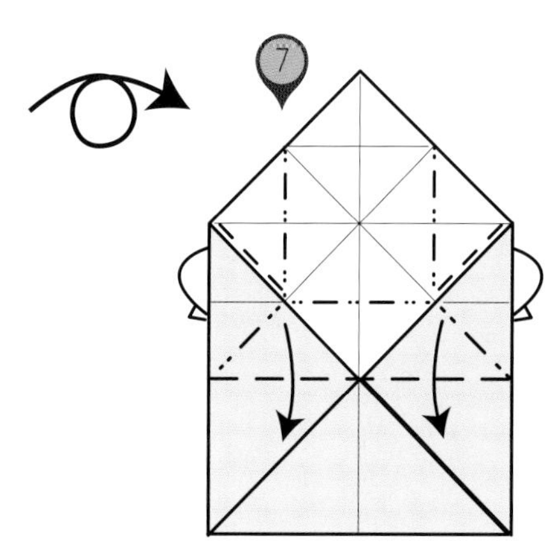

7) Carefully make these folds. The paper forms a pleat that folds downward.

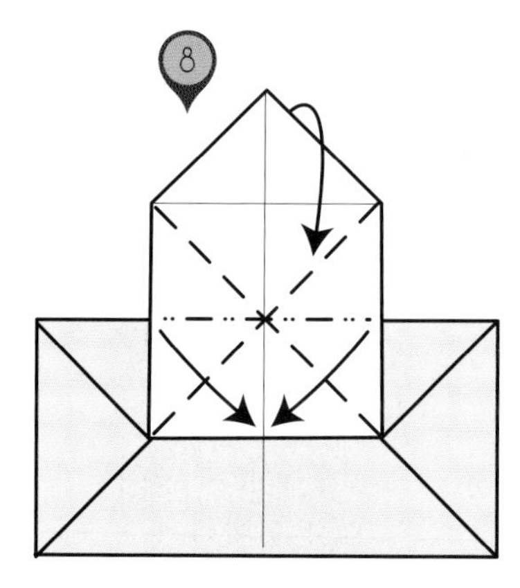

8) Collapse the paper down using these creases.

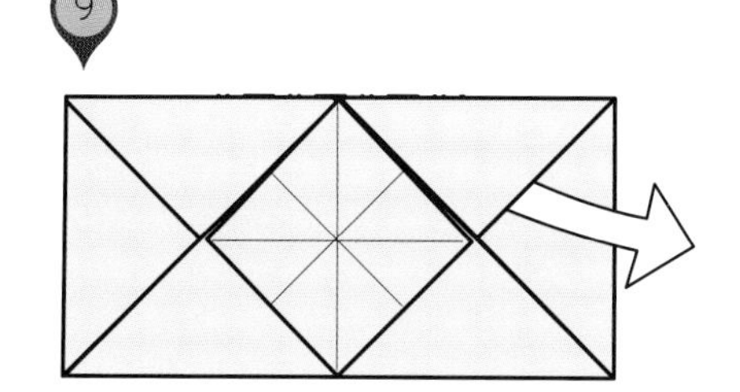

9) Open the folds slightly and ease out some paper.

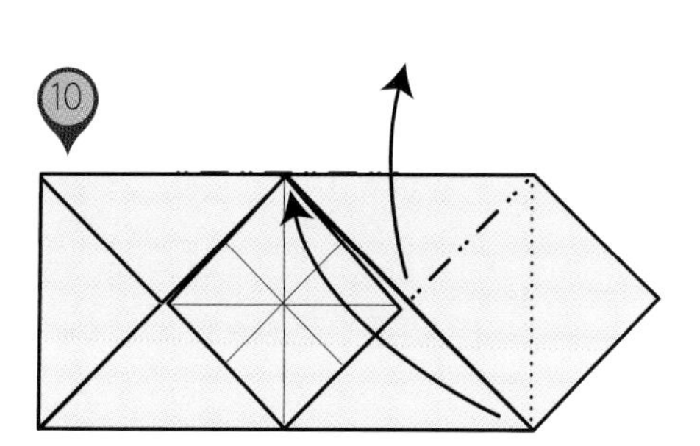

10) Fold a small triangle upward, flattening the paper.

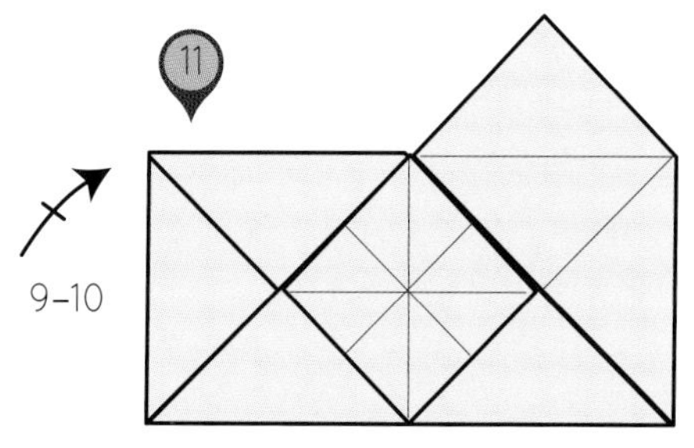

11) Repeat steps 9-10 on the left side.

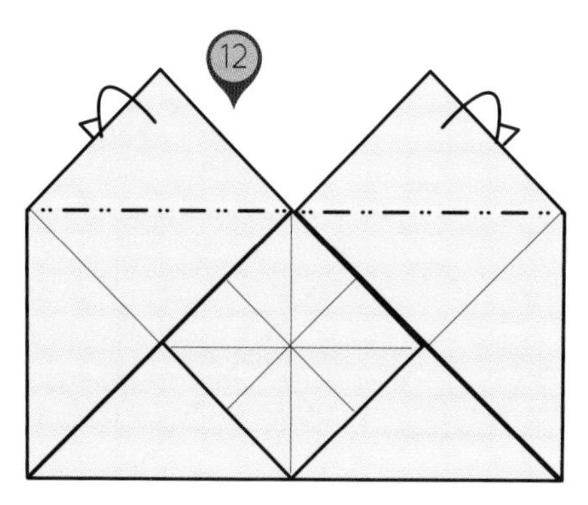

12) Tuck the flaps behind into pockets.

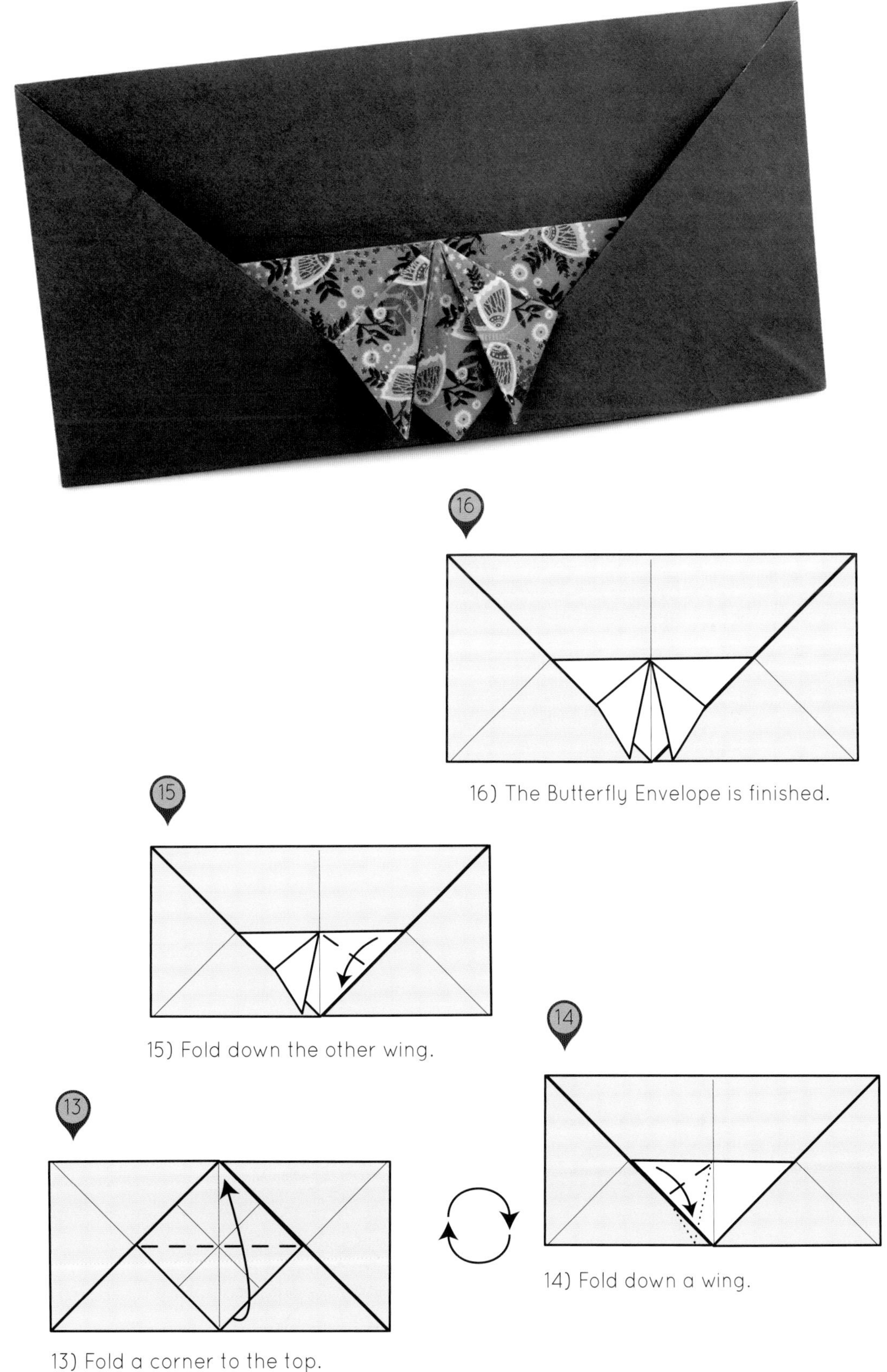

16) The Butterfly Envelope is finished.

15) Fold down the other wing.

14) Fold down a wing.

13) Fold a corner to the top.
Rotate the paper 180 degrees.

VIDEO

www.nuinui.ch/video/it/m19/farfalle/p34

Sunbathing Butterfly

Nick Robinson

This design creates the silhouette of a butterfly, which you can see by holding it toward the light. There are two variations to try.

Size of the sheet: 7 x 7 in

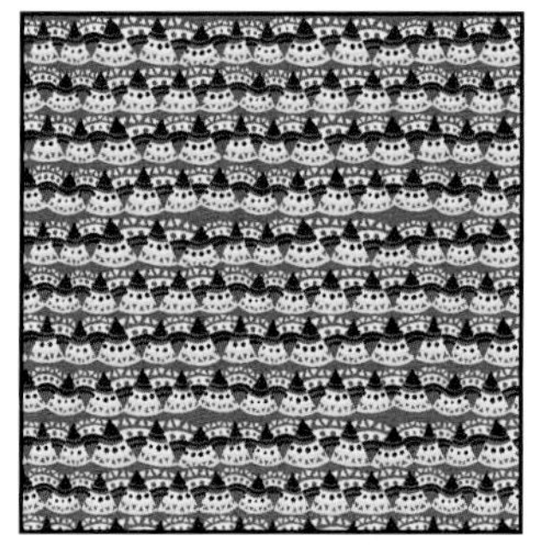

Paper

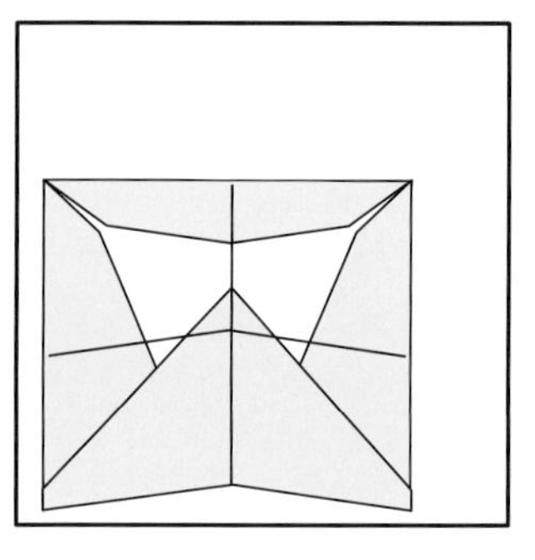

Relationship between the paper and the origami

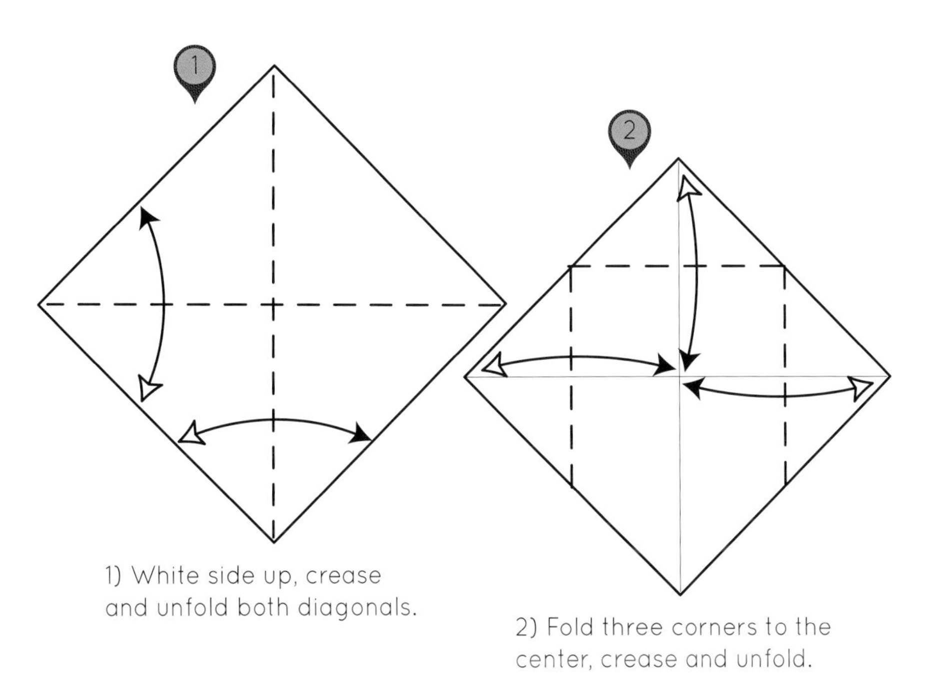

1) White side up, crease and unfold both diagonals.

2) Fold three corners to the center, crease and unfold.

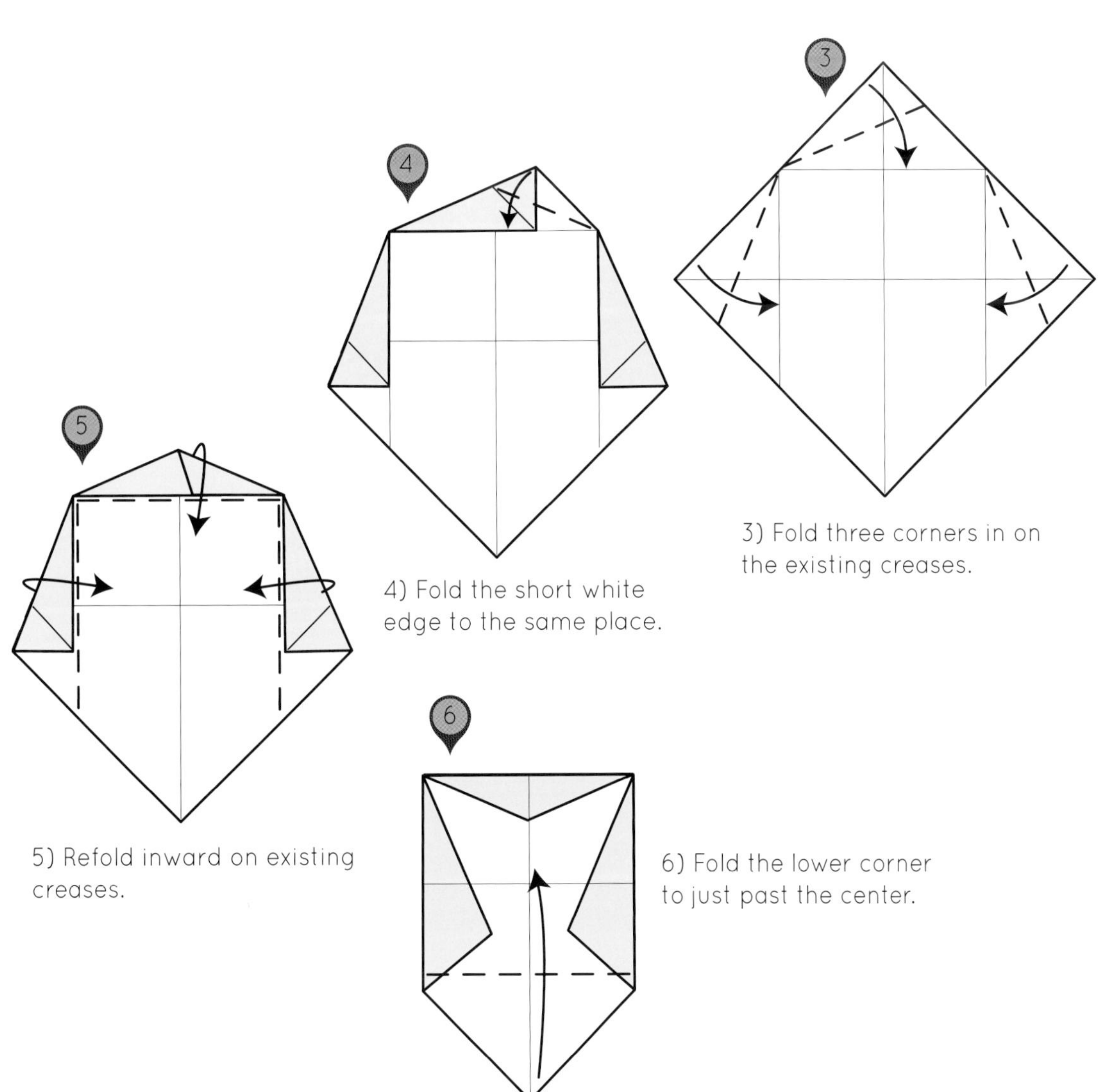

3) Fold three corners in on the existing creases.

4) Fold the short white edge to the same place.

5) Refold inward on existing creases.

6) Fold the lower corner to just past the center.

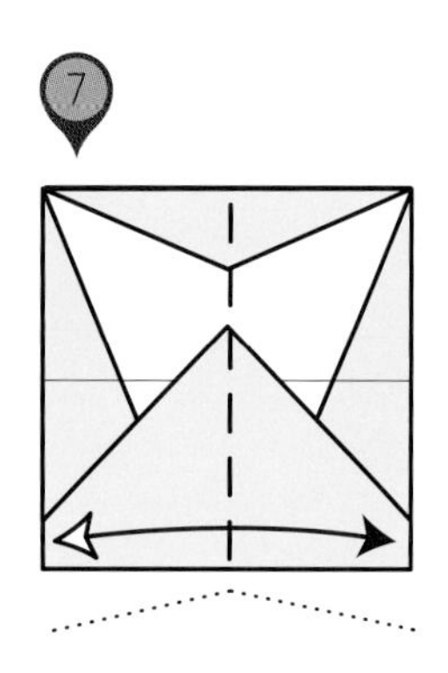

7) Reinforce the center crease and fold at a slight angle so it will stand up.

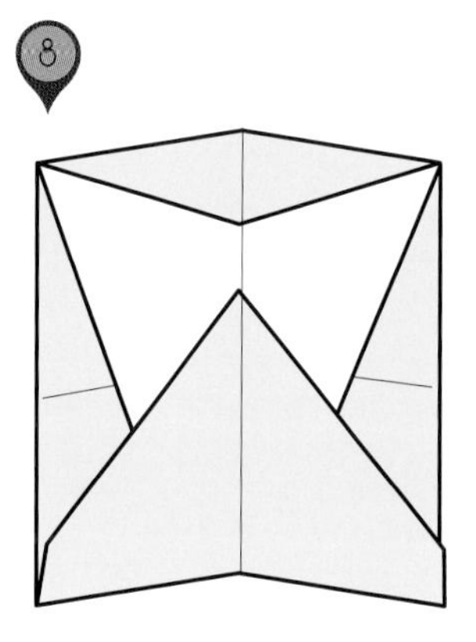

8) The Sunbathing Butterfly is finished.

VERSION 2

This gives us a butterfly further within the final square, but needs a little more work.

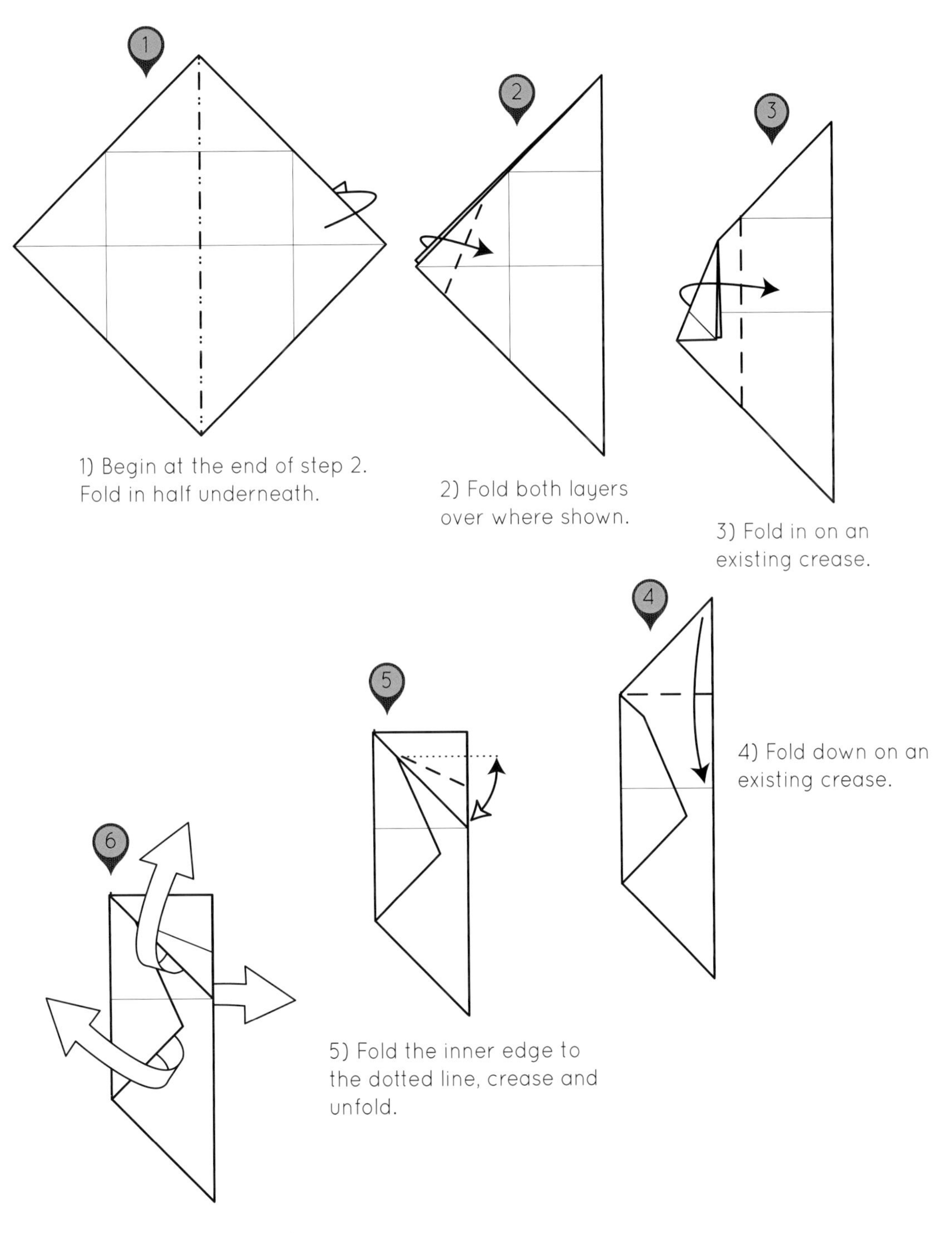

1) Begin at the end of step 2. Fold in half underneath.

2) Fold both layers over where shown.

3) Fold in on an existing crease.

4) Fold down on an existing crease.

5) Fold the inner edge to the dotted line, crease and unfold.

6) Unfold completely to the white side.

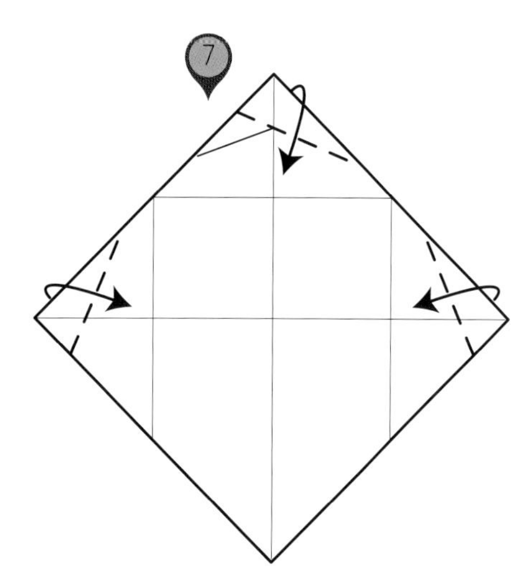

7) Fold three corners in using existing creases.

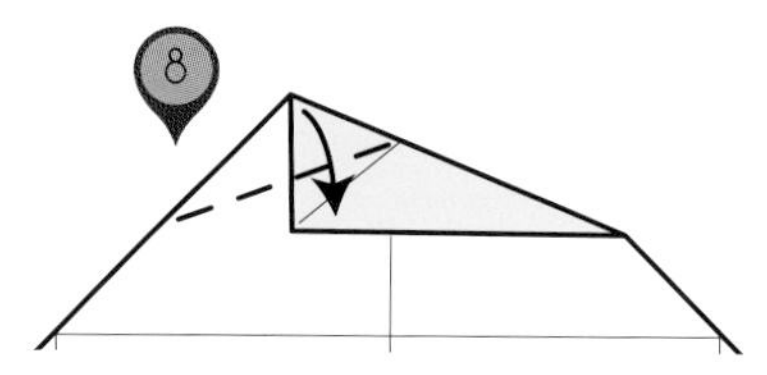

8) Fold this corner in to match up.

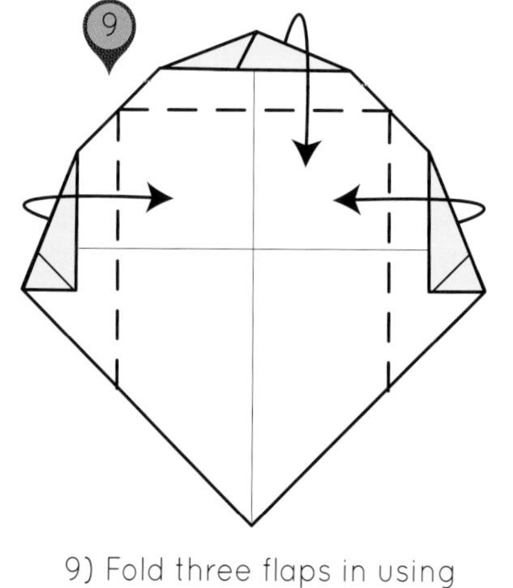

9) Fold three flaps in using existing creases.

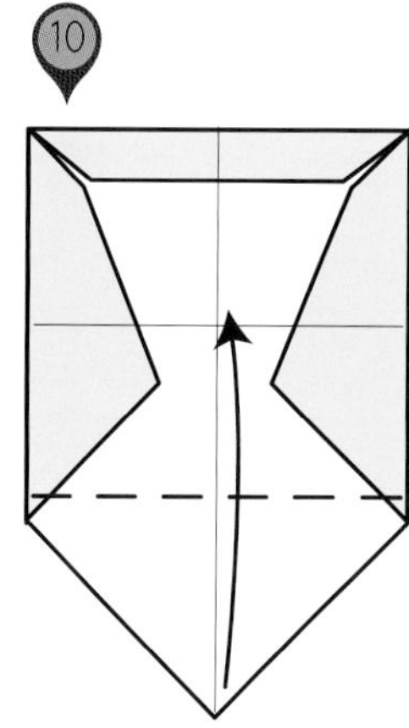

10) Fold the lower corner to just past the center.

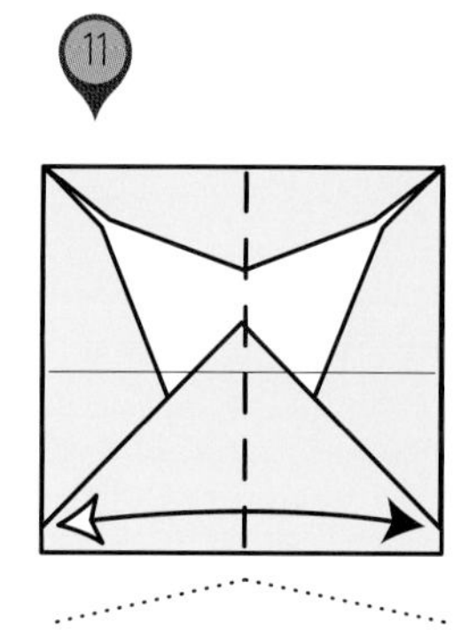

11) Reinforce the center crease and fold at a slight angle so it will stand up.

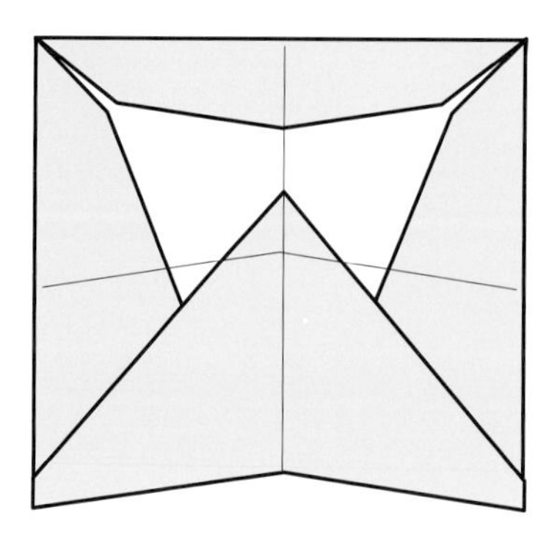

Yoshizawa's Butterfly

Akira Yoshizawa

Widely acknowledged as a founding father of origami, his work set the standards for all to follow. This design is a model of simplicity and elegance.

Size of the sheet: 7 x 7 in

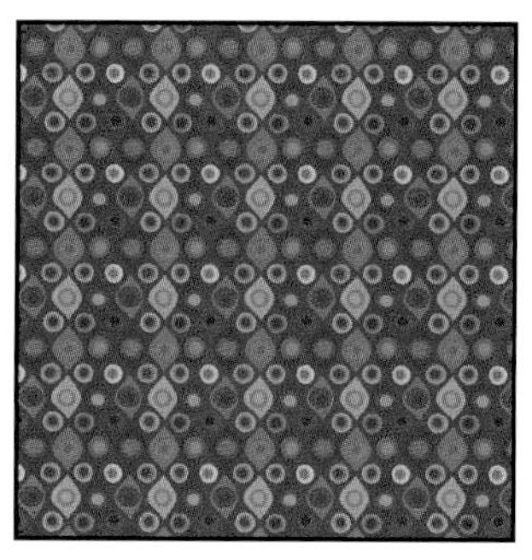

Paper

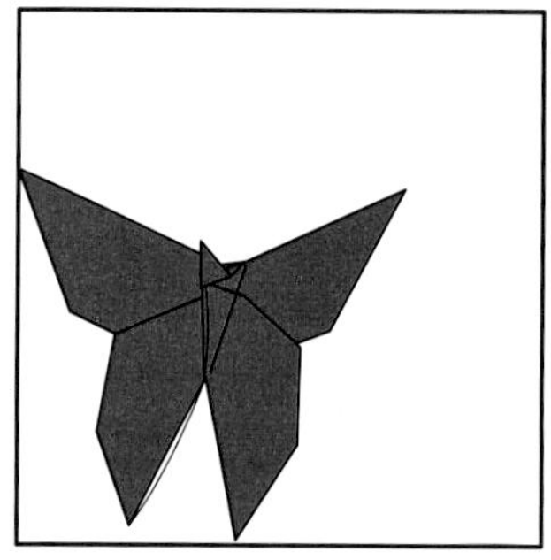

Relationship between the paper and the origami

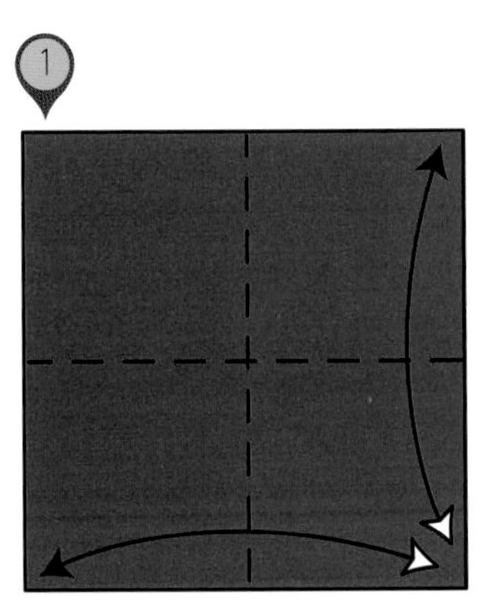

1) White side up, crease and unfold in half both ways. Turn the paper over.

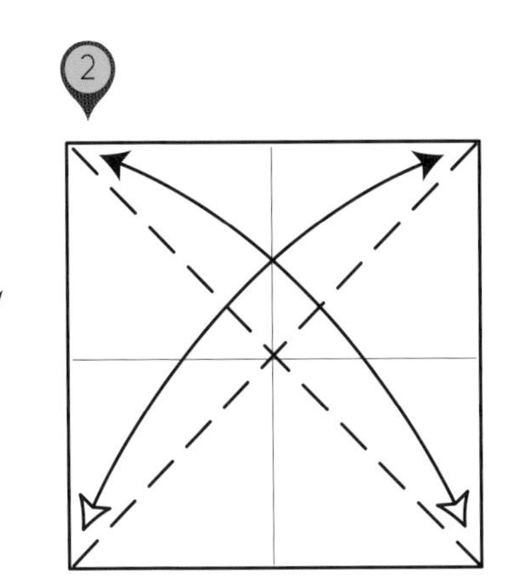

2) Crease and unfold both diagonals.

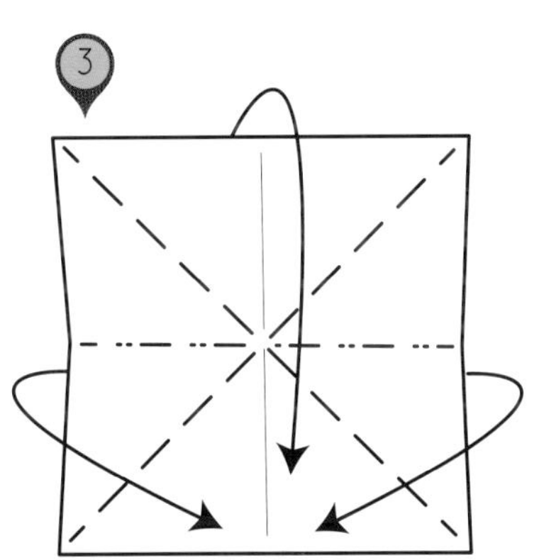

3) Collapse the paper down using these creases.

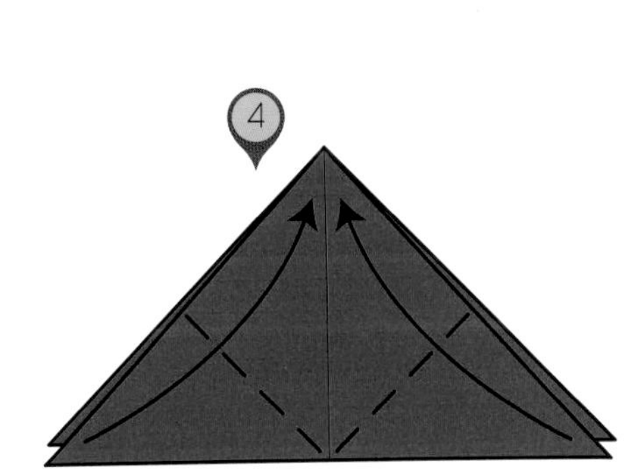

4) Fold two corners to the top corner.

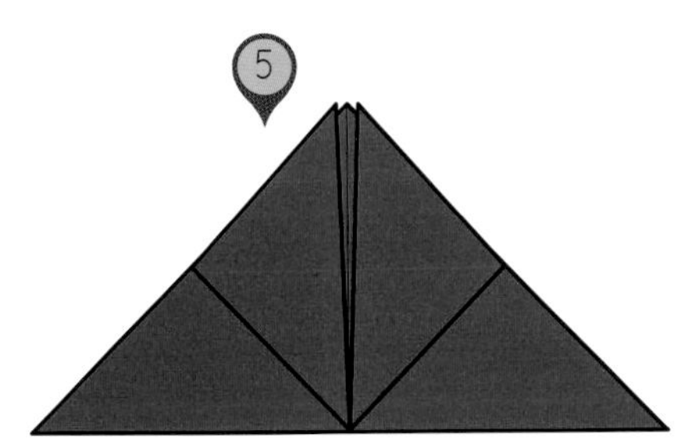

5) The result. Turn the paper over.

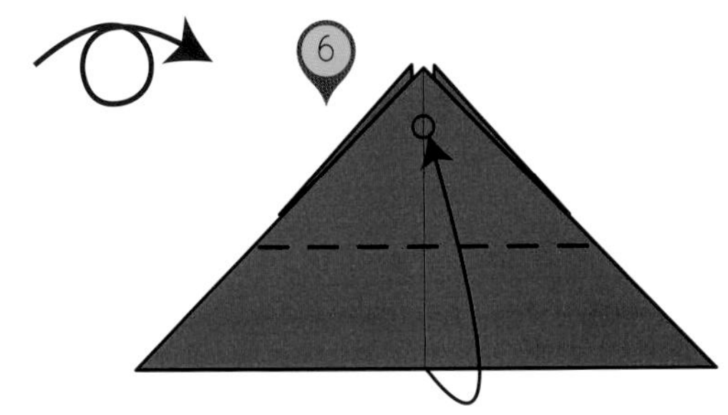

6) Fold the lower edge to the circled point.

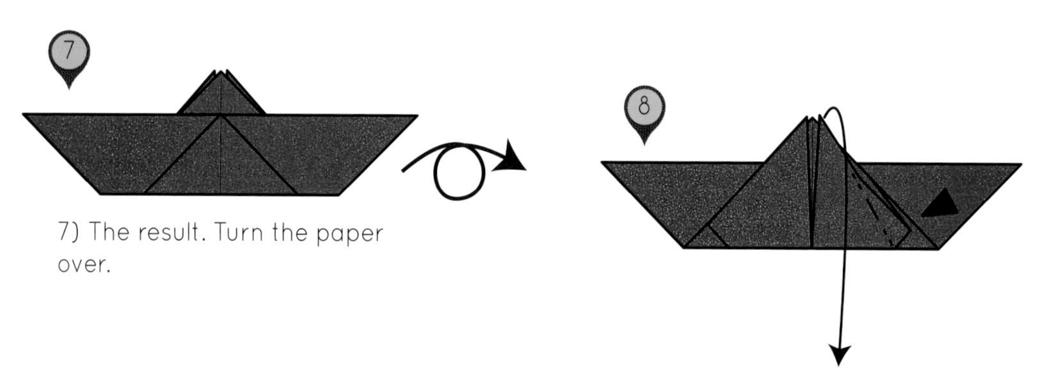

7) The result. Turn the paper over.

8) Carefully fold one flap down, squashing the corner.

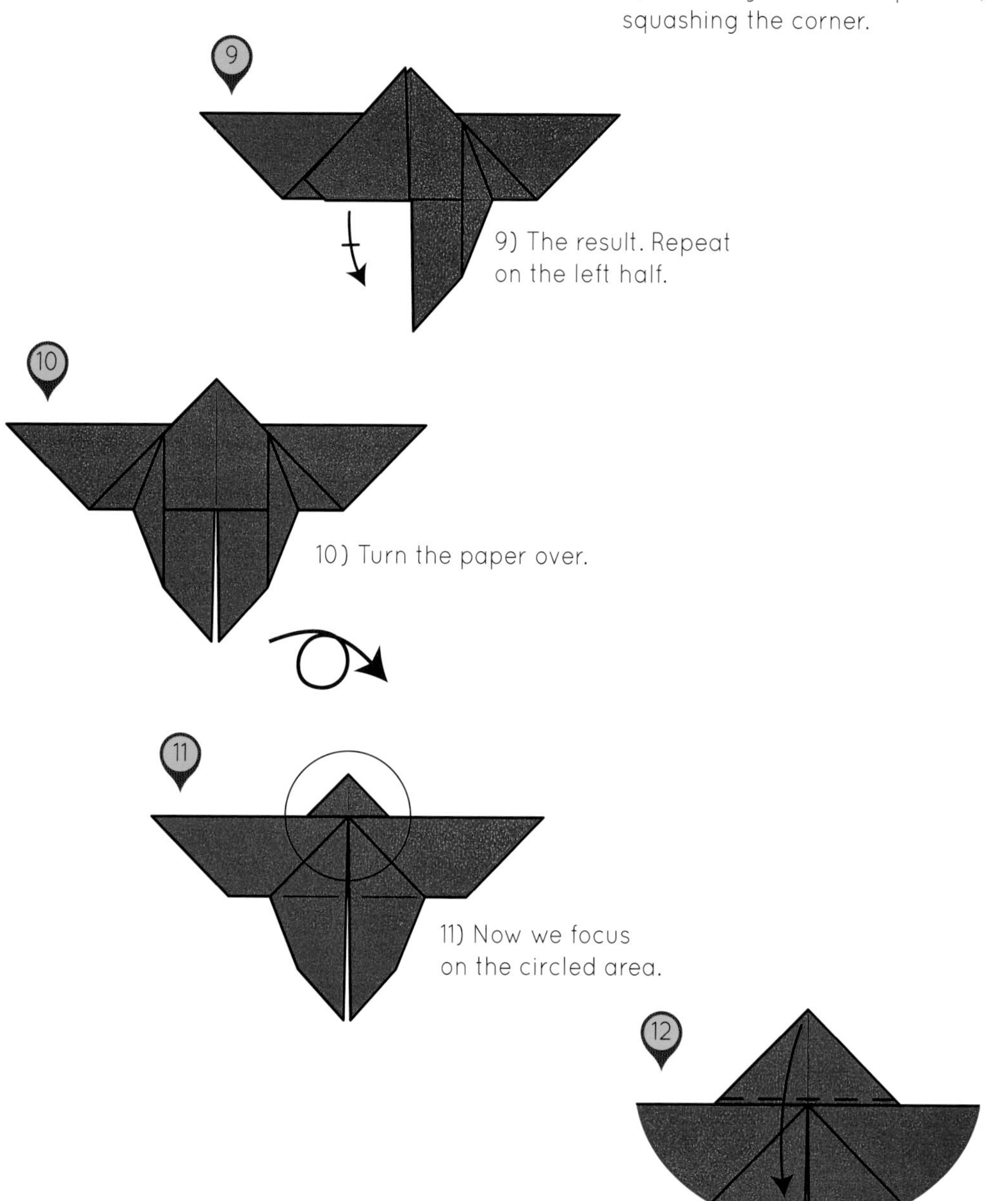

9) The result. Repeat on the left half.

10) Turn the paper over.

11) Now we focus on the circled area.

12) Fold a flap down.

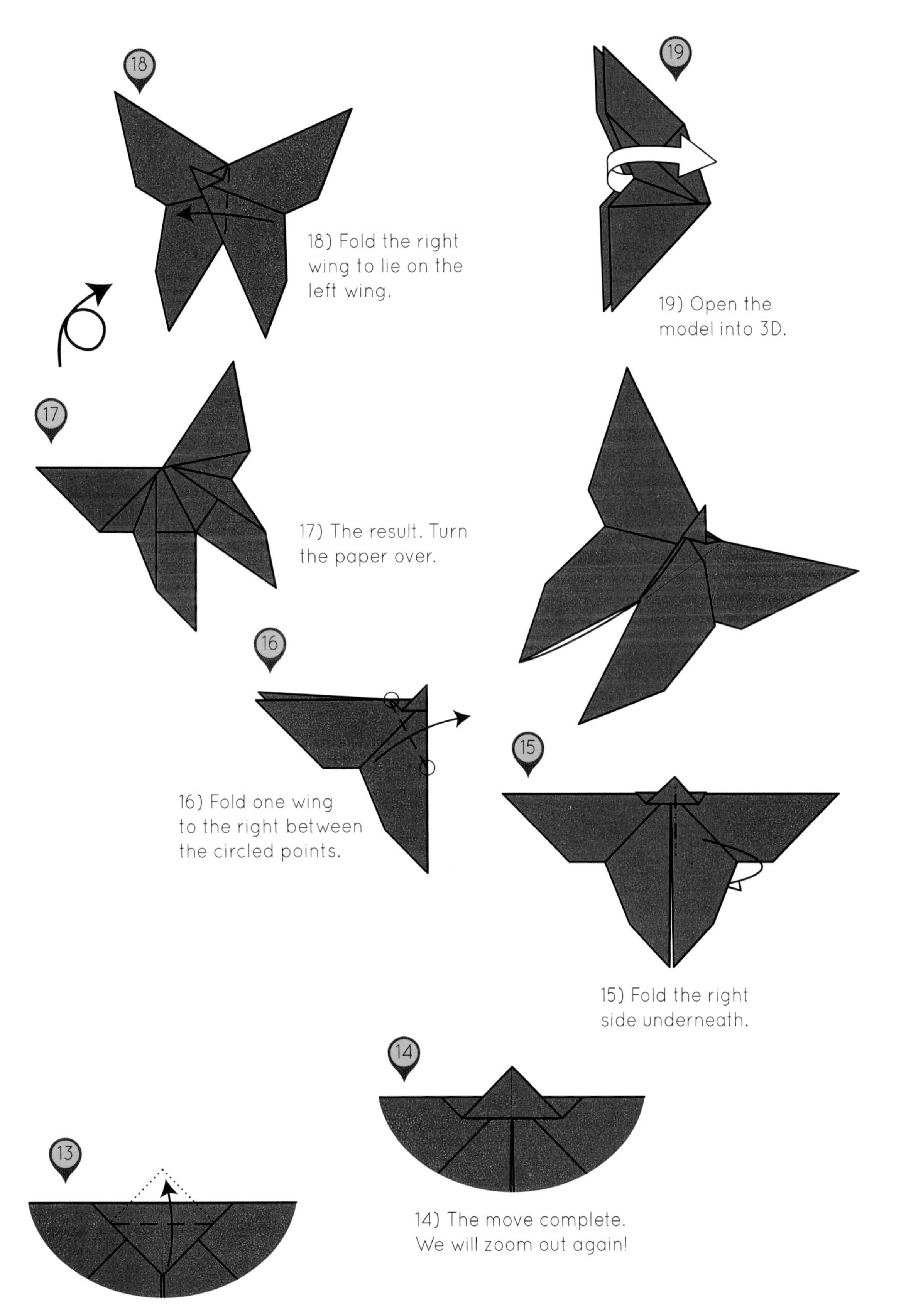

18) Fold the right wing to lie on the left wing.

19) Open the model into 3D.

17) The result. Turn the paper over.

16) Fold one wing to the right between the circled points.

15) Fold the right side underneath.

14) The move complete. We will zoom out again!

13) Fold it back up to match the dotted line.

VARIATION

Here is an elegant variation of the original design. We do not know if Yoshizawa originated it, but he would surely have approved of it!

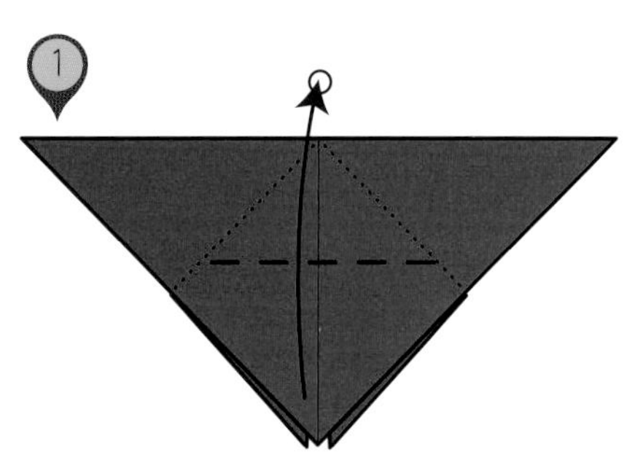

1) Start at the beginning of step 6 and rotate the paper 180 degrees. Fold a single lower corner upward; do NOT flatten the paper!

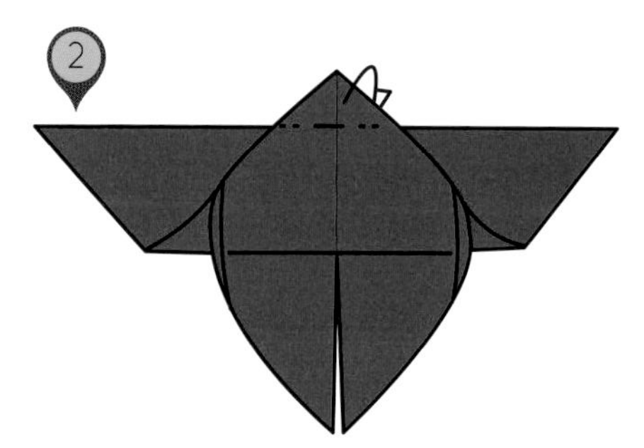

2) Fold the upper flap behind.

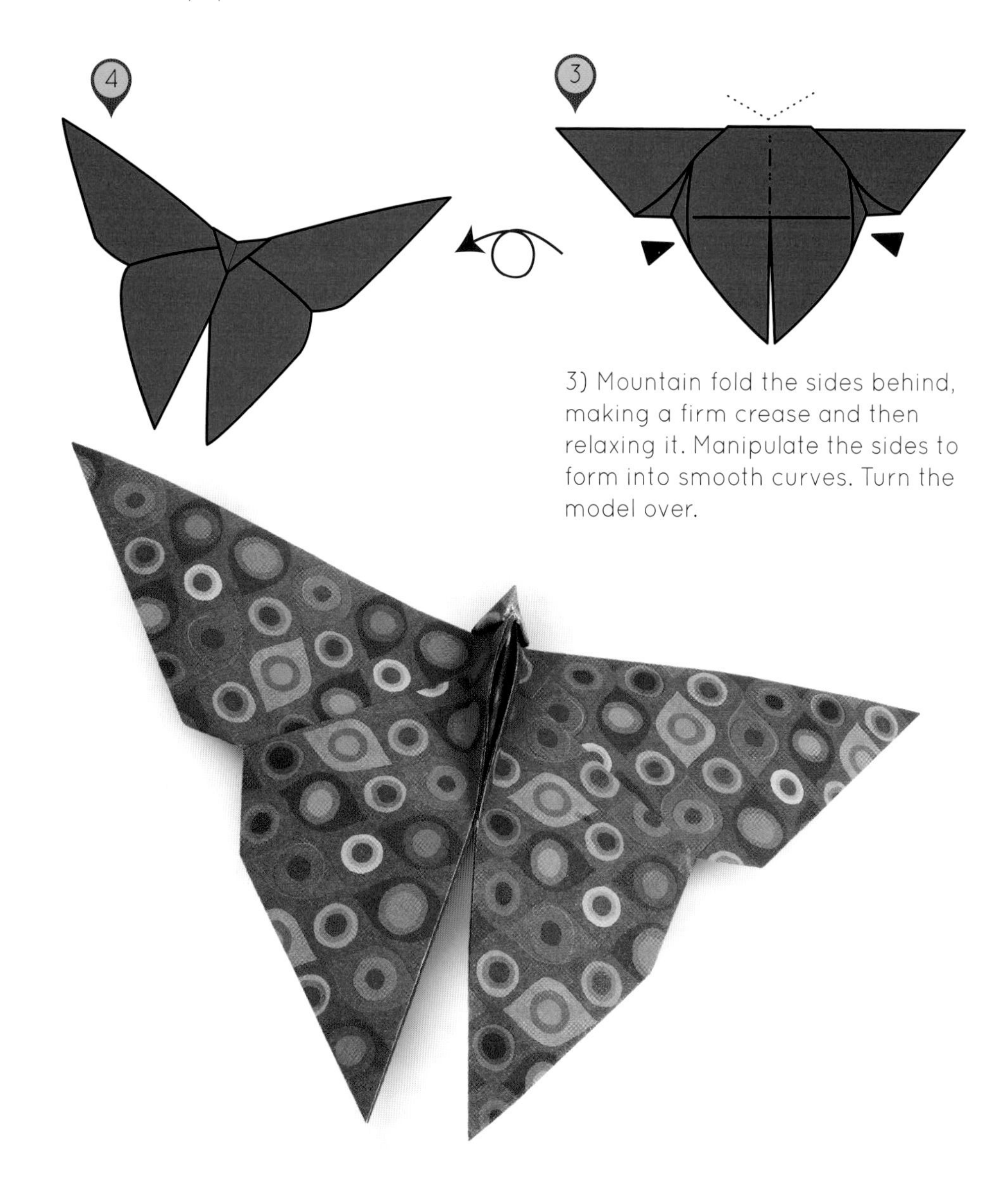

3) Mountain fold the sides behind, making a firm crease and then relaxing it. Manipulate the sides to form into smooth curves. Turn the model over.

VIDEO
www.nuinui.ch/video/it/m19/farfalle/p46

Australian Butterfly

Shoko Aoyagi

An unusual folding sequence produces a beautiful result.

Size of the sheet: 7 x 7 in

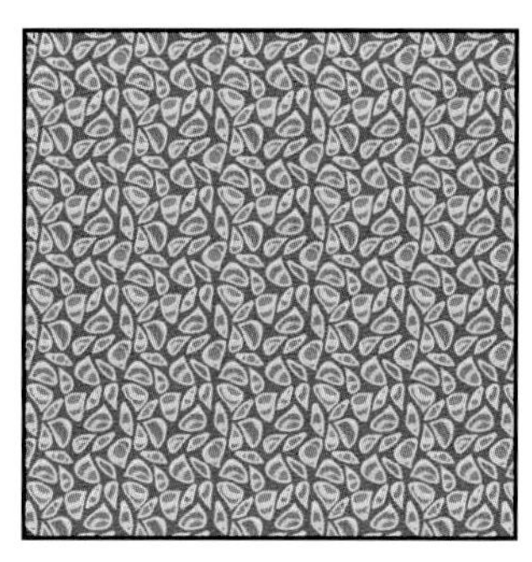

Paper

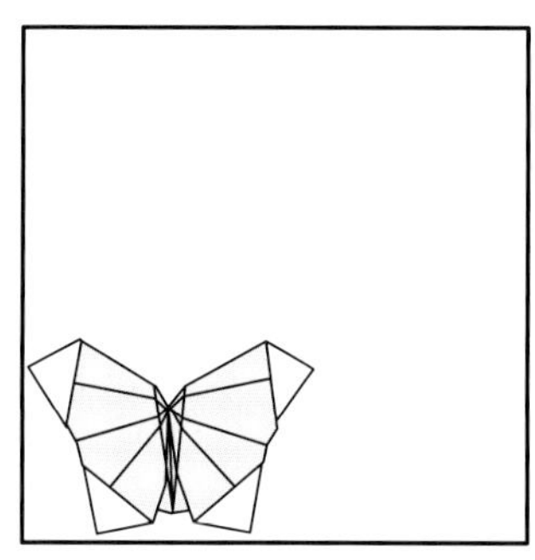

Relationship between the paper and the origami

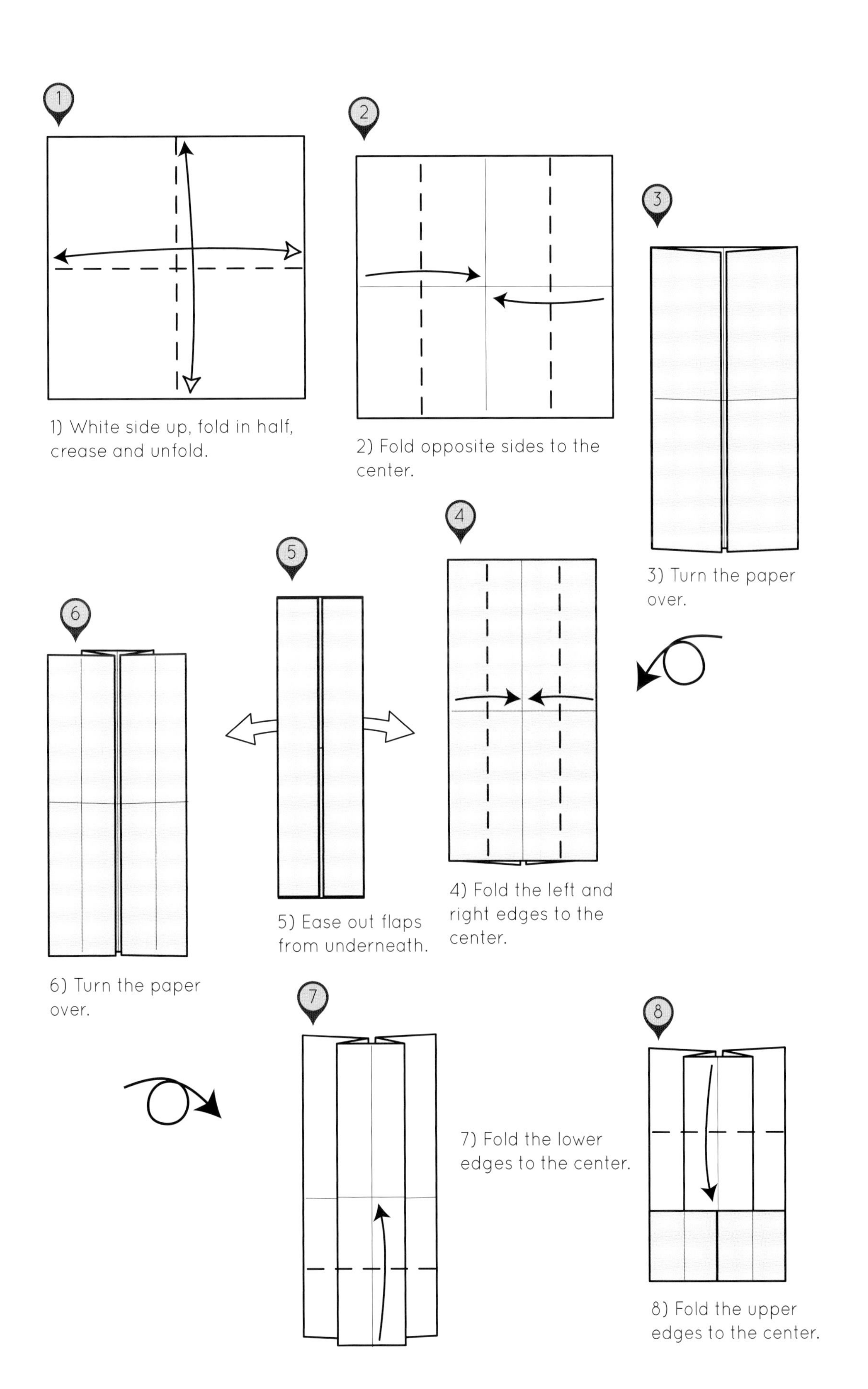

1) White side up, fold in half, crease and unfold.

2) Fold opposite sides to the center.

3) Turn the paper over.

4) Fold the left and right edges to the center.

5) Ease out flaps from underneath.

6) Turn the paper over.

7) Fold the lower edges to the center.

8) Fold the upper edges to the center.

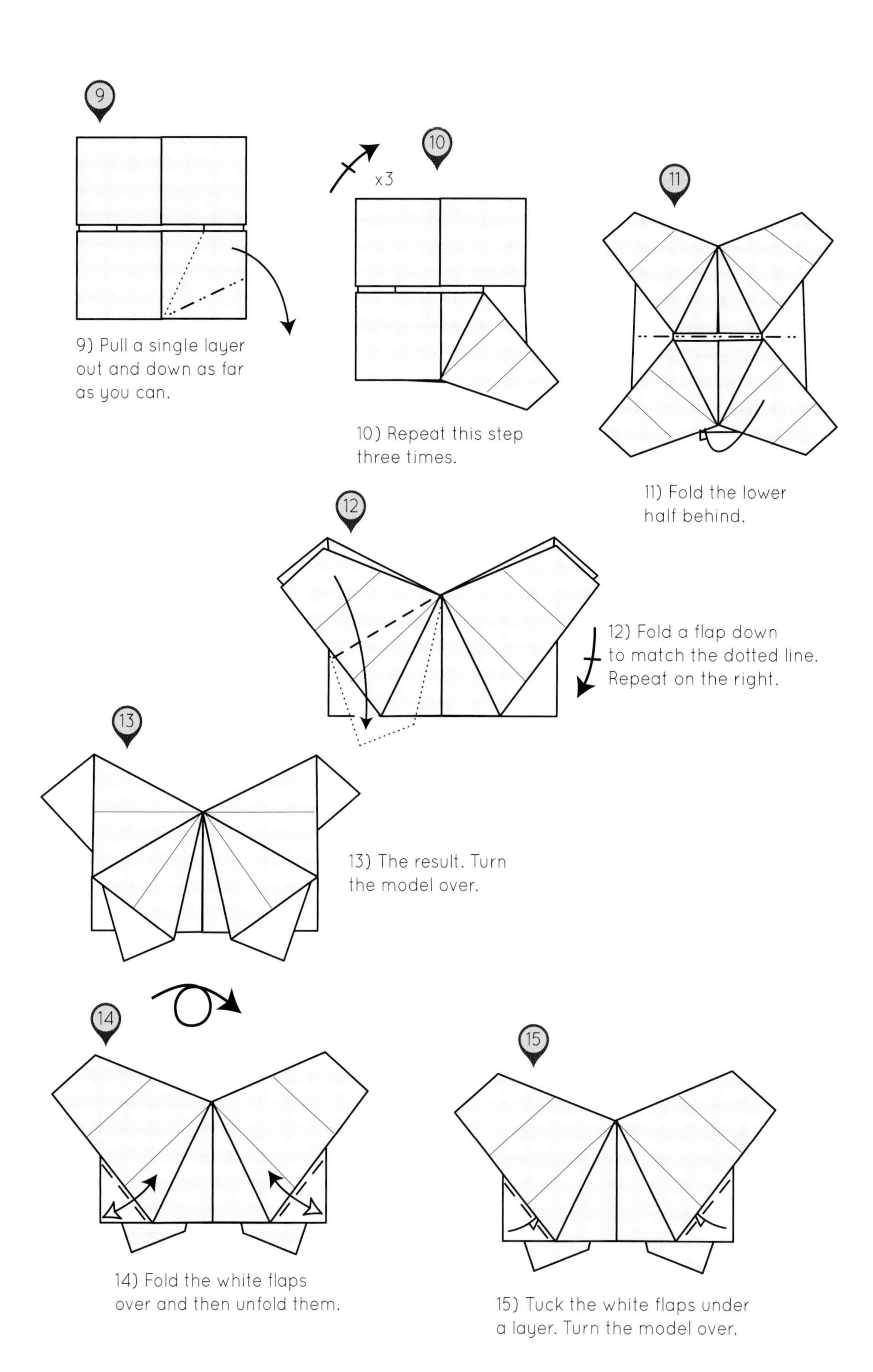

9) Pull a single layer out and down as far as you can.

10) Repeat this step three times.

11) Fold the lower half behind.

12) Fold a flap down to match the dotted line. Repeat on the right.

13) The result. Turn the model over.

14) Fold the white flaps over and then unfold them.

15) Tuck the white flaps under a layer. Turn the model over.

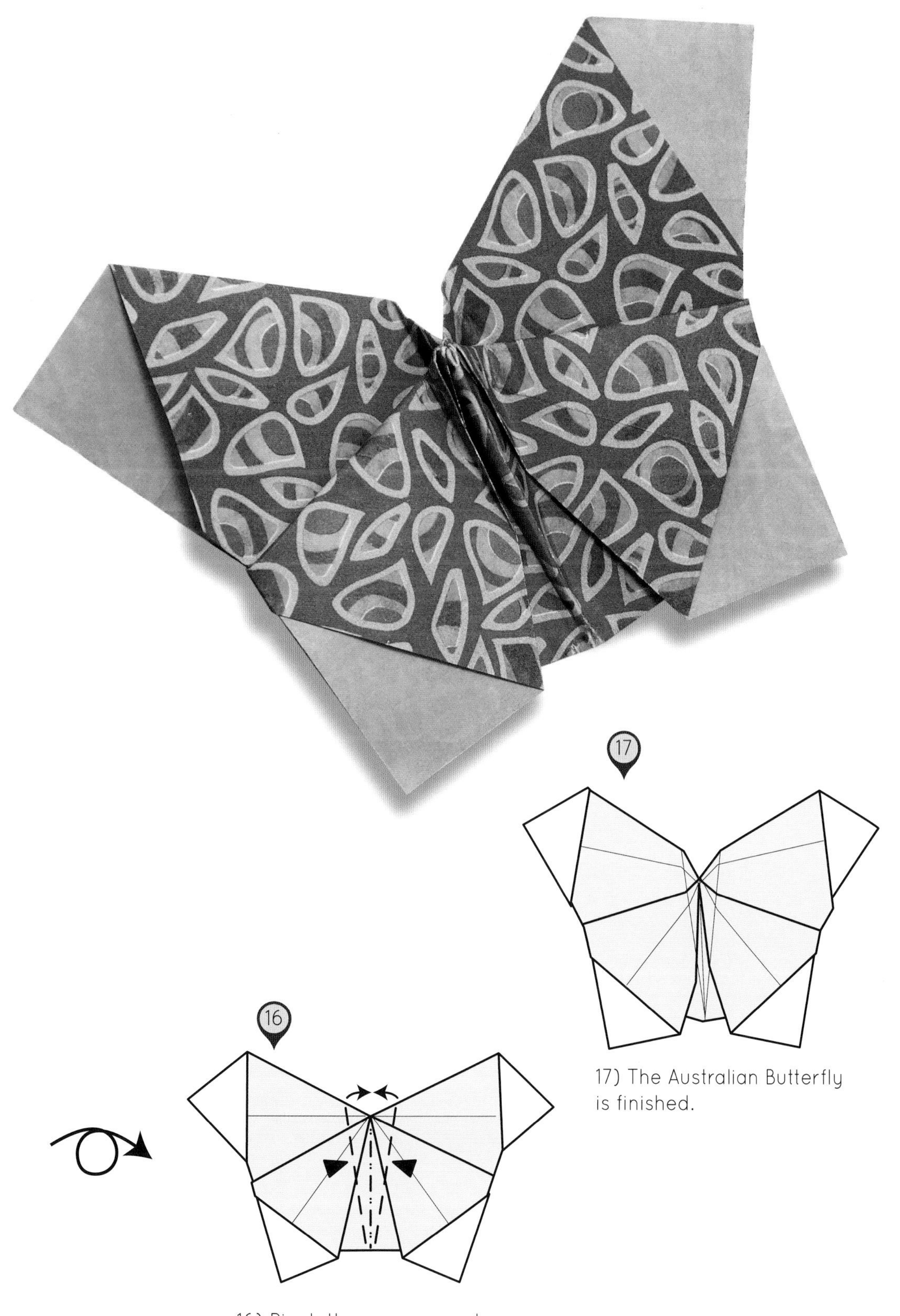

17) The Australian Butterfly is finished.

16) Pinch these creases at the center to form the body.

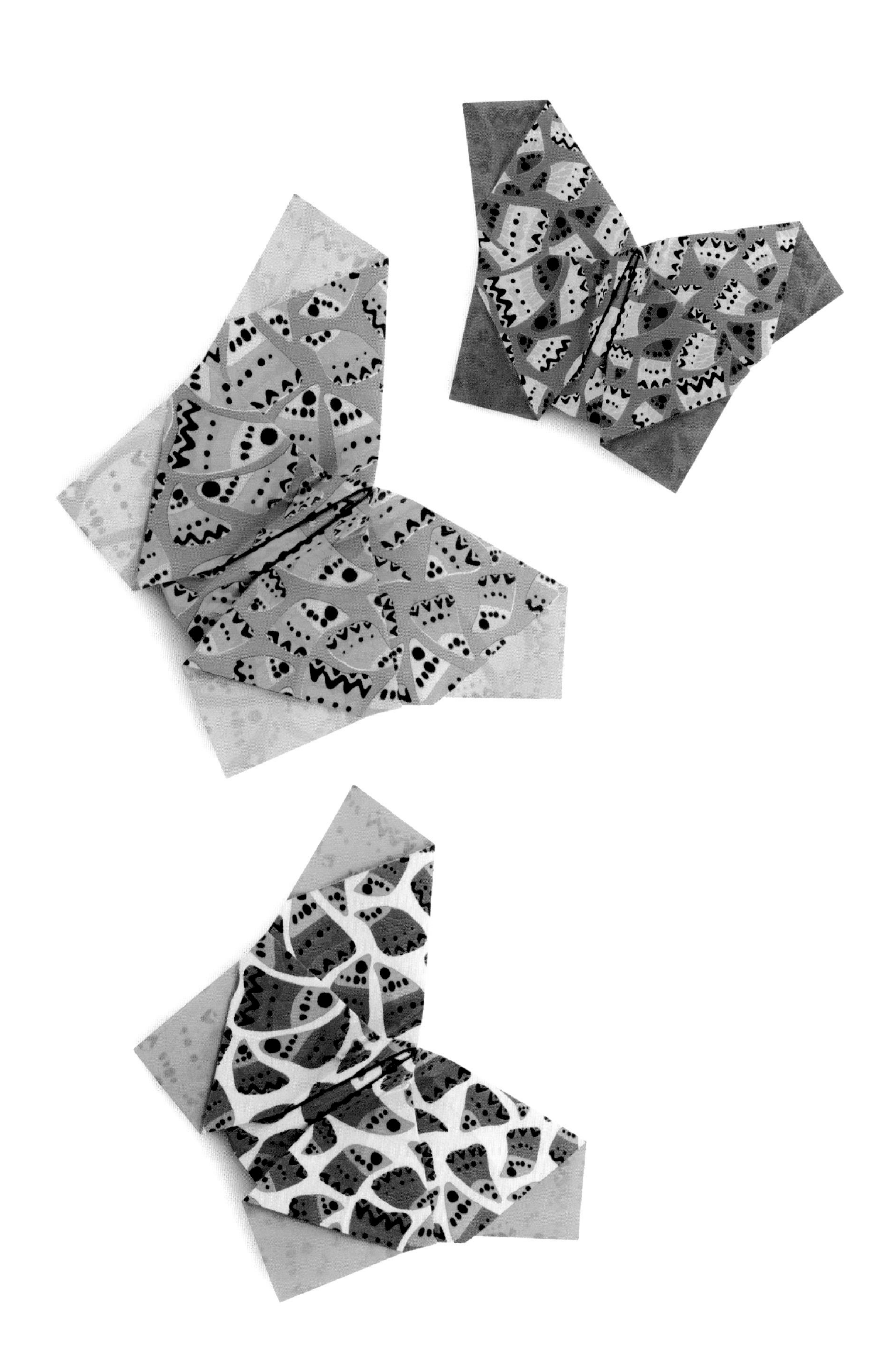

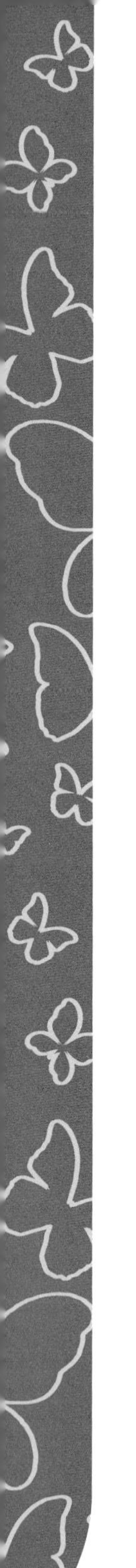

VIDEO
www.nuinui.ch/video/it/m19/farfalle/p52

Donahue's Butterfly

David Donahue

A simple, elegant design that allows for many variations in wing and body shapes.

Size of the sheet: 7 x 7 in

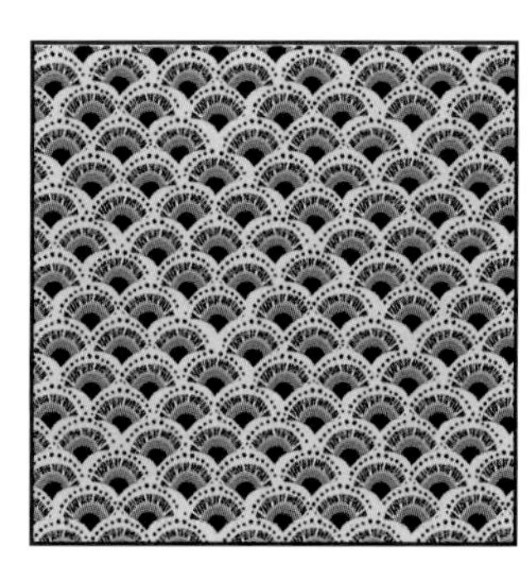

Paper

Relationship between the paper and the origami

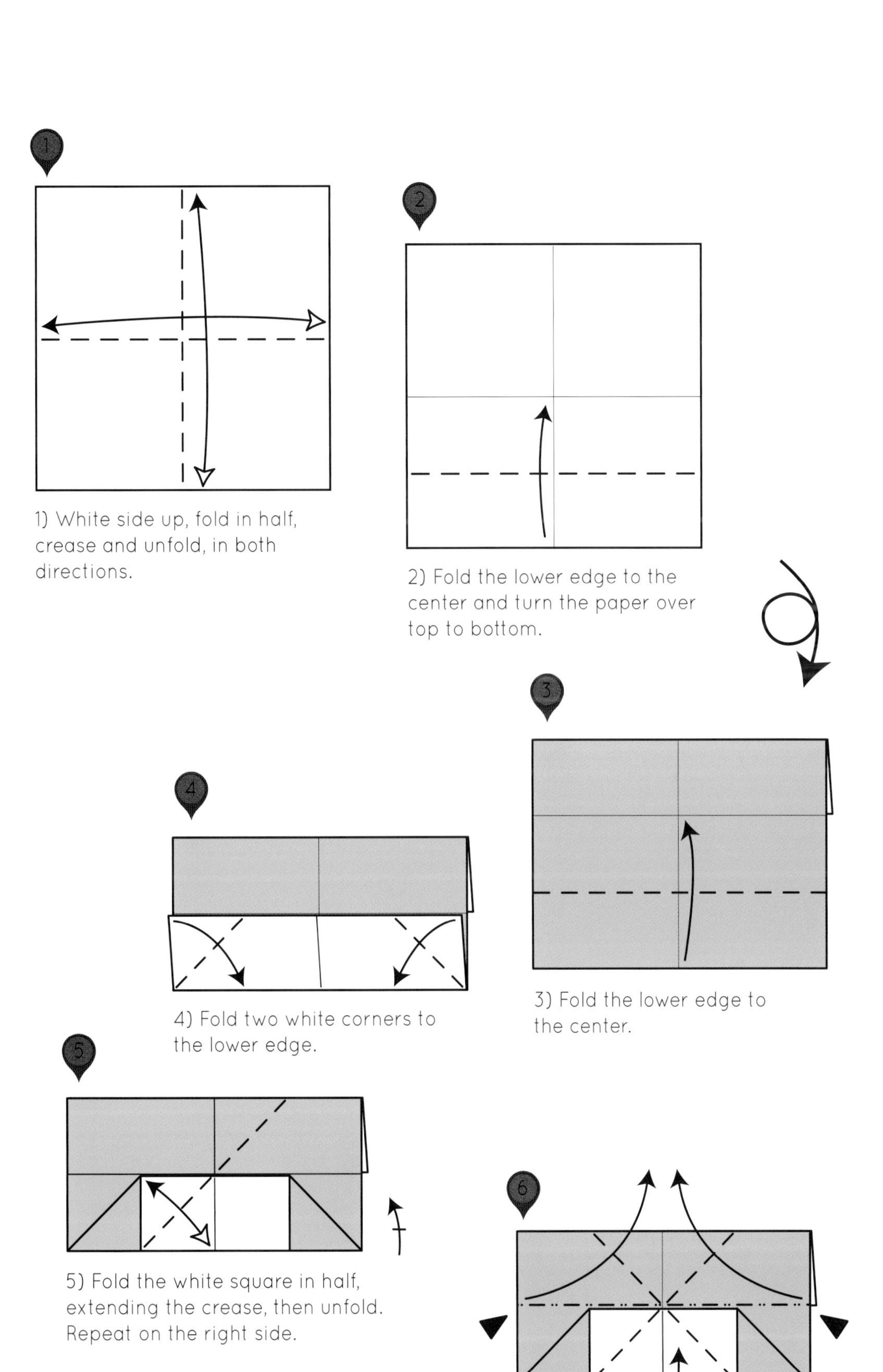

1) White side up, fold in half, crease and unfold, in both directions.

2) Fold the lower edge to the center and turn the paper over top to bottom.

3) Fold the lower edge to the center.

4) Fold two white corners to the lower edge.

5) Fold the white square in half, extending the crease, then unfold. Repeat on the right side.

6) Use these creases to fold the short edges upward.

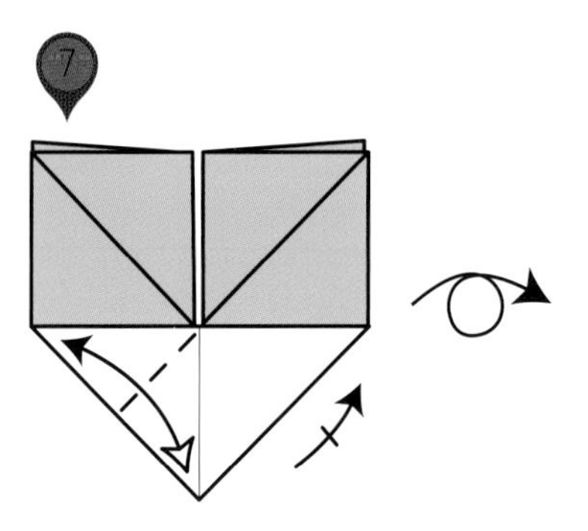

7) Crease and unfold.
Repeat on the right.
Turn the paper over.

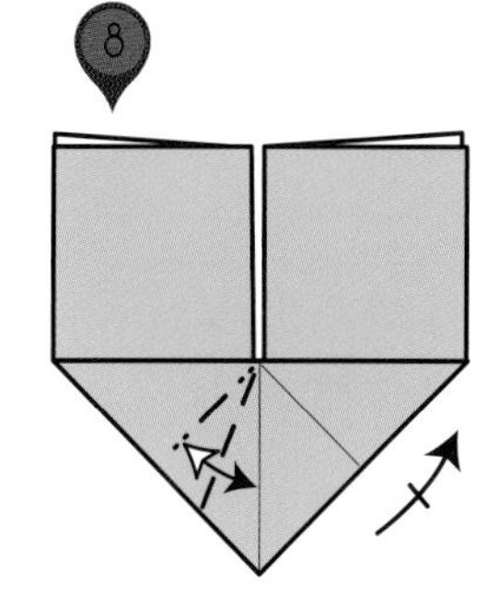

8) Crease and unfold.
Repeat on the right.
Turn the paper over.

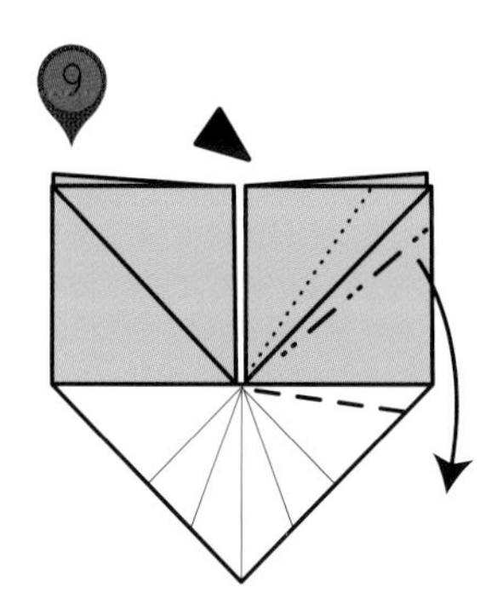

9) Form the valley fold, and flatten the mountain crease in place. The dotted line is a hidden mountain fold.

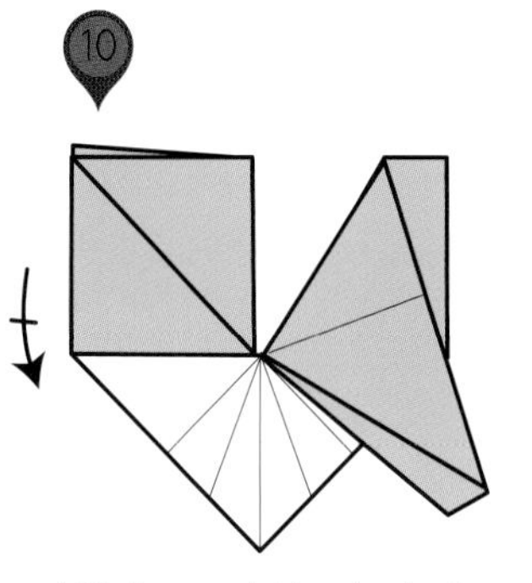

10) Repeat the last step on the left.

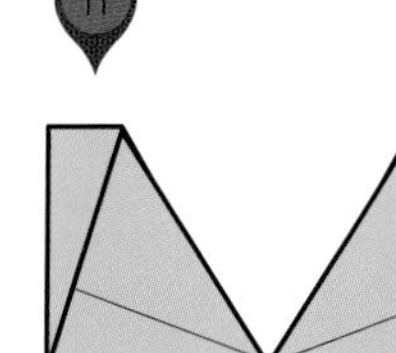

11) Put in existing creases.

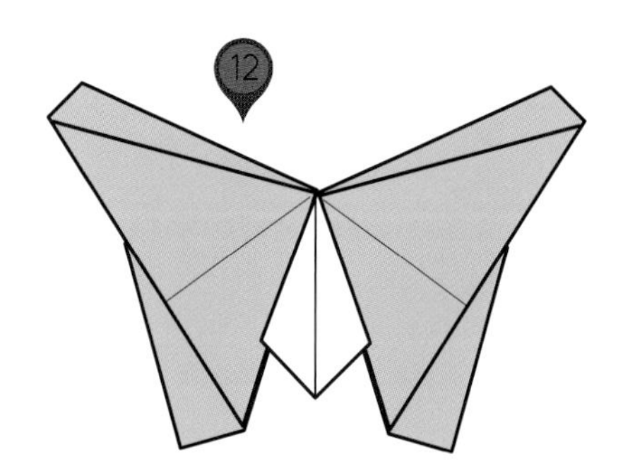

12) The Donahue's Butterfly is finished.

VIDEO
www.nuinui.ch/video/it/m19/farfalle/p56

Meadow Brown

Wayne Brown

A masterpiece of simplicity that truly captures the ephemeral nature of this beautiful insect.

Size of the sheet: 7 x 7 in

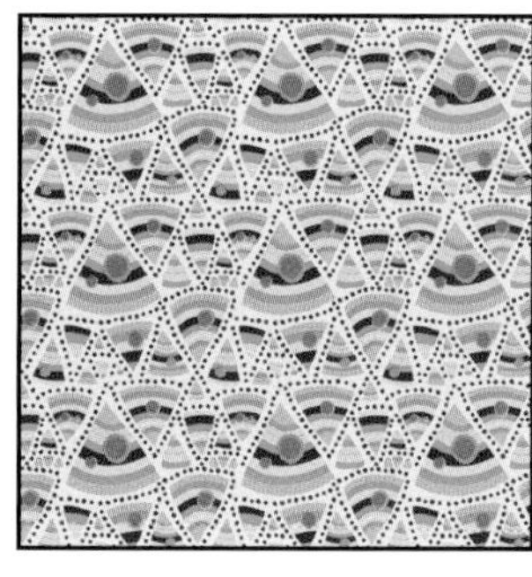

Paper

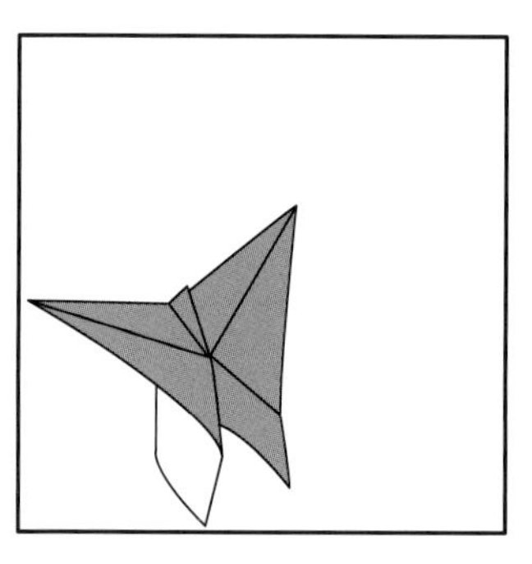

Relationship between the paper and the origami

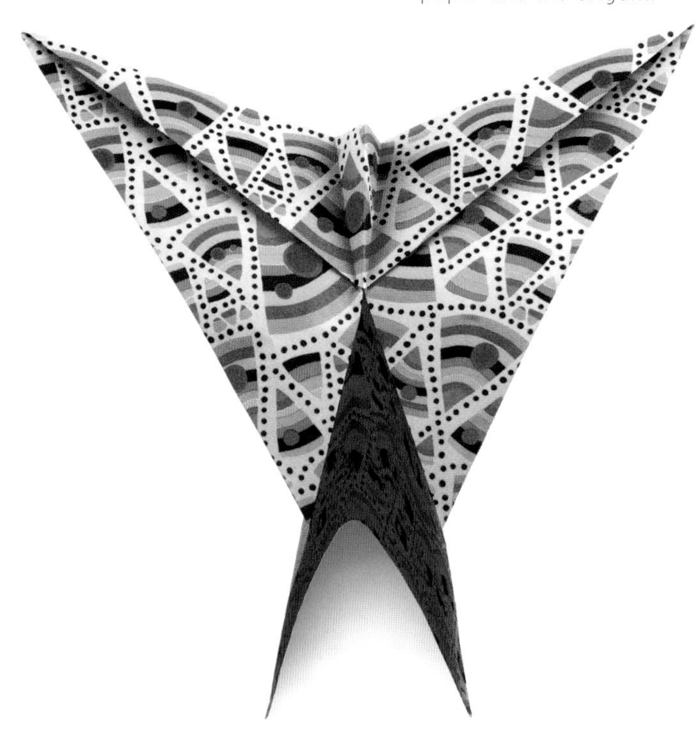

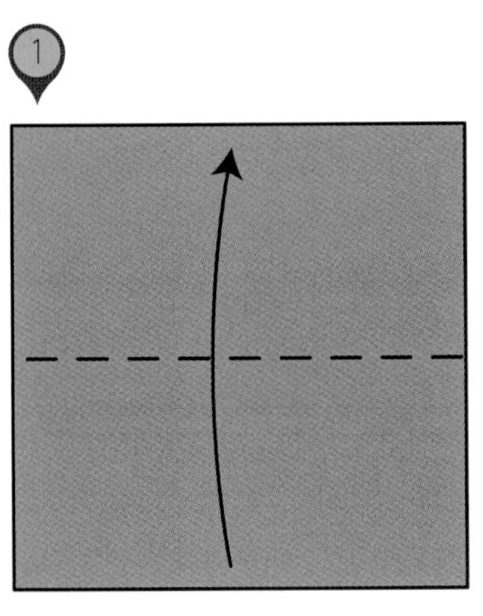

1) Colored side upward, fold in half upward.

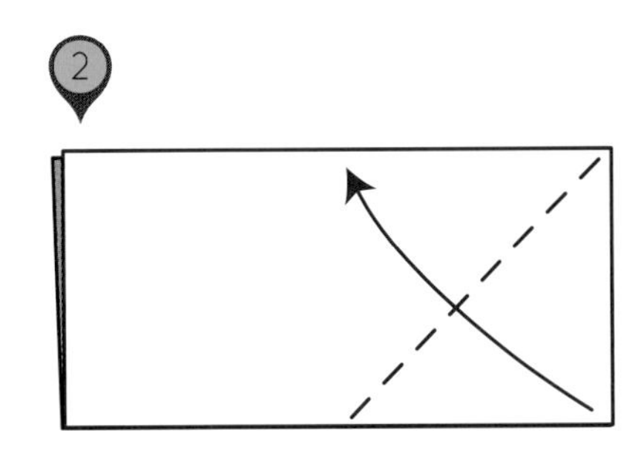

2) Fold the lower right corner to lie on the upper edge.

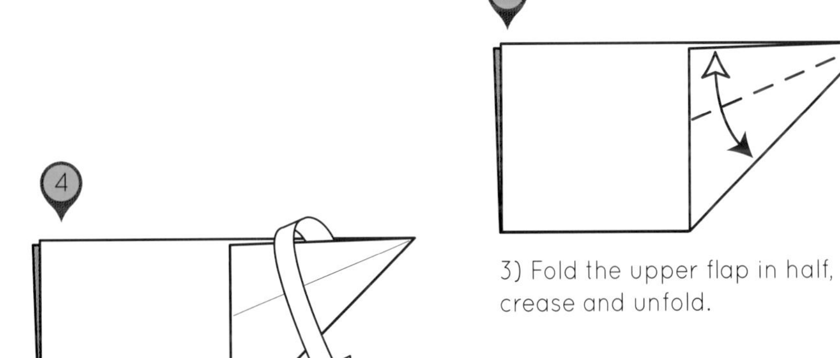

3) Fold the upper flap in half, crease and unfold.

4) Unfold the upper flap.

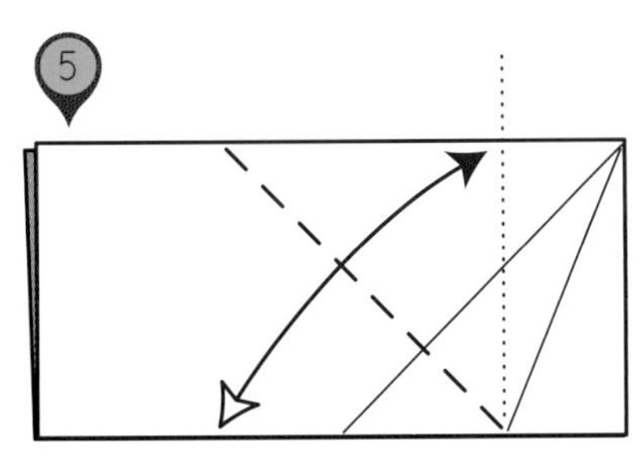

5) Fold to the dotted line, crease and unfold.

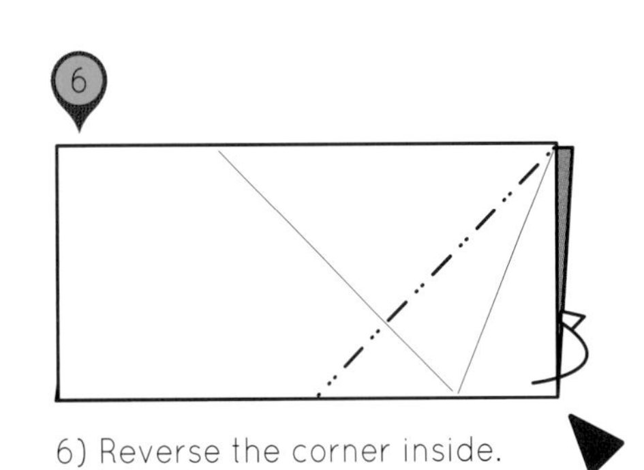

6) Reverse the corner inside.

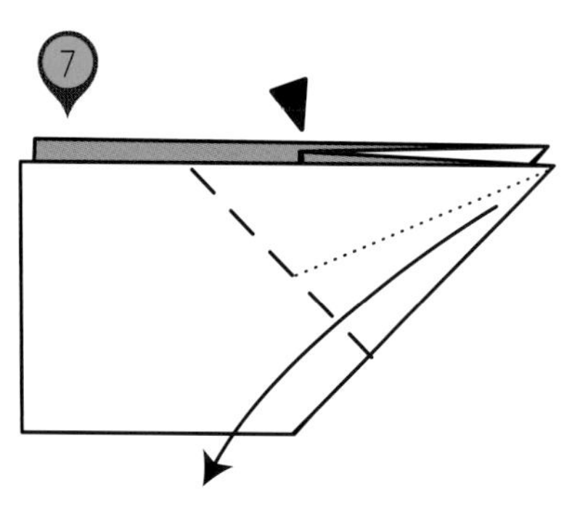

7) Fold one point down, flattening the inside flap.

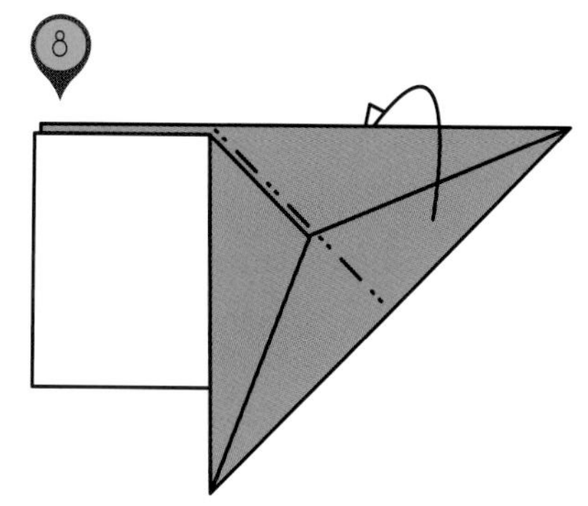

8) Fold half of the flap behind. Rotate the model.

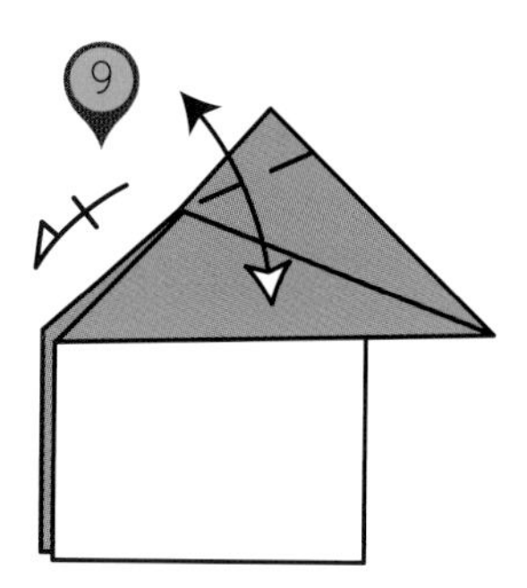

9) Carefully fold the blue flap upward, flattening on the crease, then unfolding. Repeat underneath.

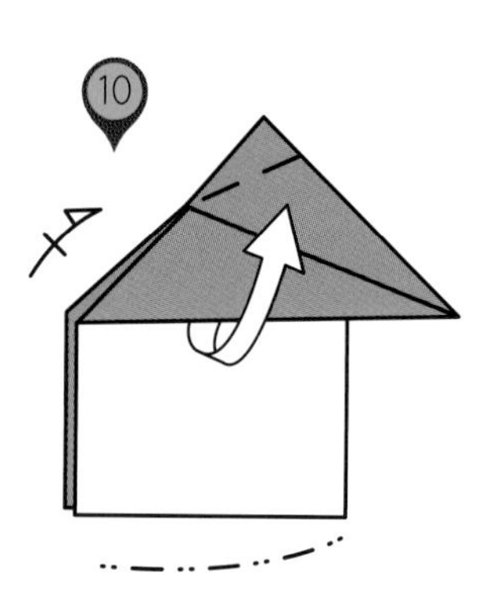

10) Open out the sides and form the body with valley creases on either side.

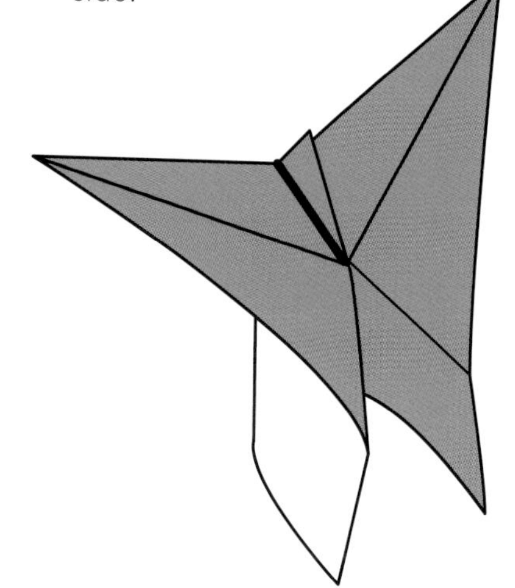

Moth Silhouette

Thea Anning

The basic proportions of this model can be altered to produce many variations.

Size of the sheet: 7 x 7 in

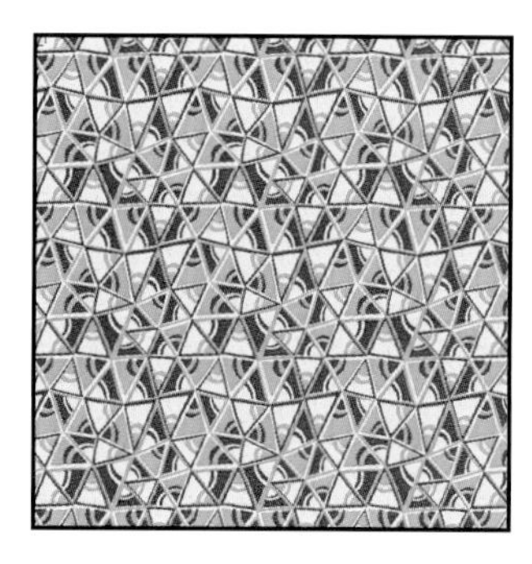

Paper

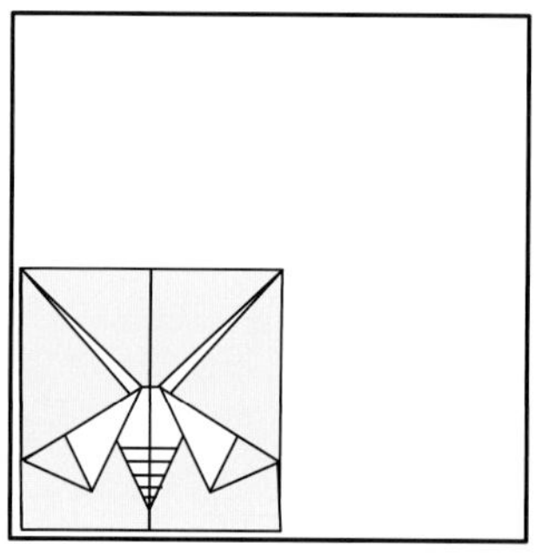

Relationship between the paper and the origami

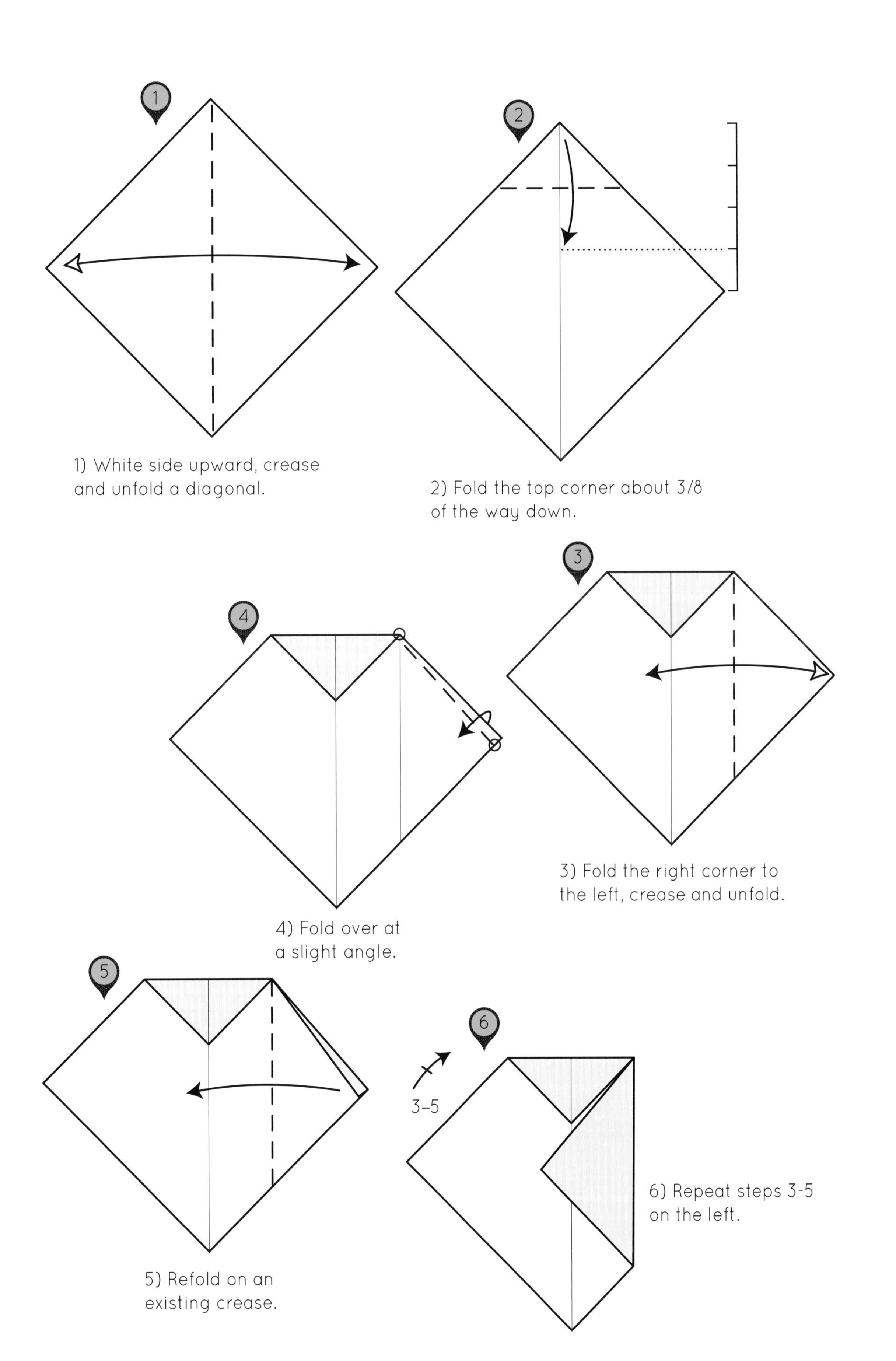

1) White side upward, crease and unfold a diagonal.

2) Fold the top corner about 3/8 of the way down.

3) Fold the right corner to the left, crease and unfold.

4) Fold over at a slight angle.

5) Refold on an existing crease.

6) Repeat steps 3-5 on the left.

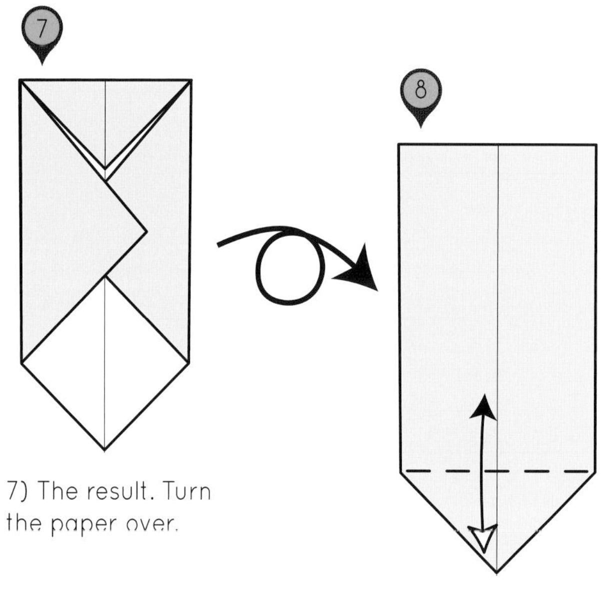

7) The result. Turn the paper over.

8) Crease and unfold where shown.

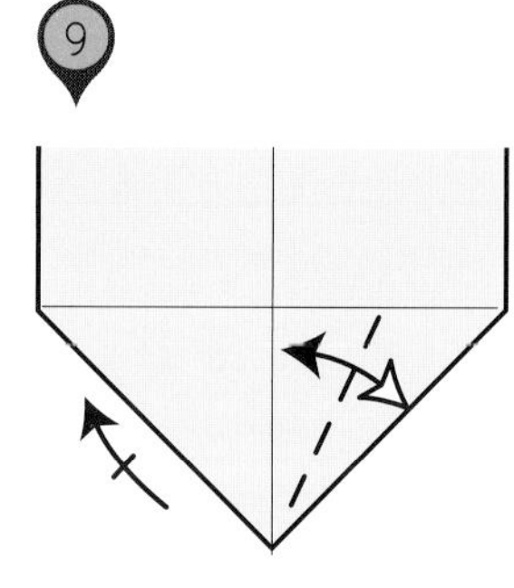

9) Crease and unfold. Repeat on the left.

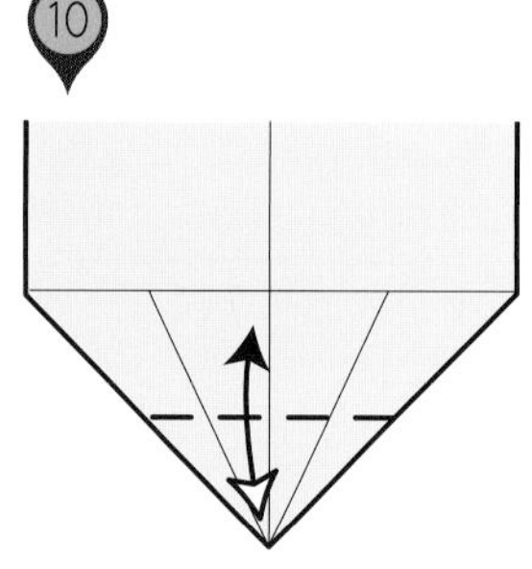

10) Fold the triangular flap in half, then unfold.

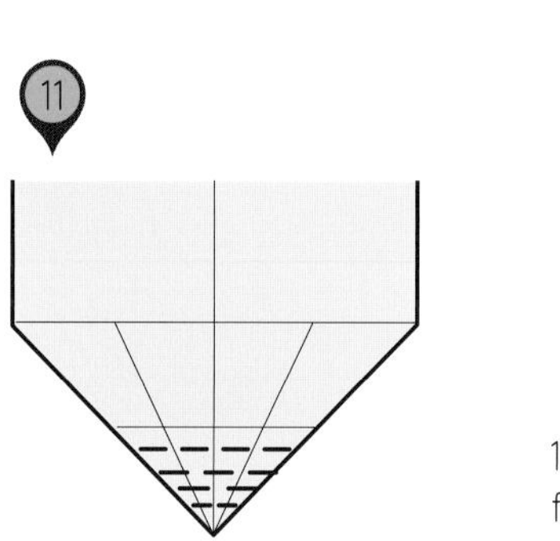

11) Add more creases.

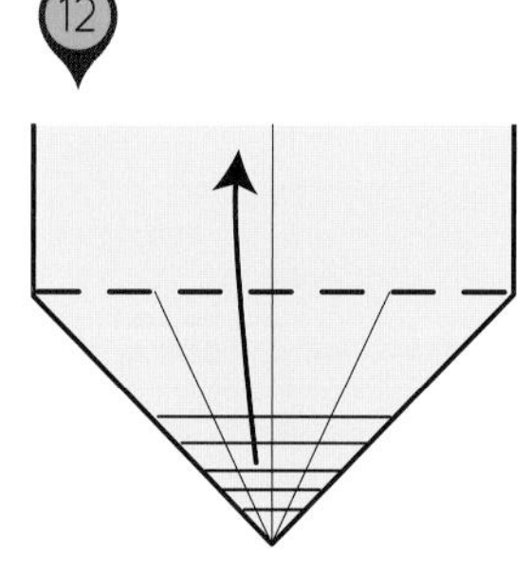

12) Fold up on an existing crease and turn the paper over.

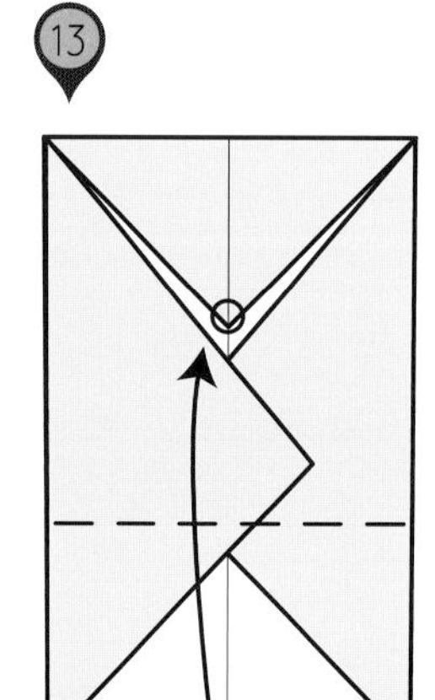

13) Fold so the lower edge lies slightly above the circled corner.

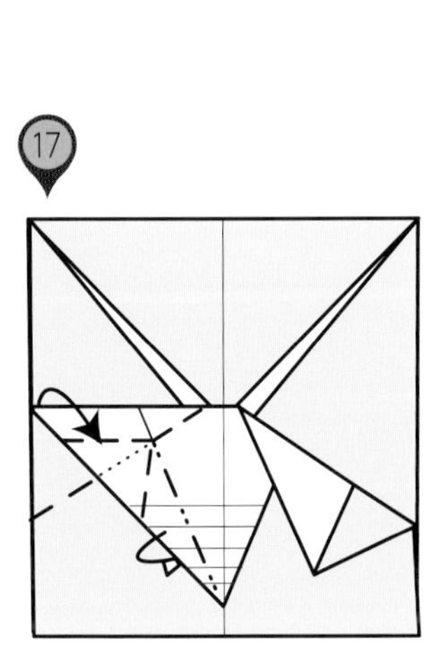

17) Repeat on the left.

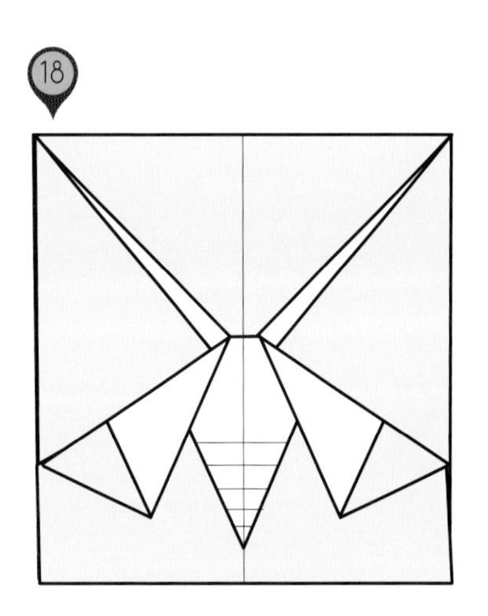

18) The Moth Silhouette is finished.

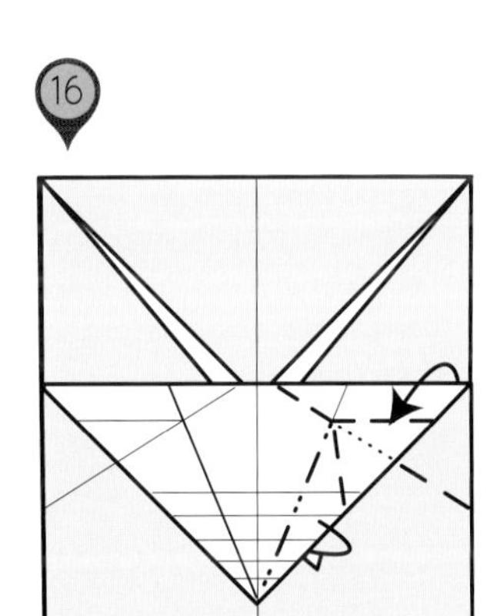

16) Take a deep breath! Fold the upper right corner down; at the same time, wrap the lower white edge underneath. A new small valley crease is formed as you flatten the paper.

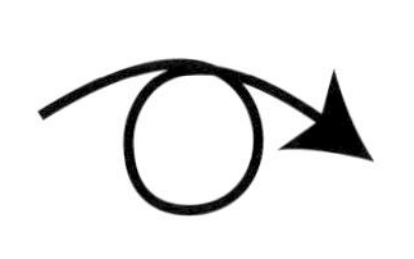

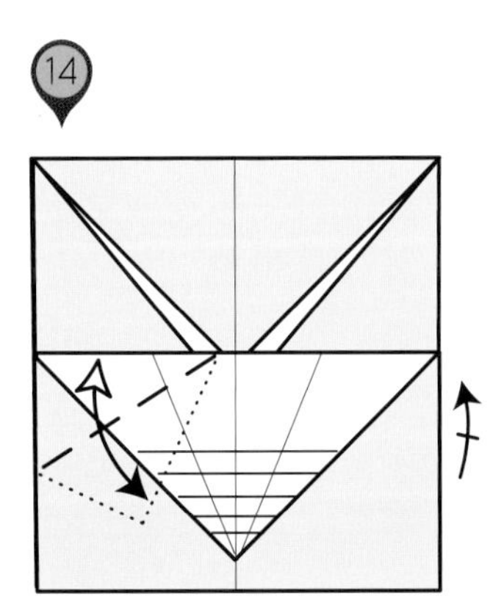

14) Fold to the dotted line, crease and unfold. Repeat on the right.

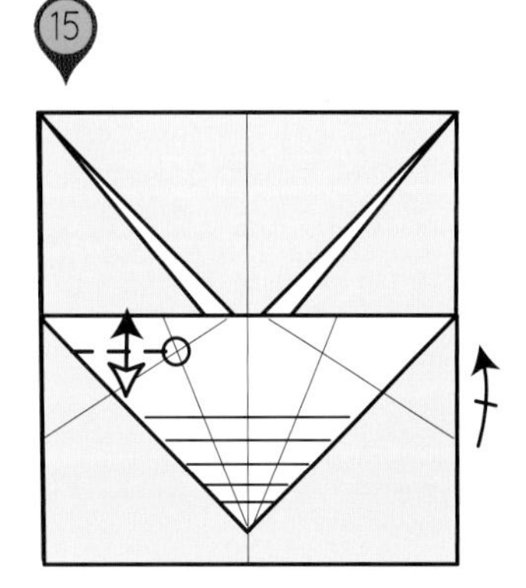

15) Make a horizontal crease starting at the circled point. Repeat on the right.

Other possibilities—
please experiment!

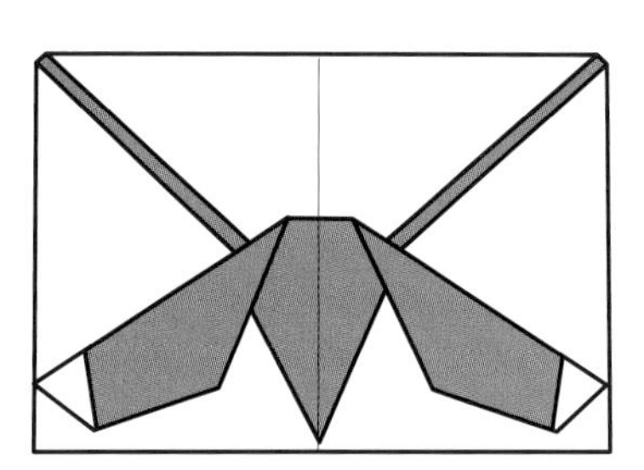

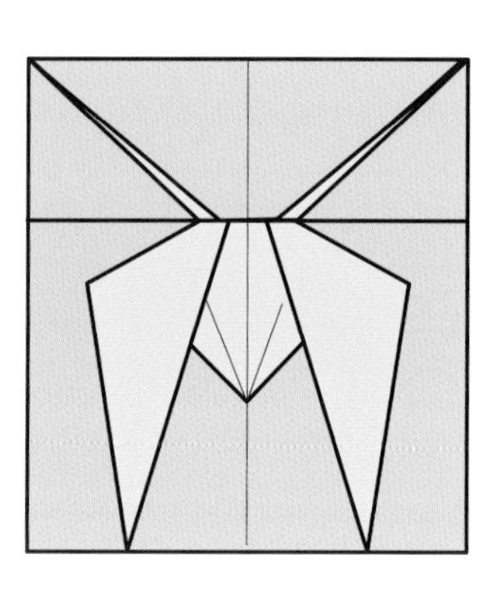

Daisy Butterfly

Nick Robinson

This design uses colors on both sides of the sheet of paper.
Try making the folds in step 3 larger or smaller
and see how the result changes.

Size of the sheet: 7 x 7 in

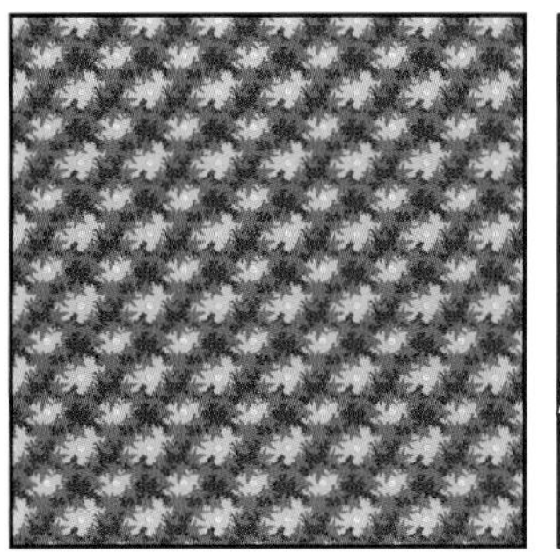

Paper

Relationship between the paper and the origami

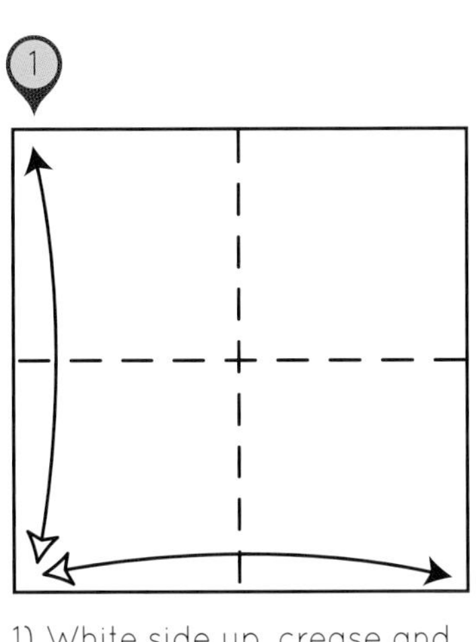

1) White side up, crease and unfold in half both ways.

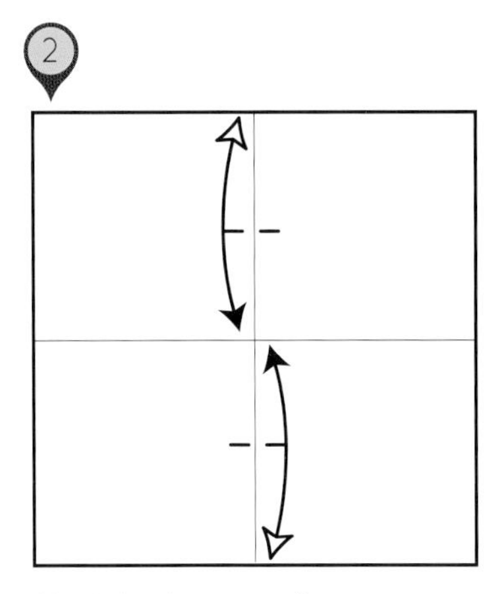

2) Make two small pinches.

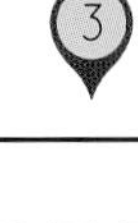

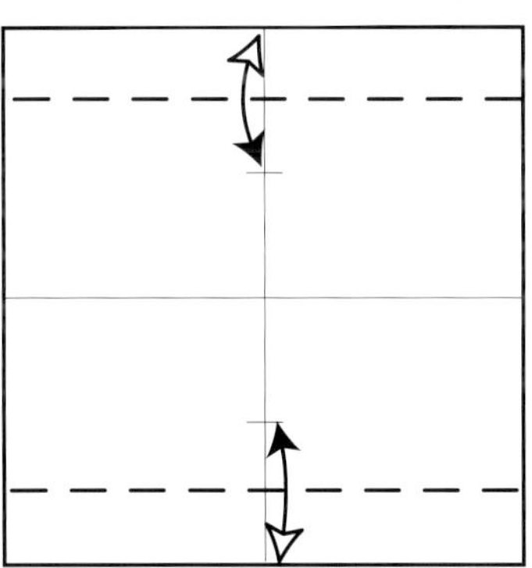

3) Fold upper and lower edges to the pinch marks; crease and unfold.

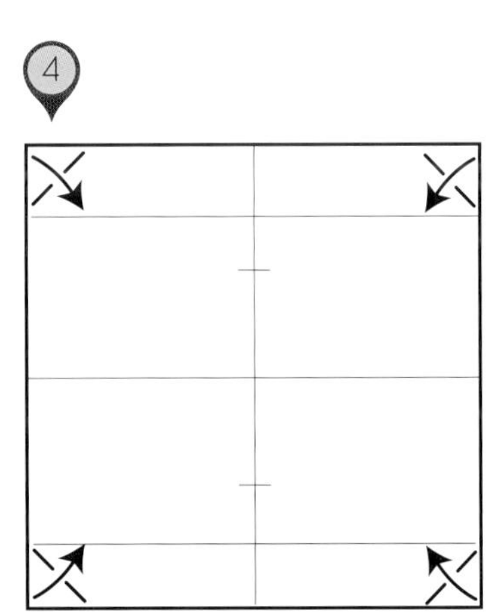

4) Fold the corners to lie on the creases.

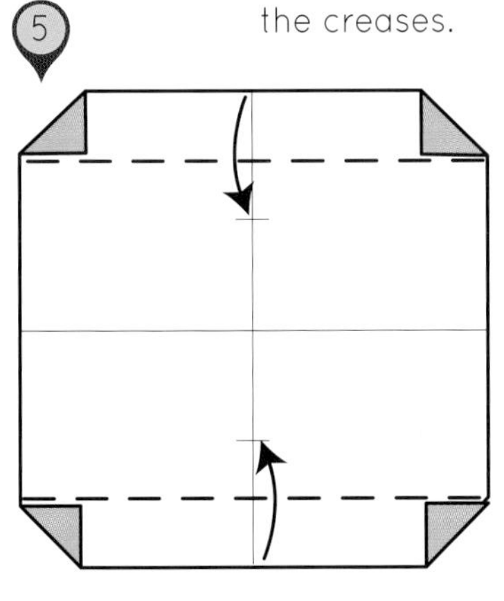

5) Refold inward on existing creases.

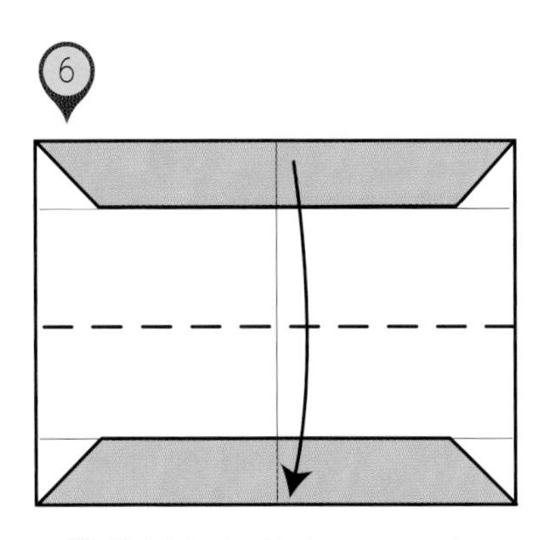

6) Fold in half downward.

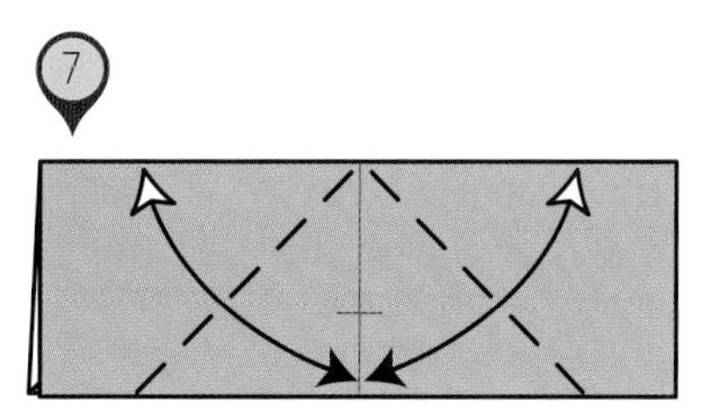

7) Fold each half of the upper edge to the vertical center; crease and unfold.

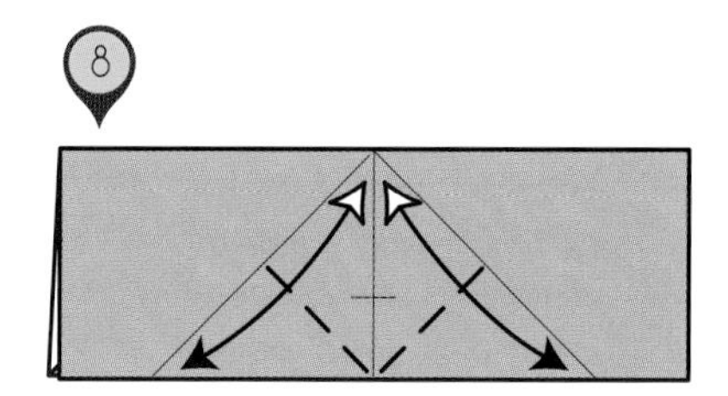

8) Make two precreases where shown, through all layers.

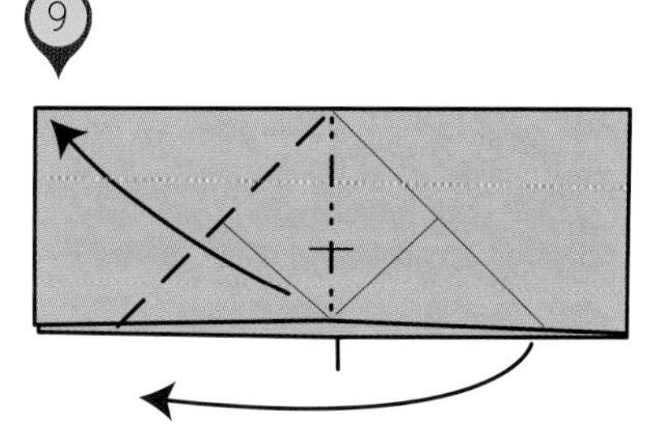

9) Open the layers and squash to the left.

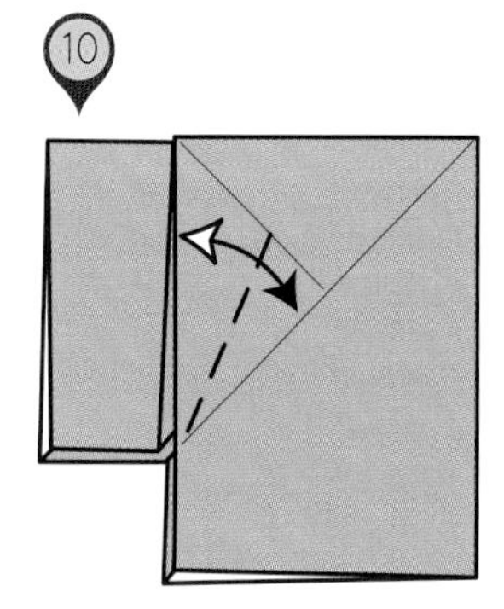

10) Precrease where shown.

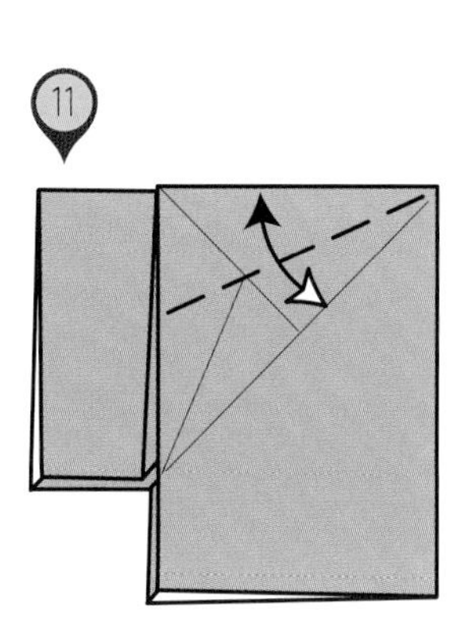

11) Another precrease.

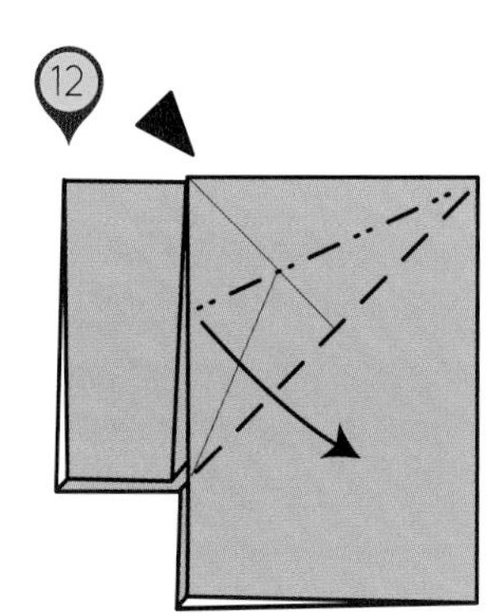

12) Open and squash the flap evenly.

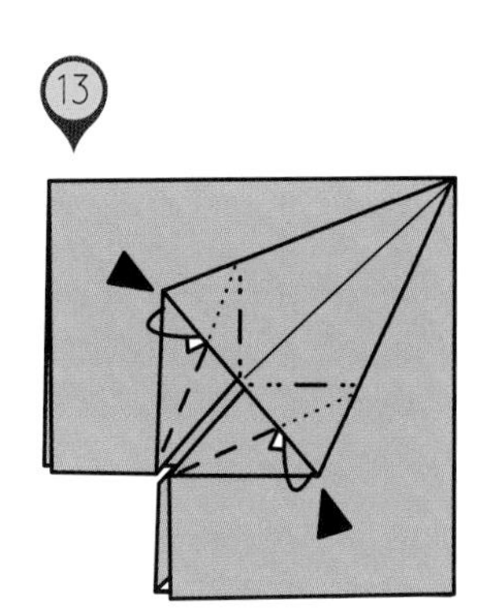

13) Reverse the corners inside.

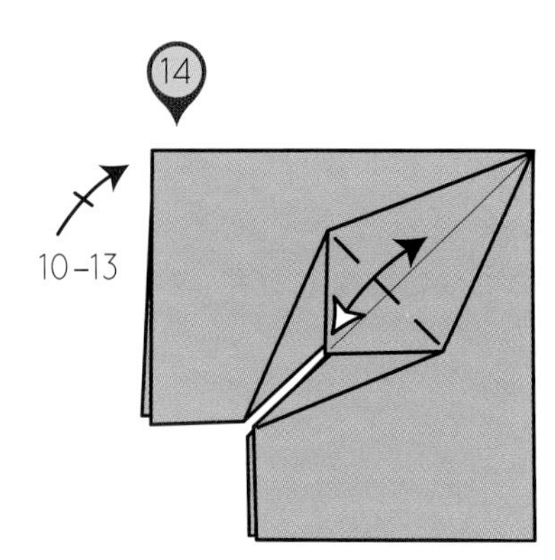

14) Repeat steps 10-13 on the underside. Fold a flap over, crease and unfold.

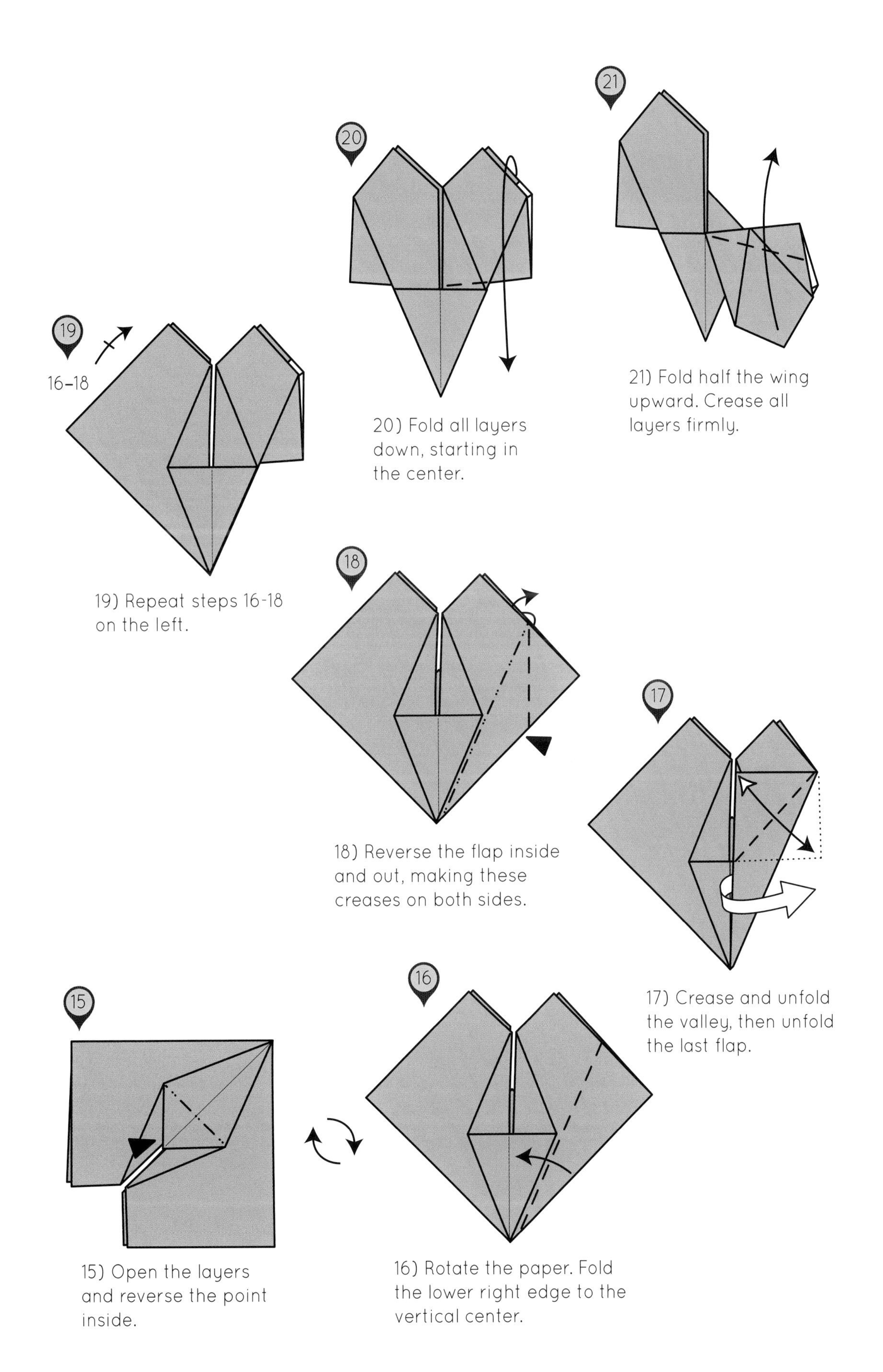

15) Open the layers and reverse the point inside.

16) Rotate the paper. Fold the lower right edge to the vertical center.

17) Crease and unfold the valley, then unfold the last flap.

18) Reverse the flap inside and out, making these creases on both sides.

19) Repeat steps 16-18 on the left.

20) Fold all layers down, starting in the center.

21) Fold half the wing upward. Crease all layers firmly.

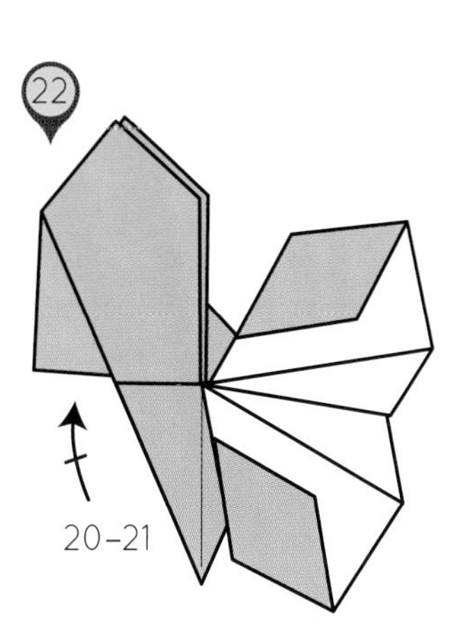

22) Repeat steps 20-21 on the left.

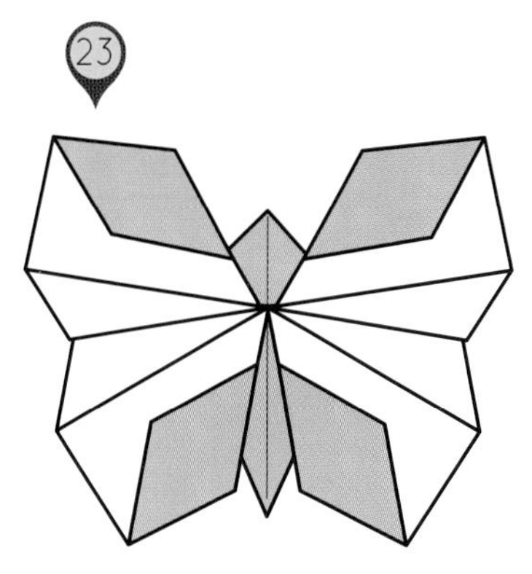

23) The result. Turn the paper over.

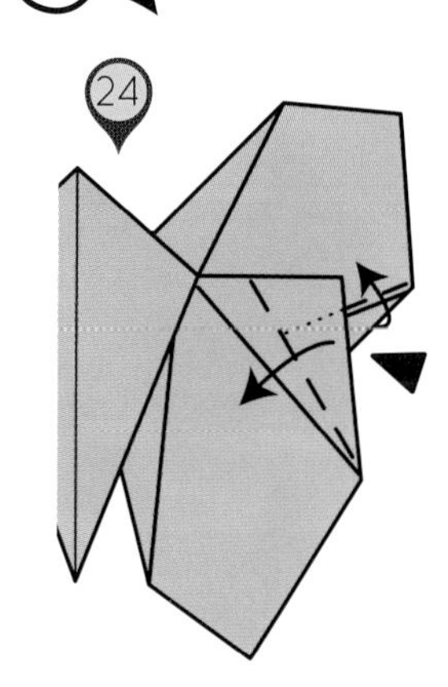

24) Fold the flap inward, making a squash fold underneath.

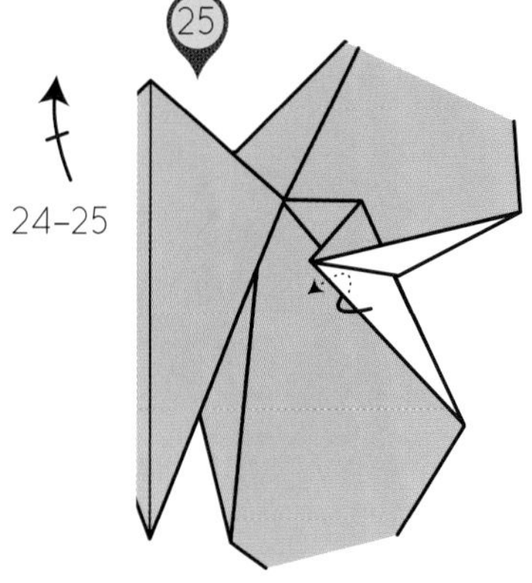

25) Tuck the flap under a layer. Repeat steps 24-25 on the left.

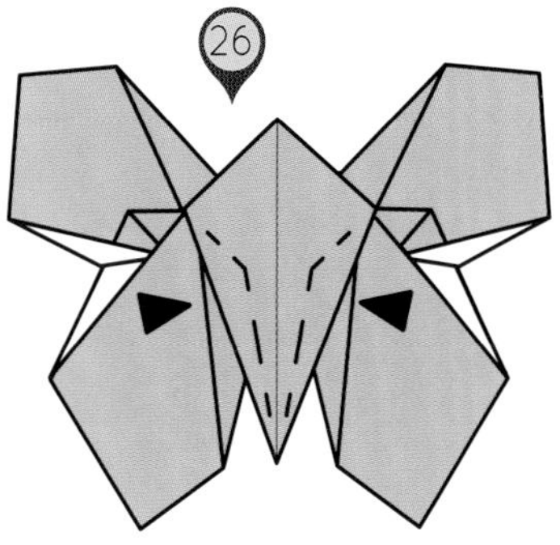

26) Gently shape the body, then turn the model over.

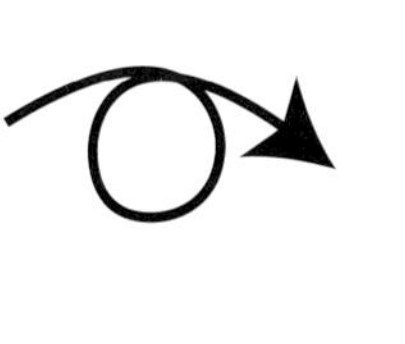

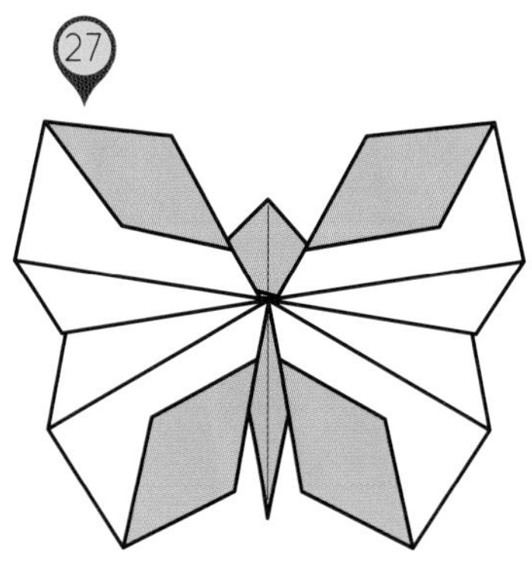

27) The Daisy Butterfly is finished.

Snyder Butterfly

Rob Snyder

A neat, stylized butterfly that needs accurate folding. Try using a similar technique but divide the paper into 6 (or 7, or 9!).

Size of the sheet: 7 x 7 in

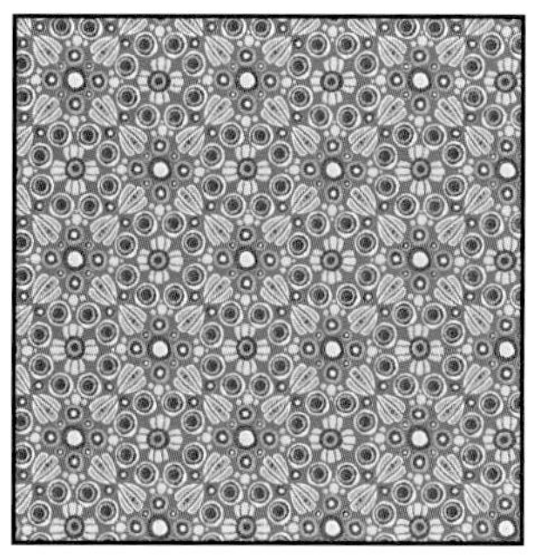

Paper

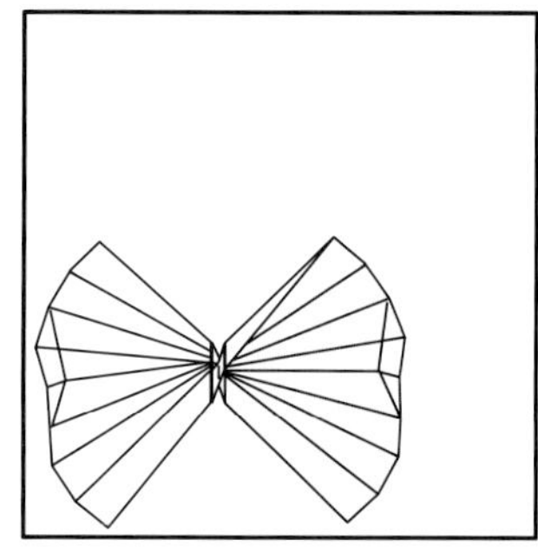

Relationship between the paper and the origami

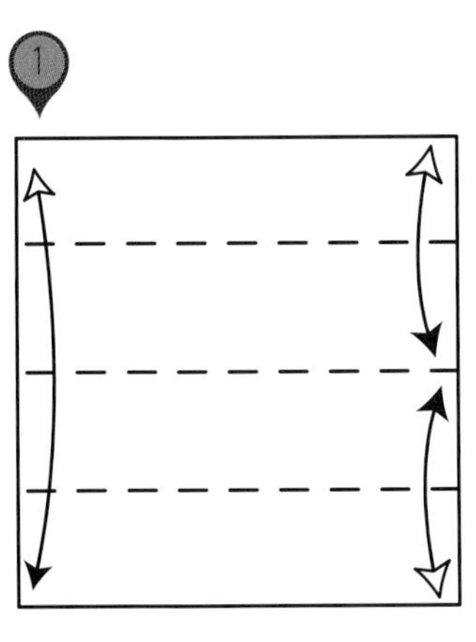

1) Add horizontal halfway and quarter creases.

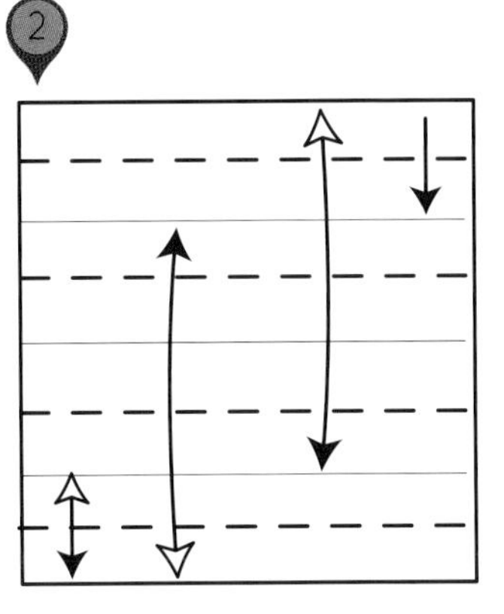

2) Add horizontal eighth creases. Leave the top crease in place.

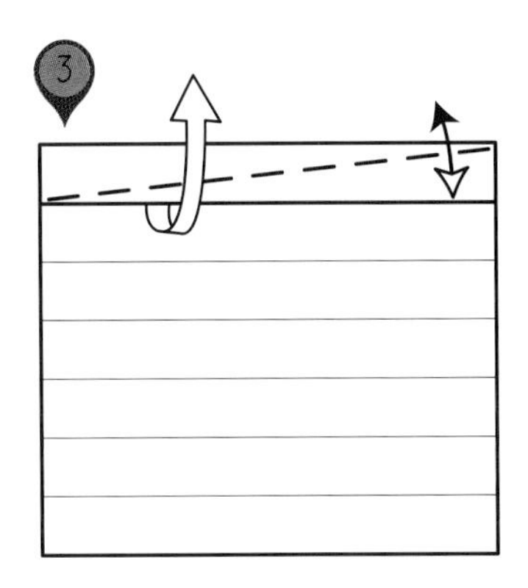

3) Fold the flap up from lower left to top right corner, then unfold.

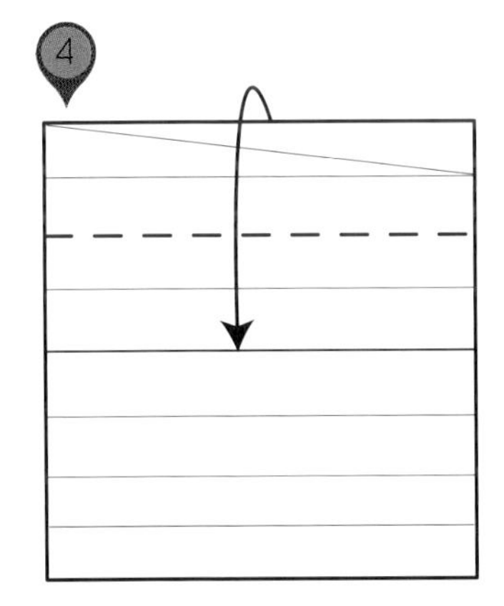

4) Fold down on the quarter crease.

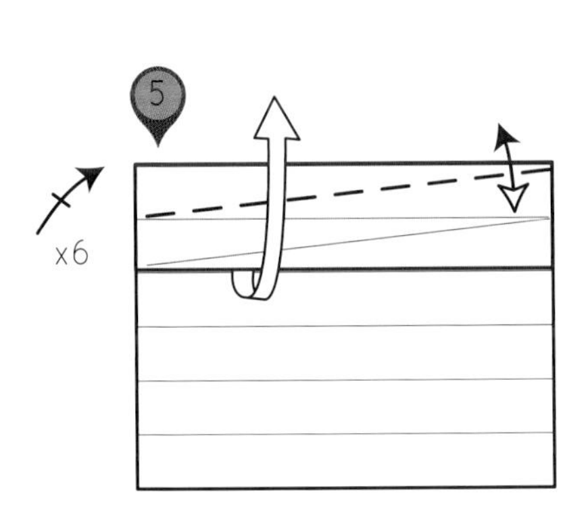

5) Add a similar crease, unfold and repeat 6 more times.

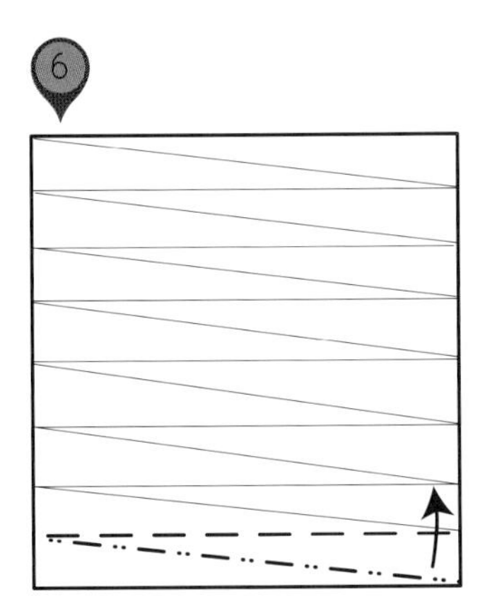

6) Put in the lower pleat.

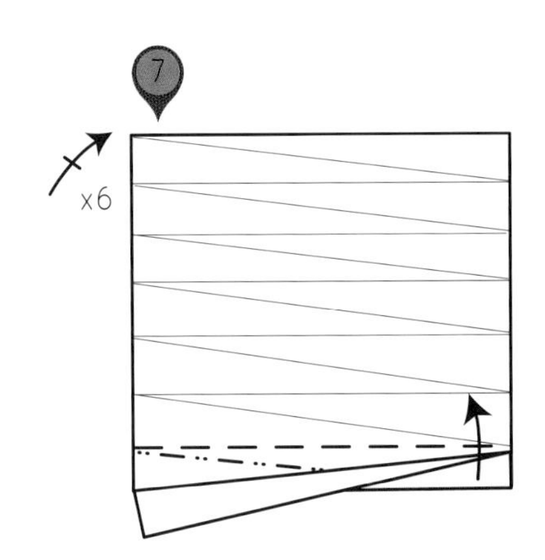

7) Continue all the way to the top.

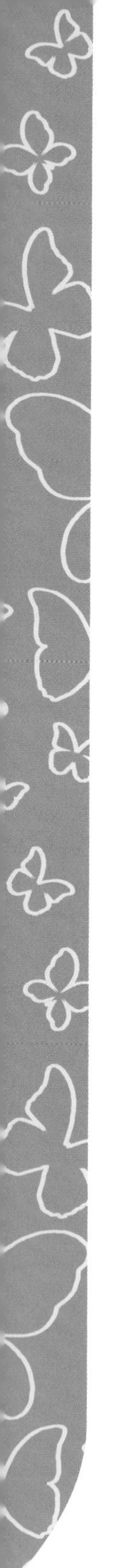

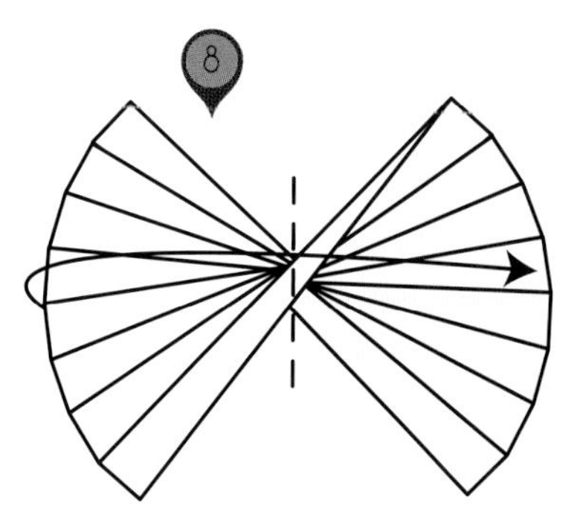

8) Carefully fold in half to the right.

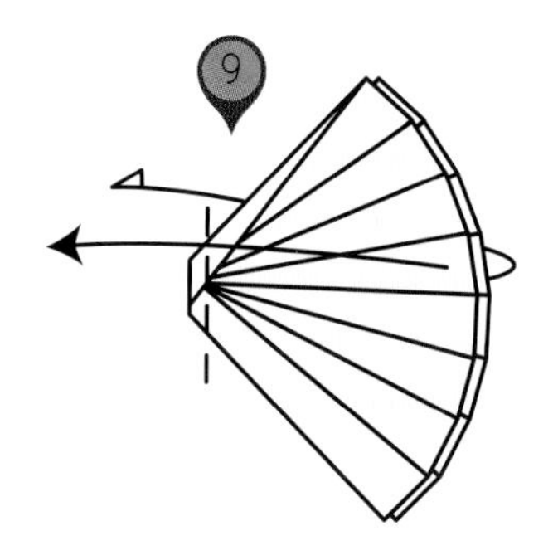

9) Leave a small gap, then fold both wings to the left.

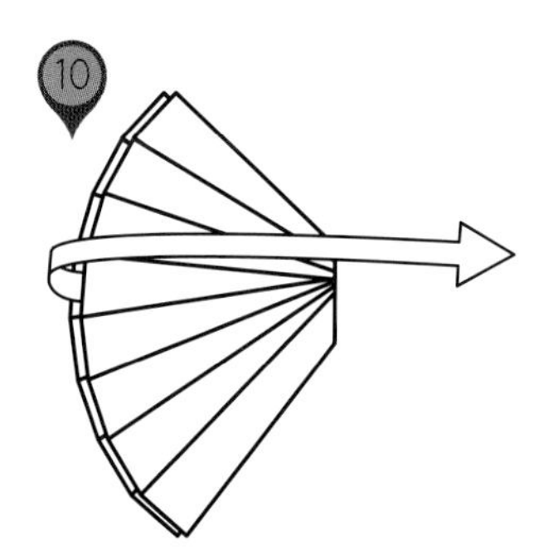

10) Open, but leave the center creases in place.

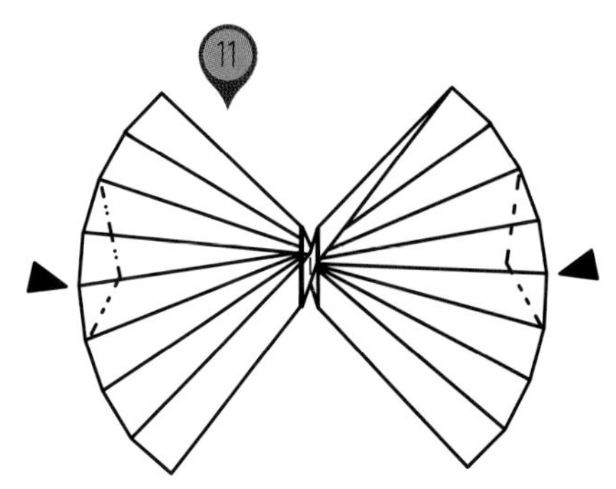

11) Gently pinch in these shaping creases.

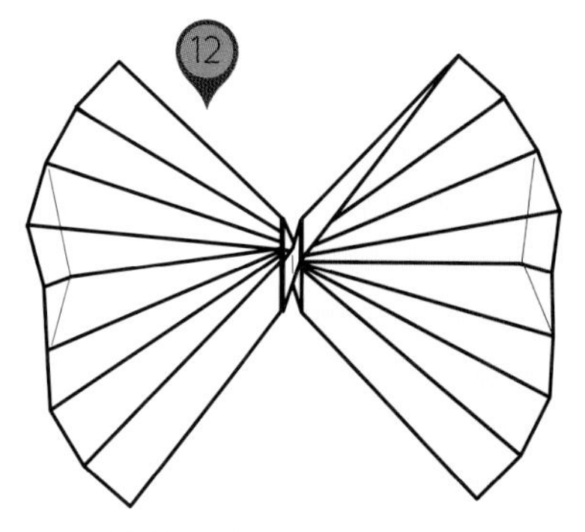

12) The Snyder Butterfly is finished.

Spotted Butterfly

Nick Robinson

This design is based on work by Jean-Pierre Wyseur.
You can make several variations between steps 10 and 12.

Size of the sheet: 7 x 7 in

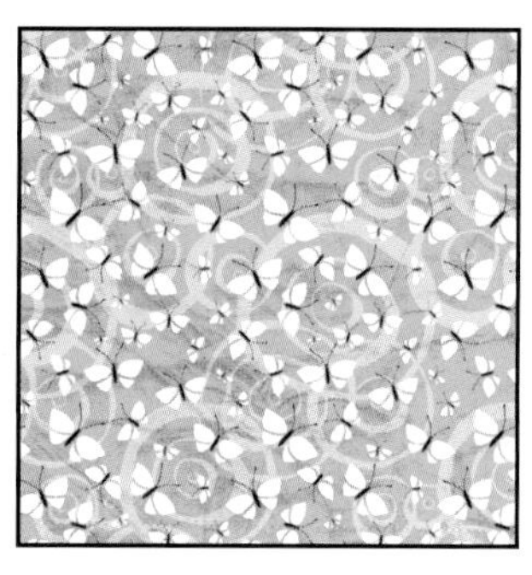

Paper

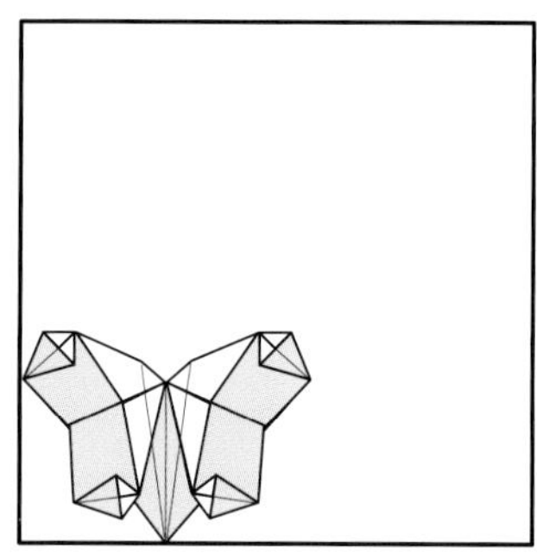

Relationship between the paper and the origami

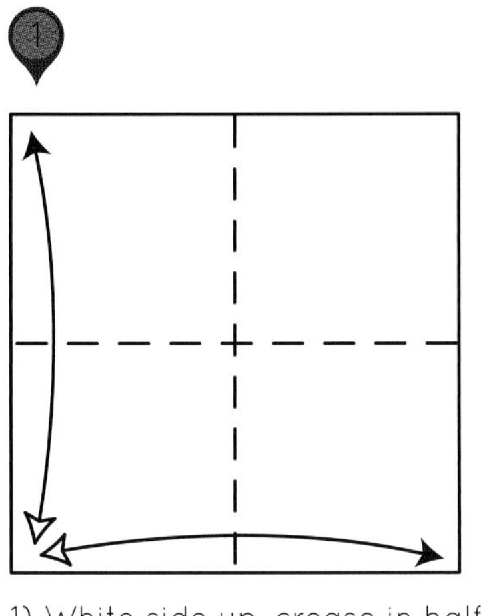

1) White side up, crease in half and unfold both ways.

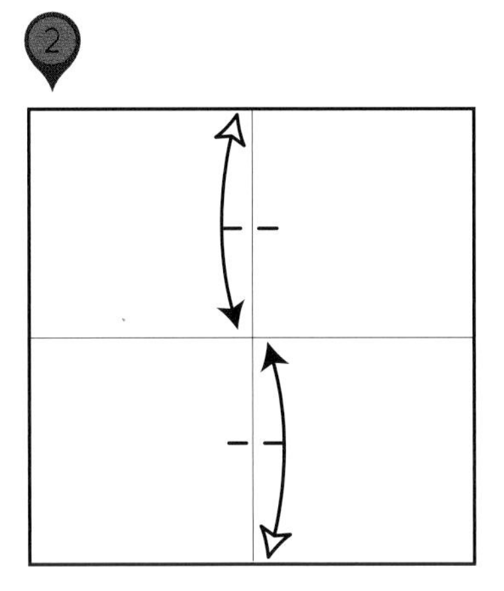

2) Make two small pinches.

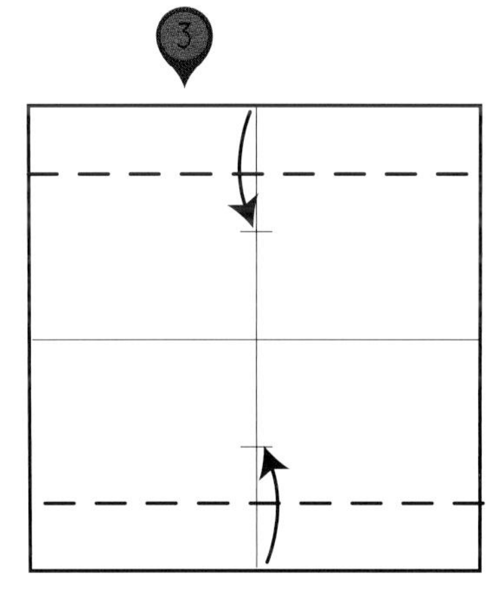

3) Fold upper and lower edges to the pinch marks.

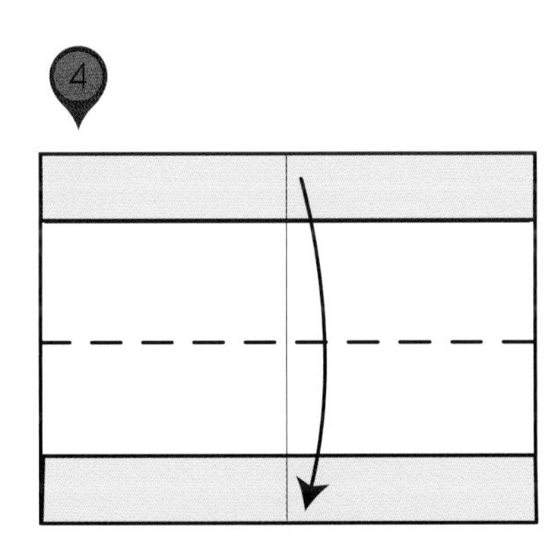

4) Fold in half downward.

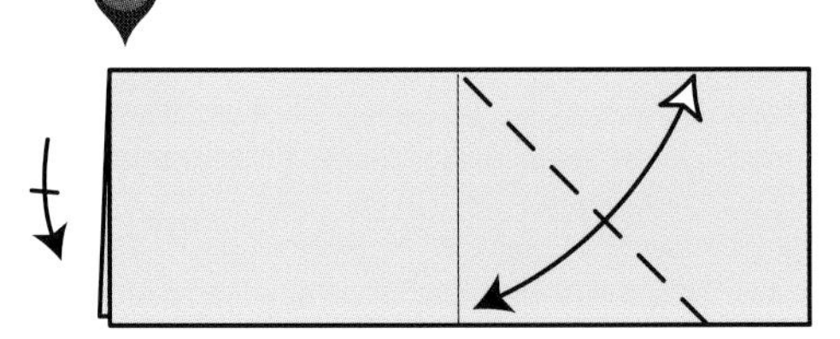

5) Crease and unfold on both sides.

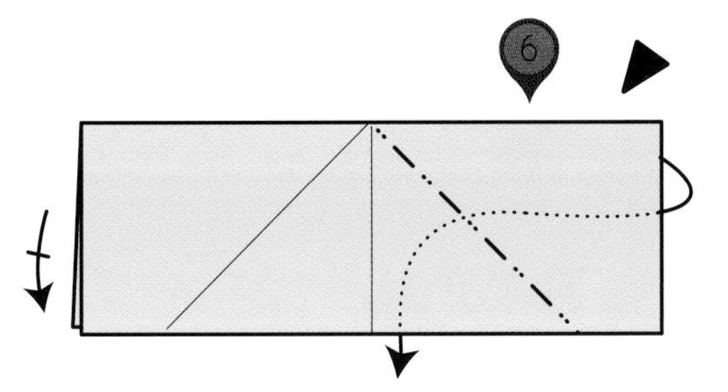

6) Reverse both upper corners inside.

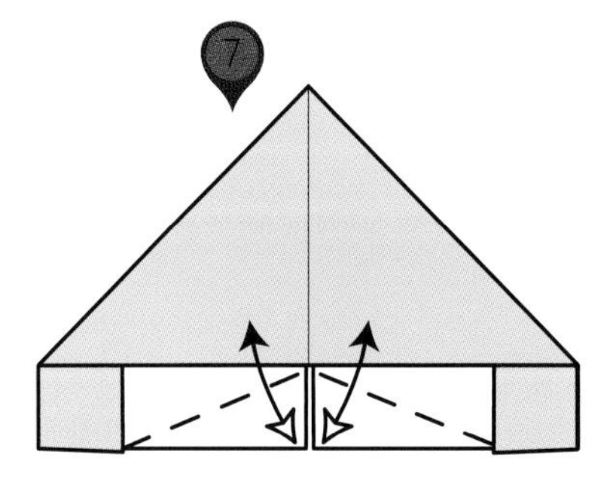

7) Crease firmly and unfold both sides.

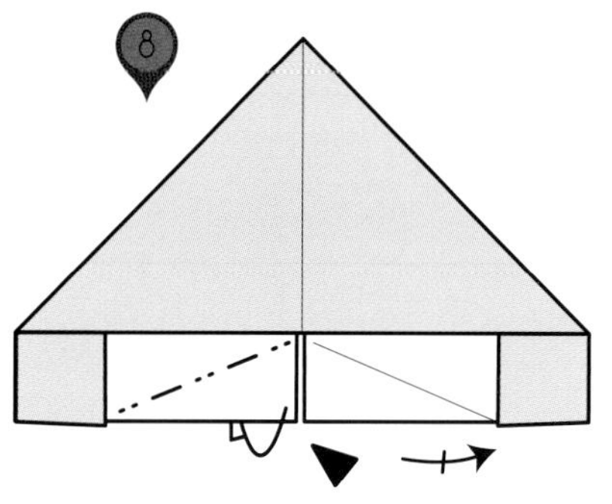

8) Reverse the left white corner inside the layers. Repeat on the right. Rotate the paper 180 degrees.

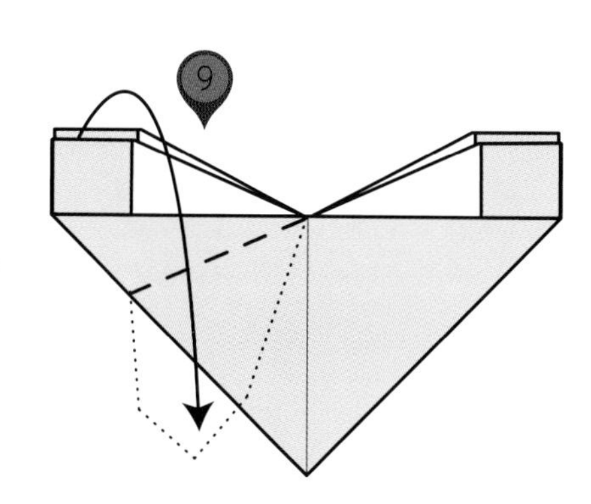

9) Fold one wing down to match the dotted line.

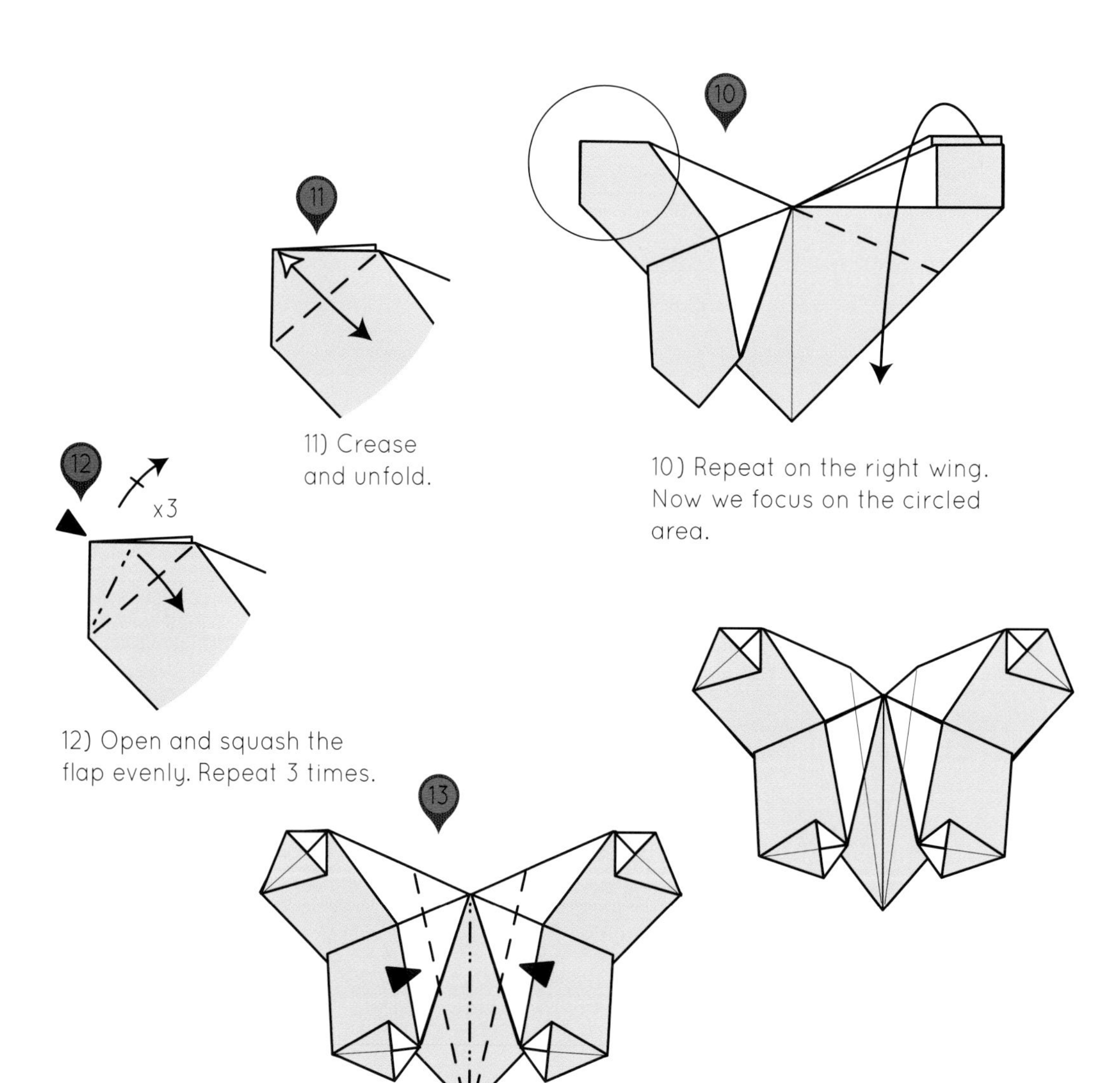

10) Repeat on the right wing. Now we focus on the circled area.

11) Crease and unfold.

12) Open and squash the flap evenly. Repeat 3 times.

13) Gently form the body into 3D.

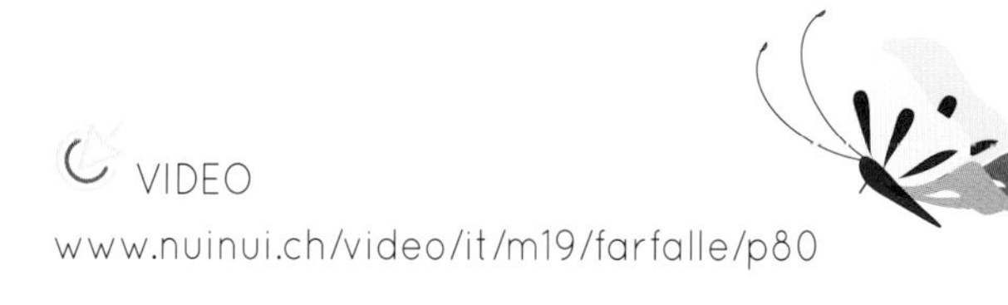

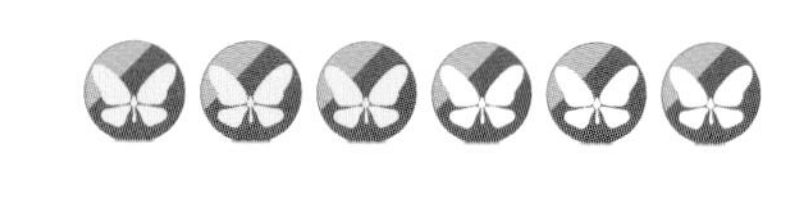

Butterfly Card

Michel Grand

Michel is a Frenchman who is fascinated with cards and envelopes. His designs are always ingenious! You can vary steps 2 and 6 to change the proportions of the butterfly.

Size of the sheet: 7 x 7 in

Paper

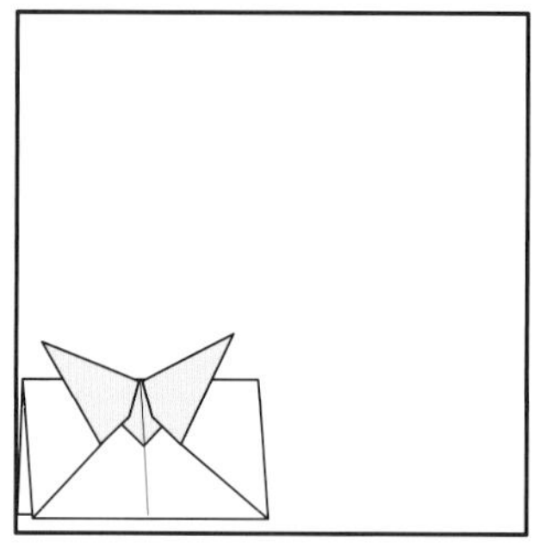

Relationship between the paper and the origami

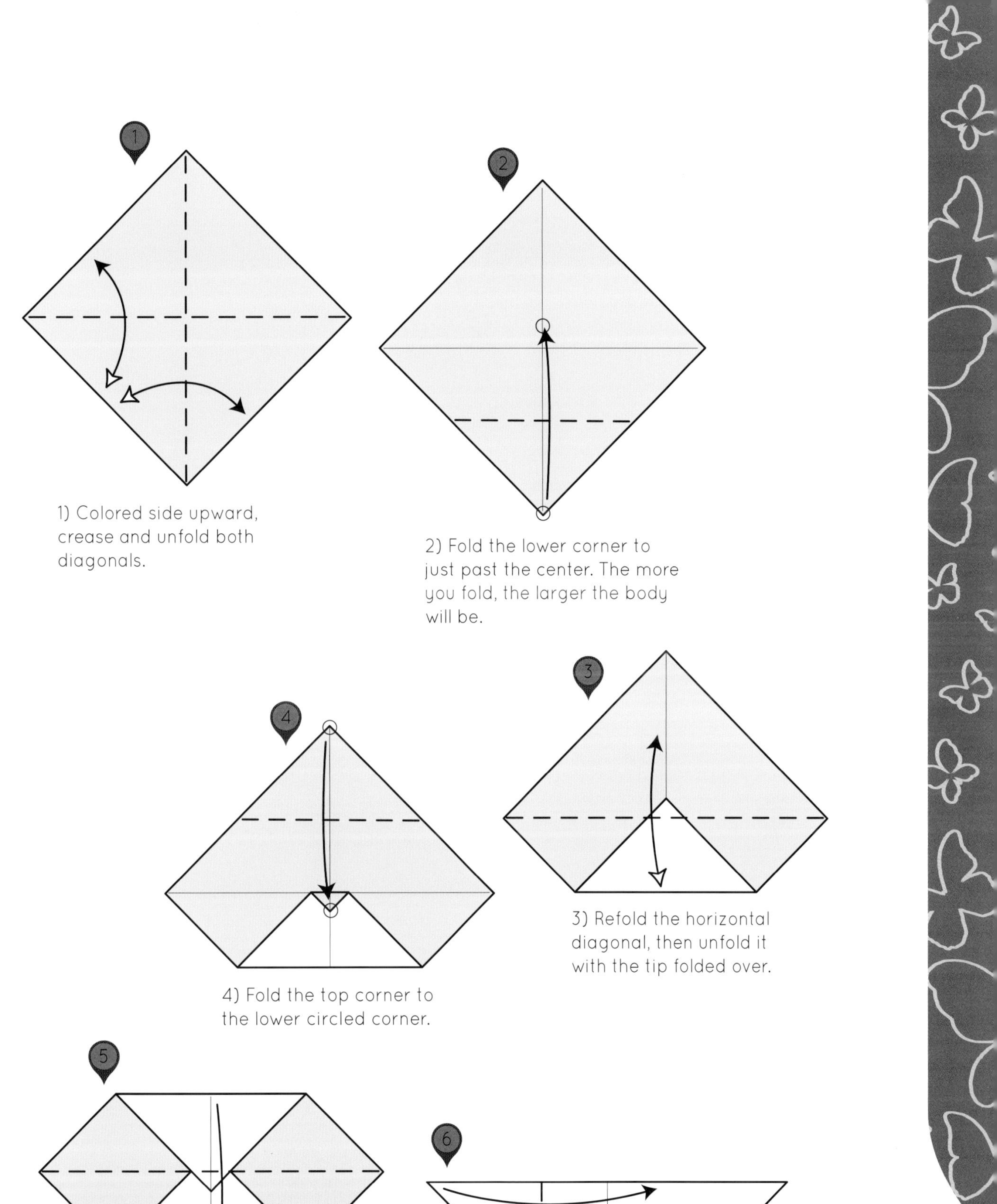

1) Colored side upward, crease and unfold both diagonals.

2) Fold the lower corner to just past the center. The more you fold, the larger the body will be.

3) Refold the horizontal diagonal, then unfold it with the tip folded over.

4) Fold the top corner to the lower circled corner.

5) Fold in half downward along the diagonal.

6) Fold the lower left corner to the position shown. The farther you fold, the larger the wings will be.

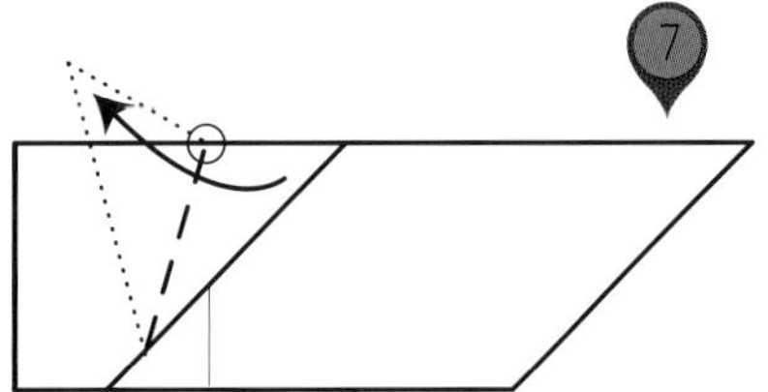

7) Fold the flap to match the dotted line. The circled point is the top of the half-way crease.

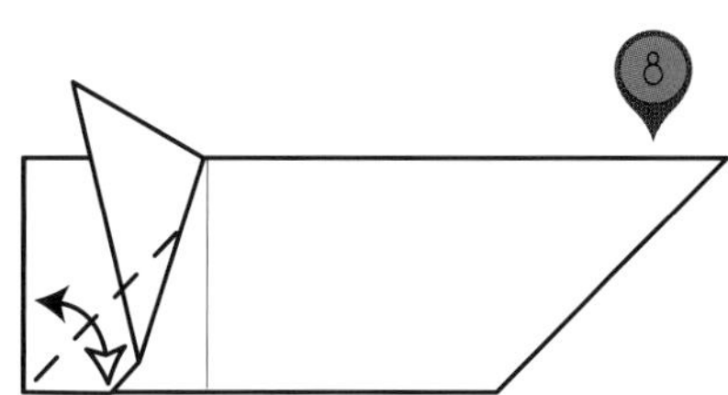

8) Fold the short lower edge to the vertical edge, crease and unfold.

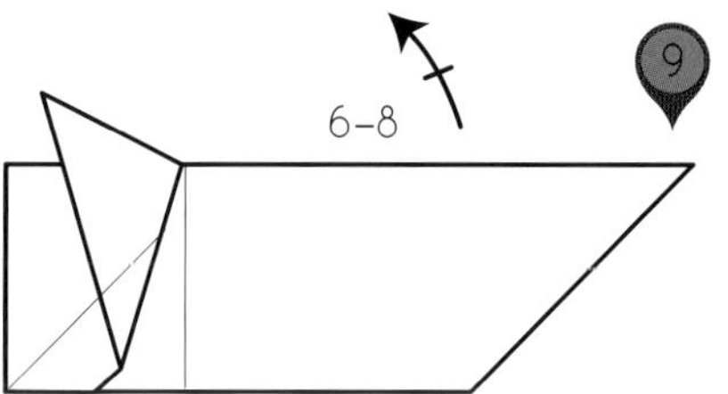

9) Repeat steps 6-8 on the right side.

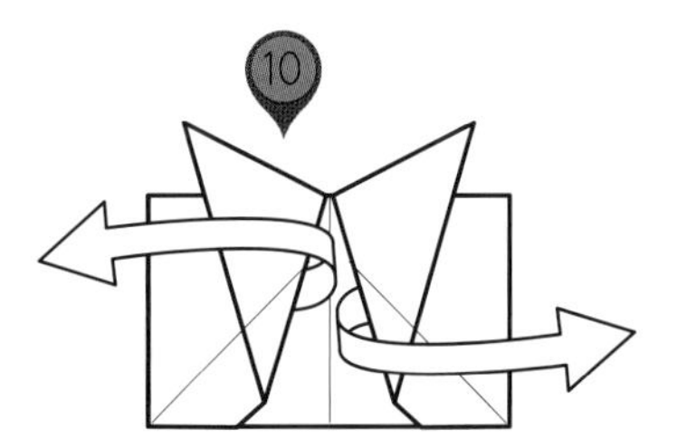

10) Fully unfold the upper flaps.

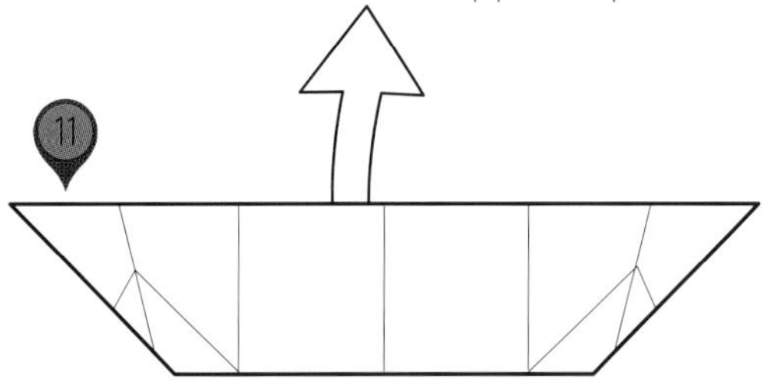

11) Unfold a layer from underneath.

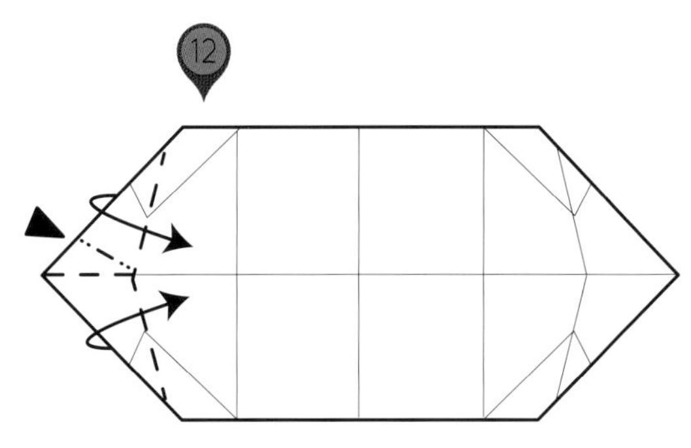

12) Fold in both sides using existing valley creases. Form a point at the center and flatten it upward.

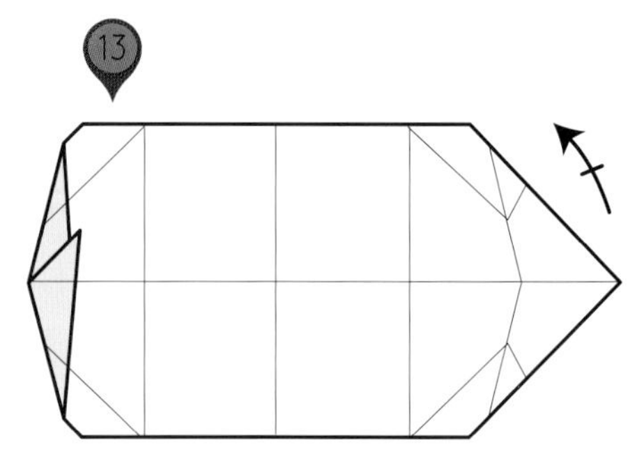

13) Repeat the last step on the right side.

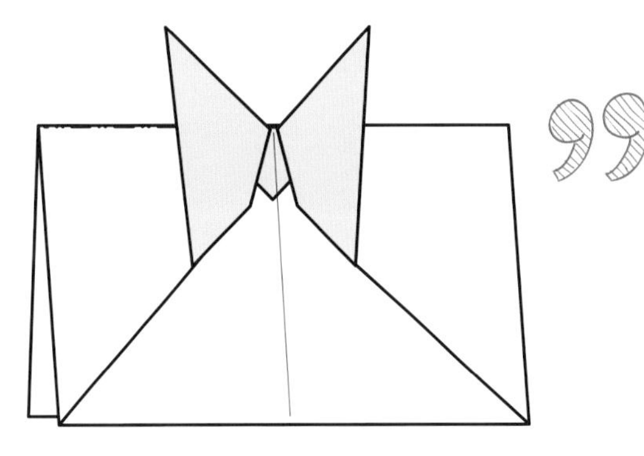

Here, steps 2 and 6
have been changed.

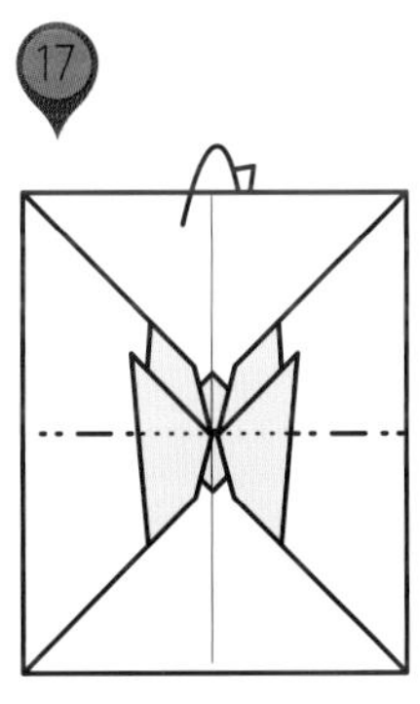

17) Fold the upper half behind, leaving the wings pointing upward.

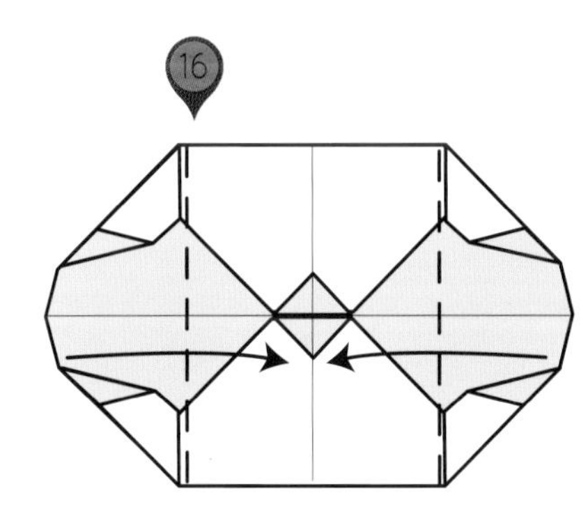

16) Fold the side in using existing creases.

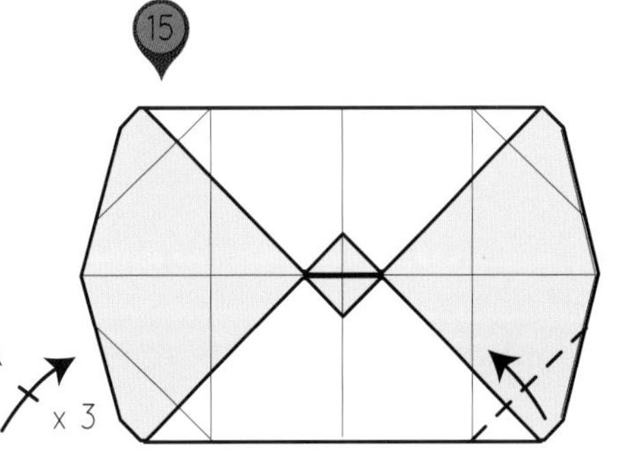

15) Fold a corner in using an existing crease. Repeat on each corner.

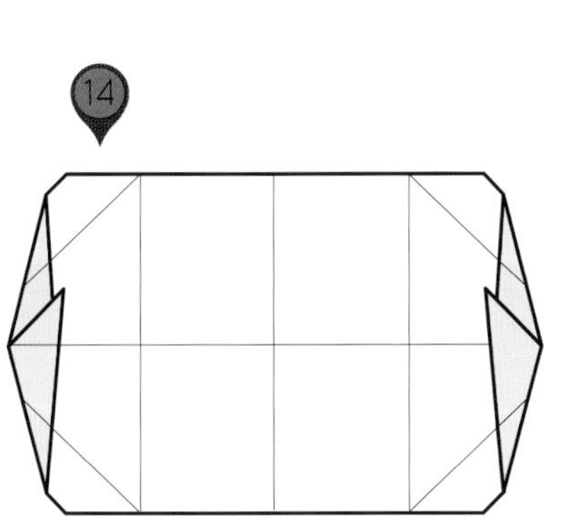

14) The result. Turn the paper over.

VIDEO
www.nuinui.ch/video/it/m19/farfalle/p86

Gigandet Butterfly

Stéphane Gigandet

You will need to fold accurately to complete this design, and crisp paper is recommended. It's worth the effort though!

Size of the sheet: 7 x 7 in

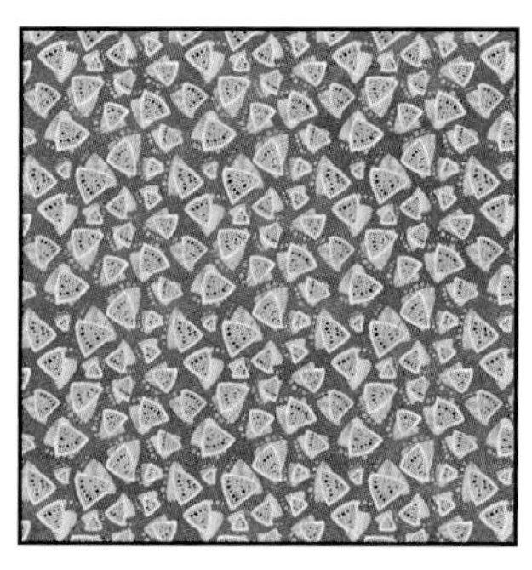

Paper

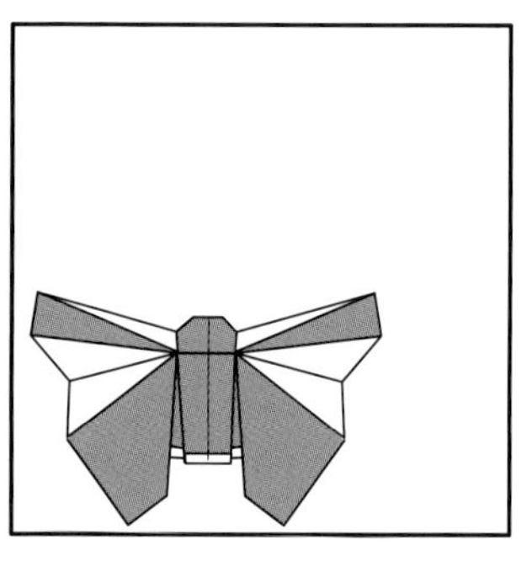

Relationship between the paper and the origami

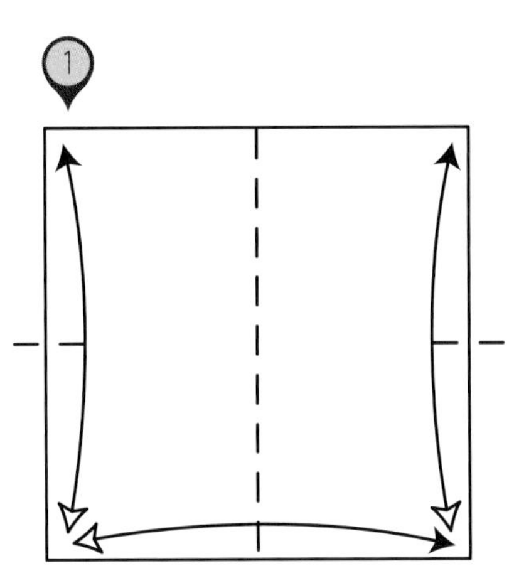

1) White side up, crease in half from side to side; pinch halfway points vertically.

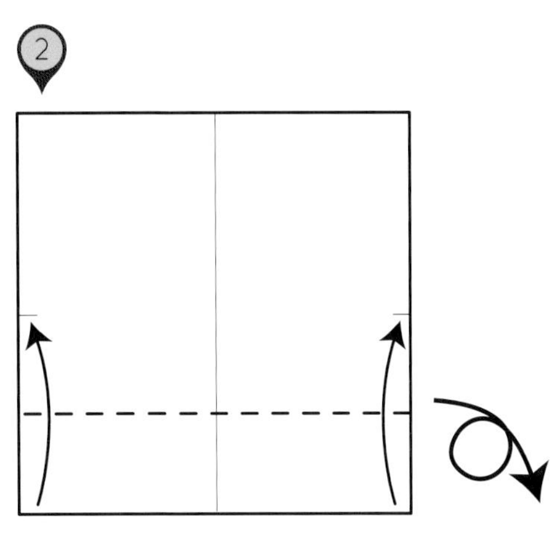

2) Fold the lower edge to the pinches. Turn the paper over.

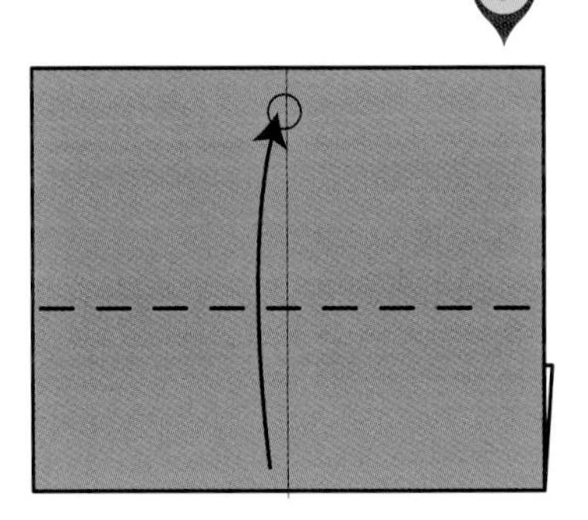

3) Fold to the circled point; see next drawing.

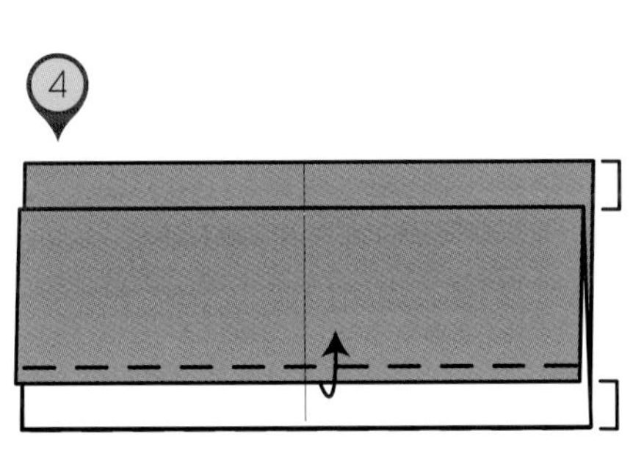

4) Check the marked areas are the same height. Fold over a very narrow flap.

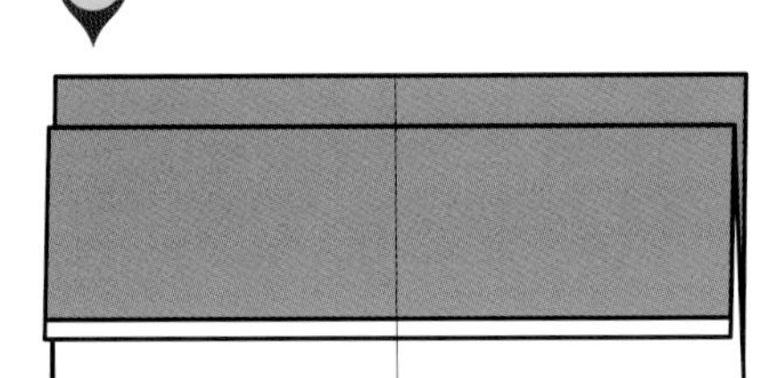

5) The result. Turn the paper over.

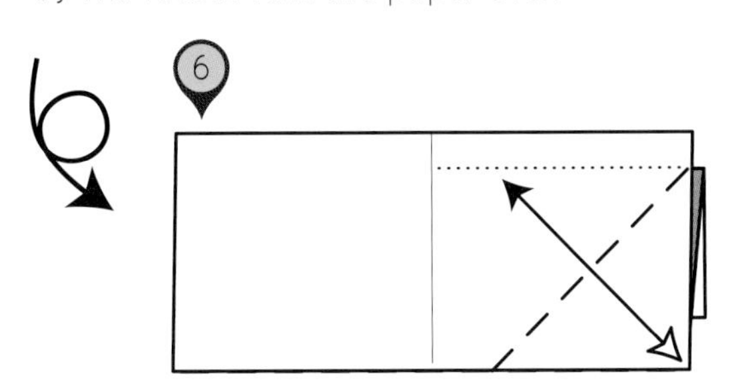

6) Fold to the hidden edge; crease and unfold.

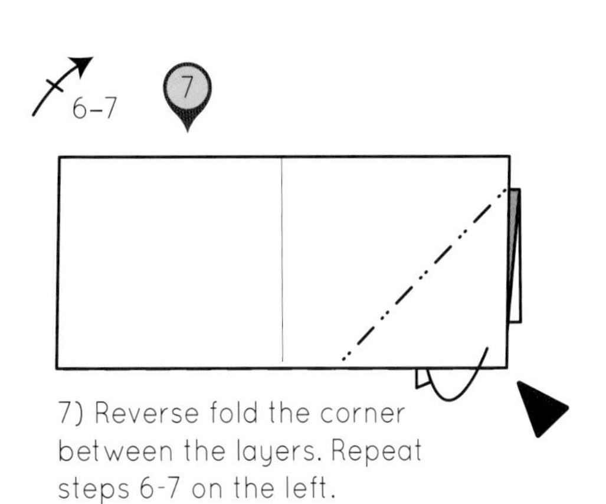

7) Reverse fold the corner between the layers. Repeat steps 6-7 on the left.

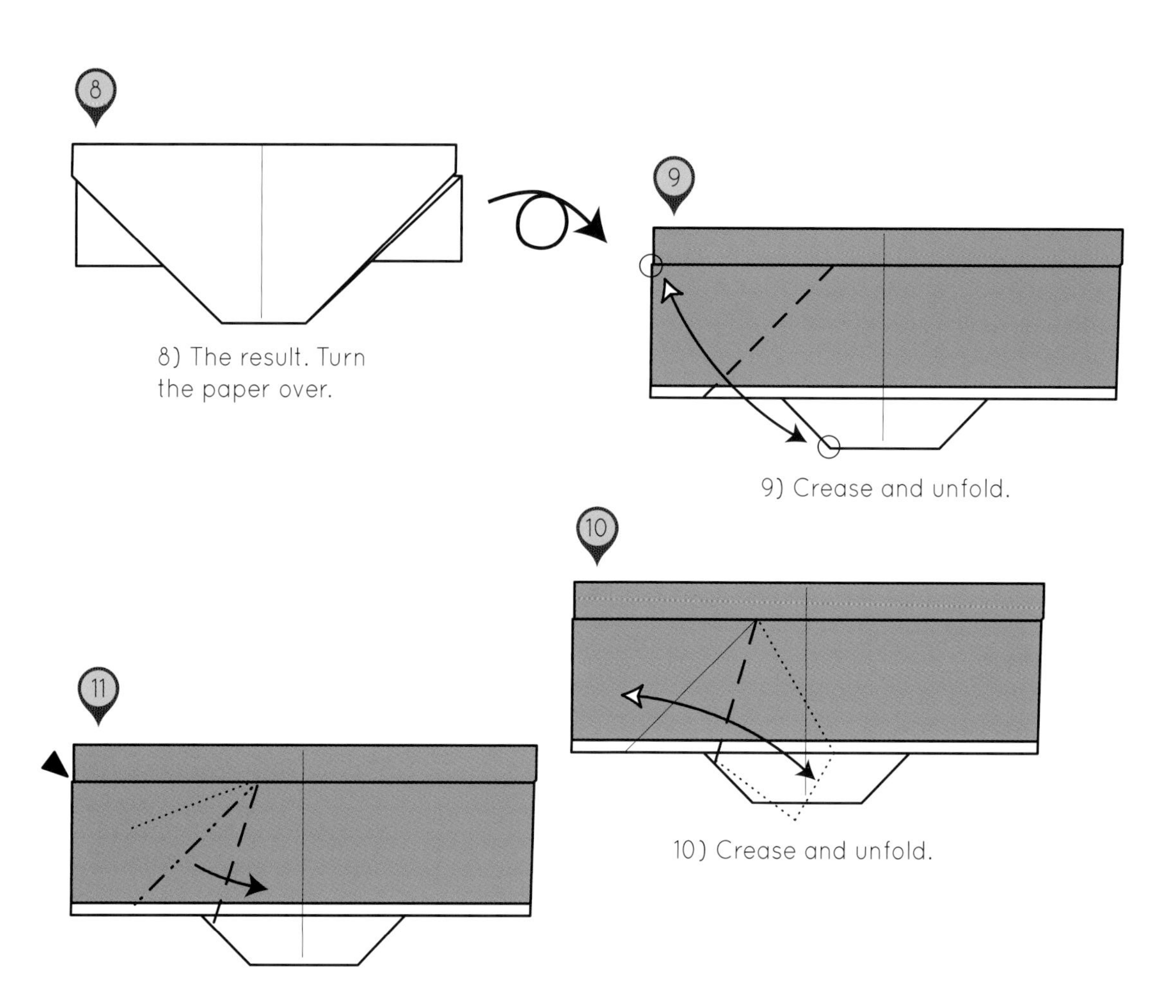

8) The result. Turn the paper over.

9) Crease and unfold.

10) Crease and unfold.

11) Make a pleat where shown, forming a new (dotted) mountain as you flatten the layers.

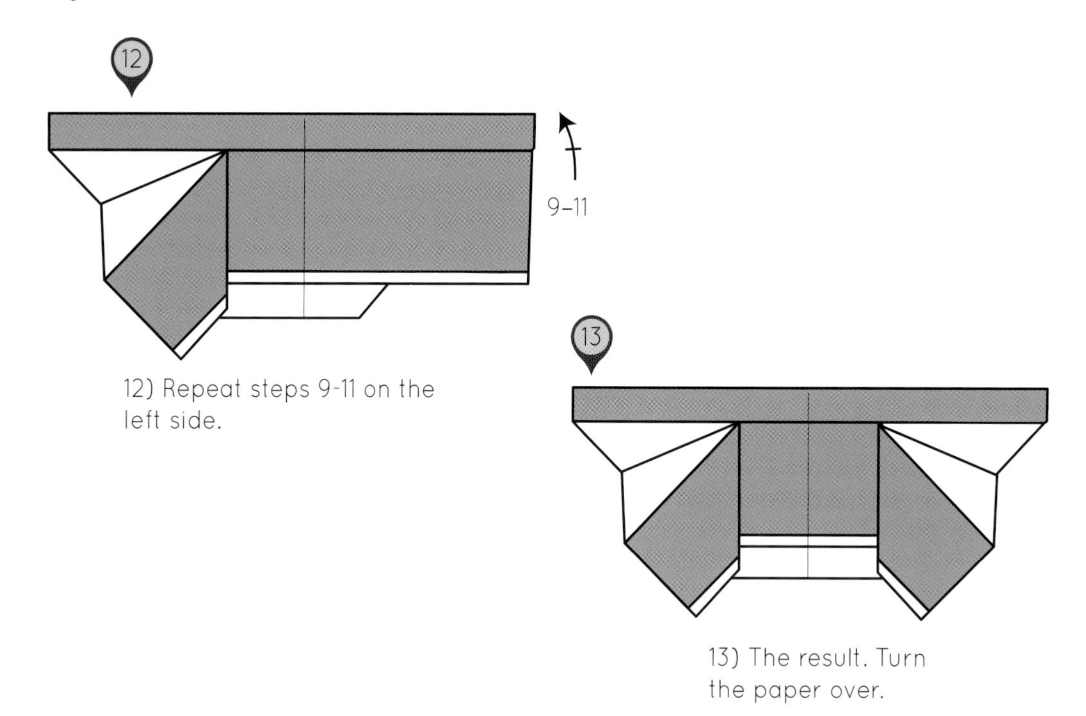

12) Repeat steps 9-11 on the left side.

13) The result. Turn the paper over.

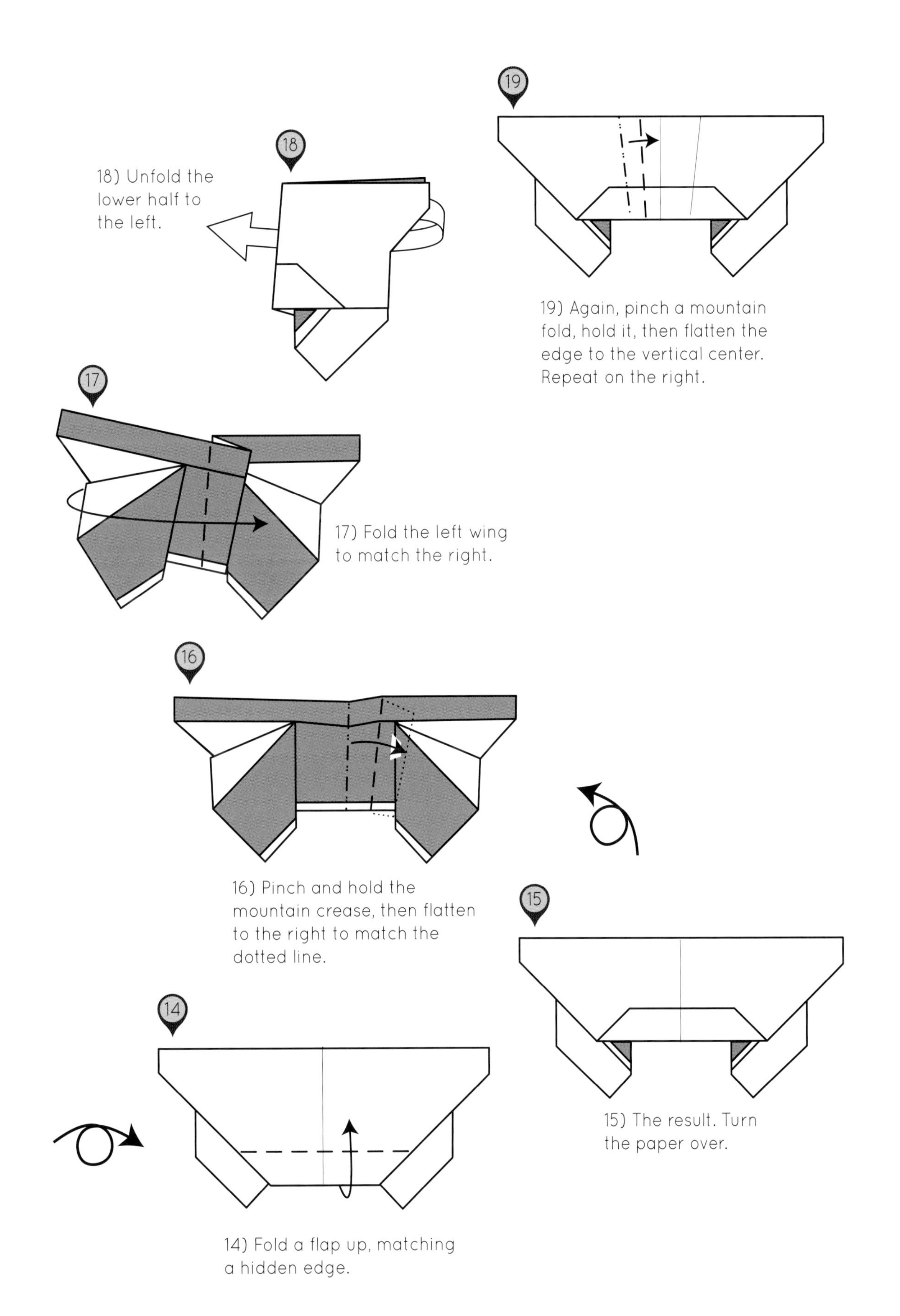
19
18
18) Unfold the lower half to the left.
19) Again, pinch a mountain fold, hold it, then flatten the edge to the vertical center. Repeat on the right.
17
17) Fold the left wing to match the right.
16
16) Pinch and hold the mountain crease, then flatten to the right to match the dotted line.
15
14
15) The result. Turn the paper over.
14) Fold a flap up, matching a hidden edge.

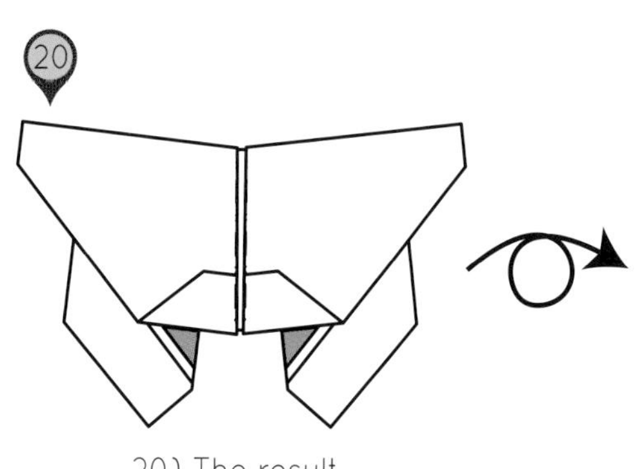

20) The result.
Turn the paper
over.

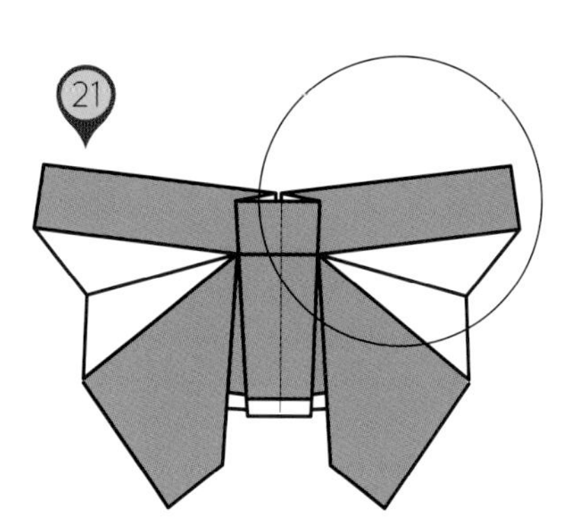

21) Now we focus
on the circled area.

> If you find the last few steps
> a struggle, stop at step 21!

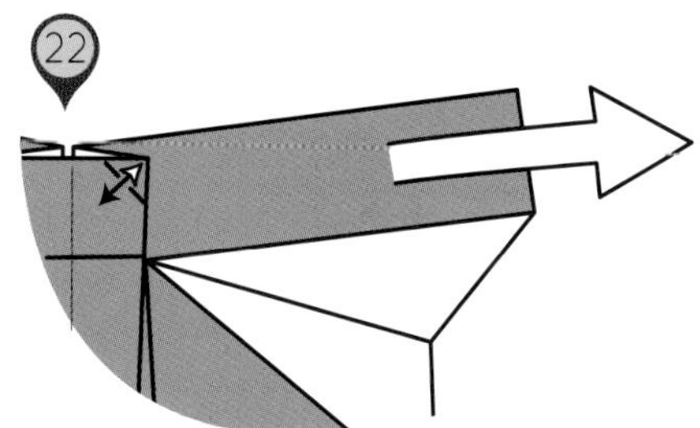

22) Make a tiny precrease,
then open out the right half.

23) Precrease where shown.

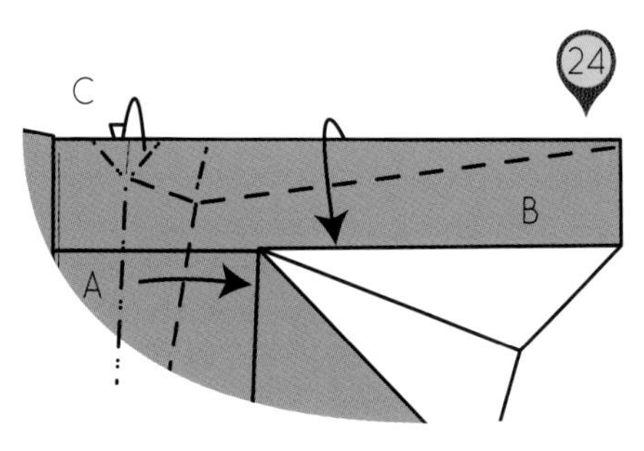

24) Take a deep breath! Start to make
fold A, then fold down B. As the two
moves are near completion, carefully
wrap the white triangle behind (C).

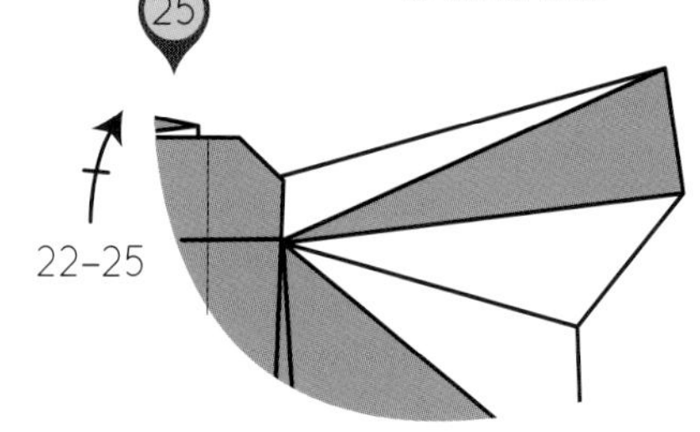

25) Repeat steps 22-25
on the left side.

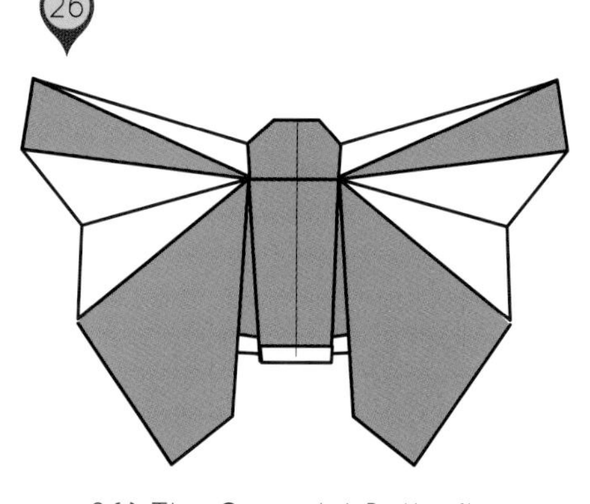

26) The Gigandet Butterfly
is finished.

Loving Butterflies

Mick Guy

This elegant design is a butterfly made from two heart shapes.
It can also be used to create many fascinating tessellations.

Size of the sheet: 7 x 7 in

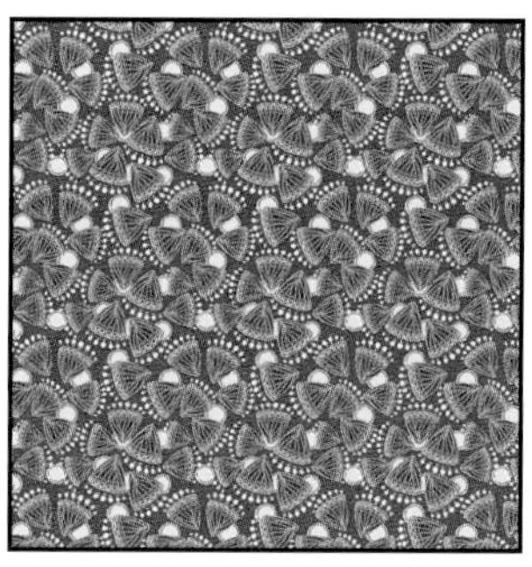

Paper

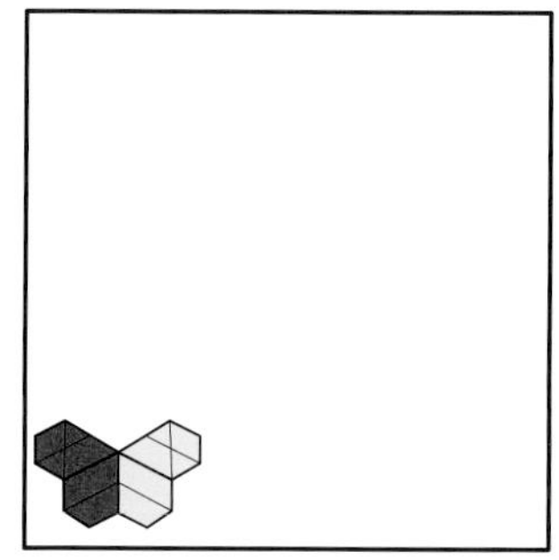

Relationship between the paper and the origami

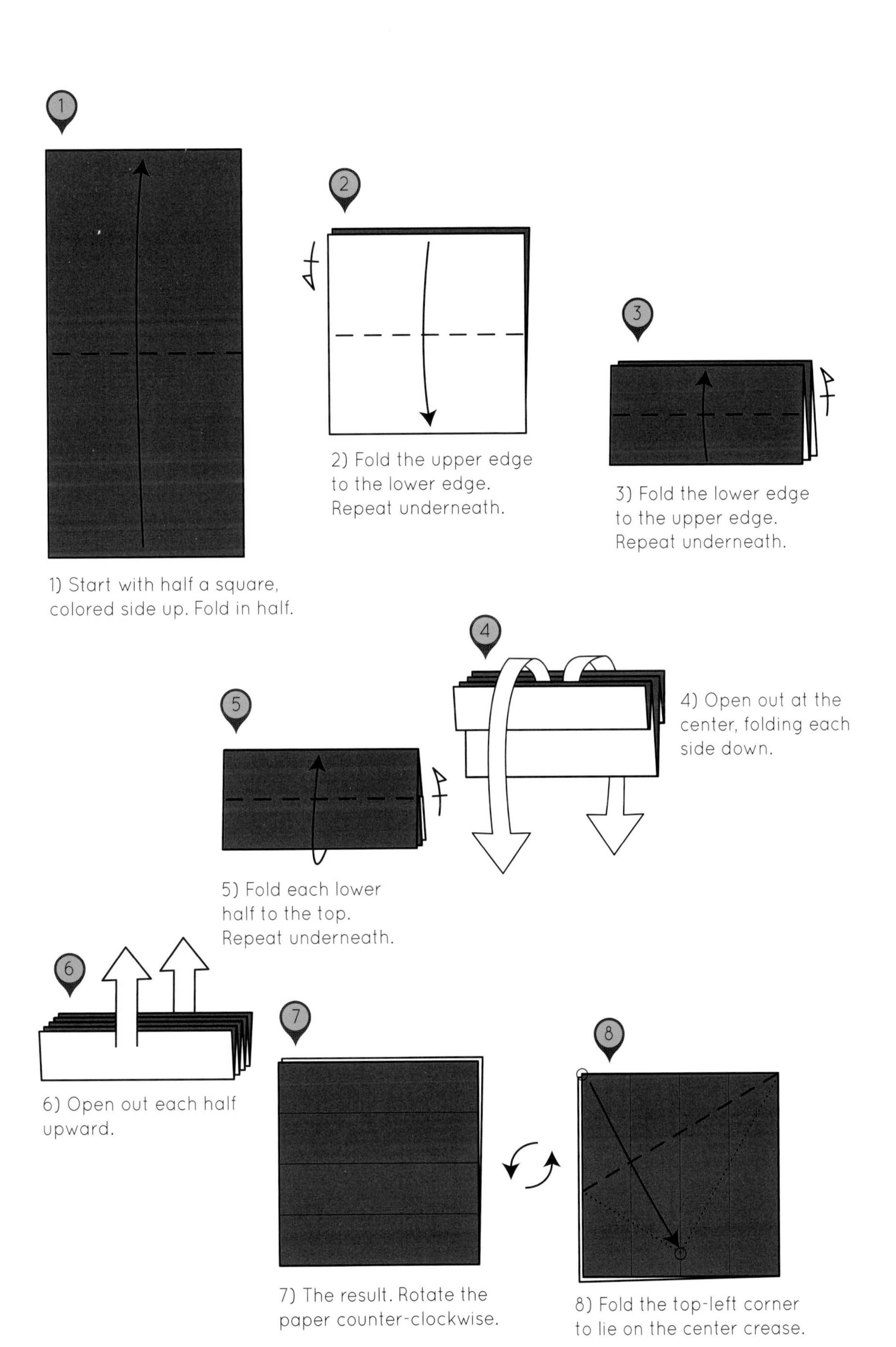

1) Start with half a square, colored side up. Fold in half.

2) Fold the upper edge to the lower edge. Repeat underneath.

3) Fold the lower edge to the upper edge. Repeat underneath.

4) Open out at the center, folding each side down.

5) Fold each lower half to the top. Repeat underneath.

6) Open out each half upward.

7) The result. Rotate the paper counter-clockwise.

8) Fold the top-left corner to lie on the center crease.

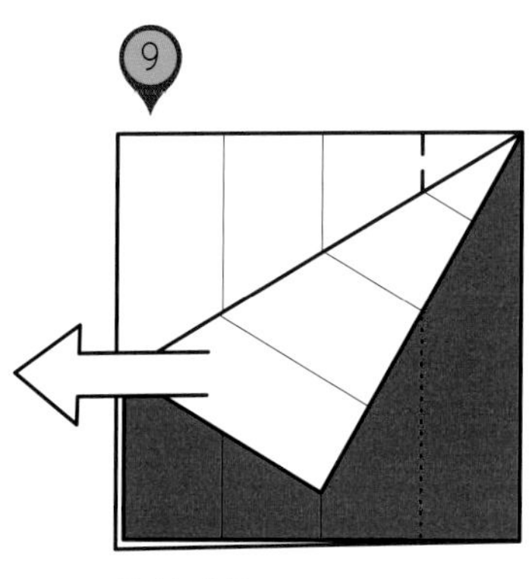

9) Pull the upper layers to the left using the hidden eighth crease.

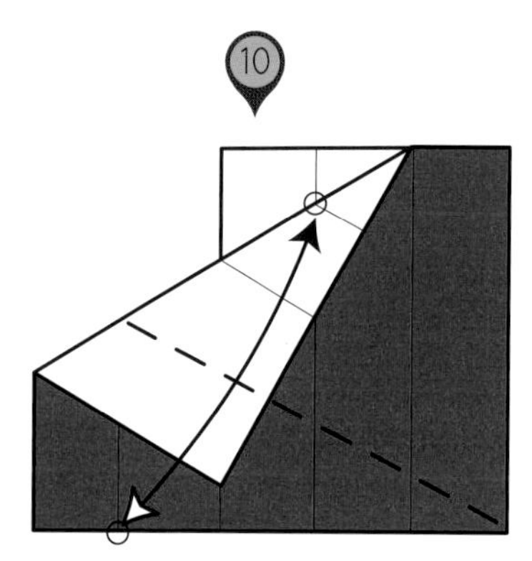

10) Fold so the circled points meet. Crease and unfold.

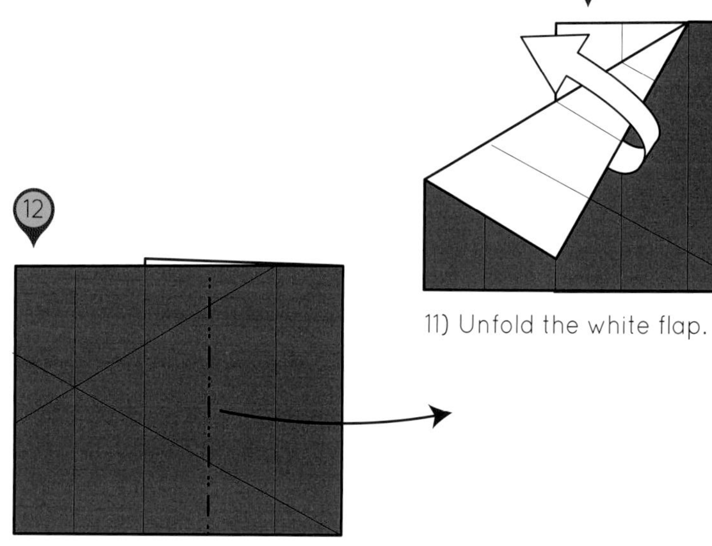

11) Unfold the white flap.

12) Fold three eighths to the right.

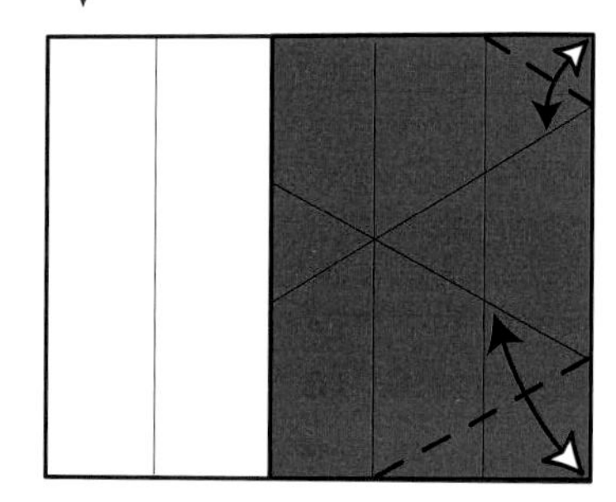

13) Make two creases, then unfold.

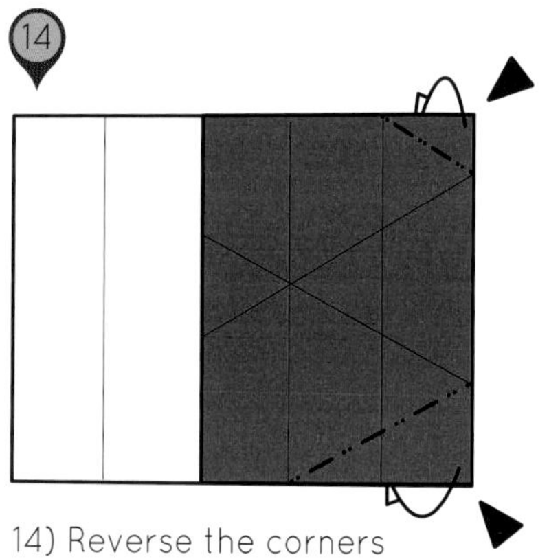

14) Reverse the corners inside.

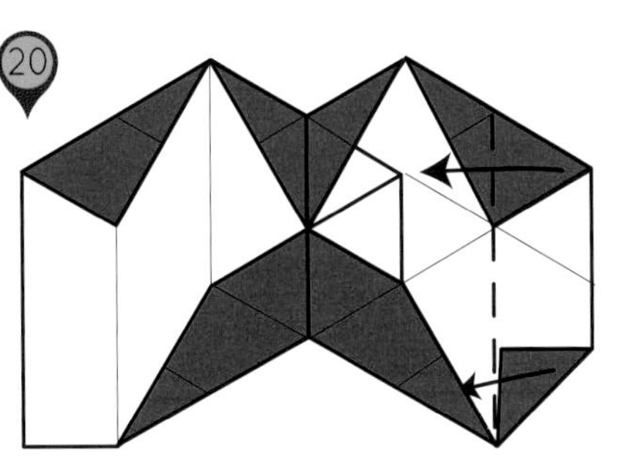

20) Fold over the flap on the right.

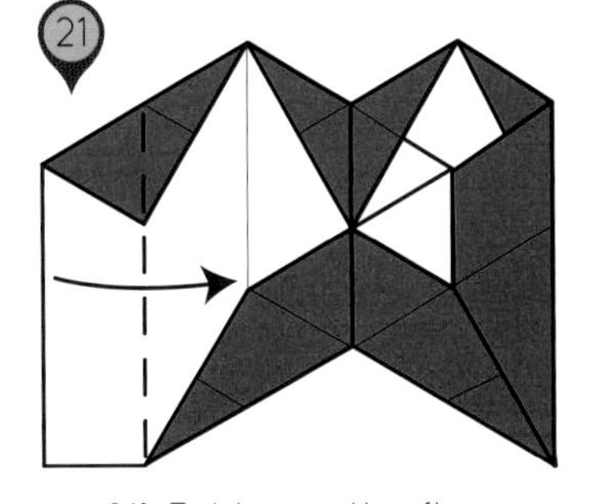

21) Fold over the flap on the left.

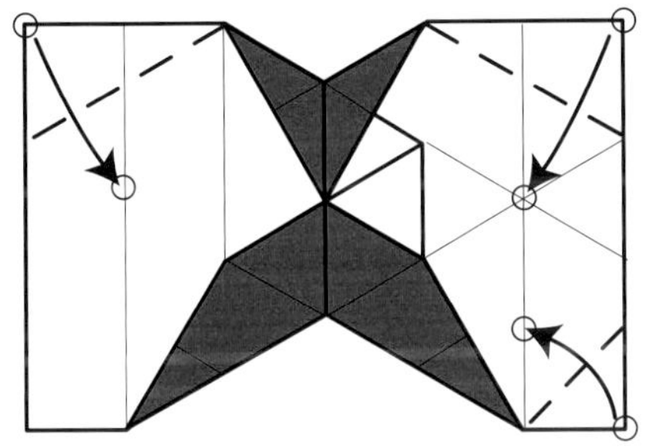

19) Fold in three corners.

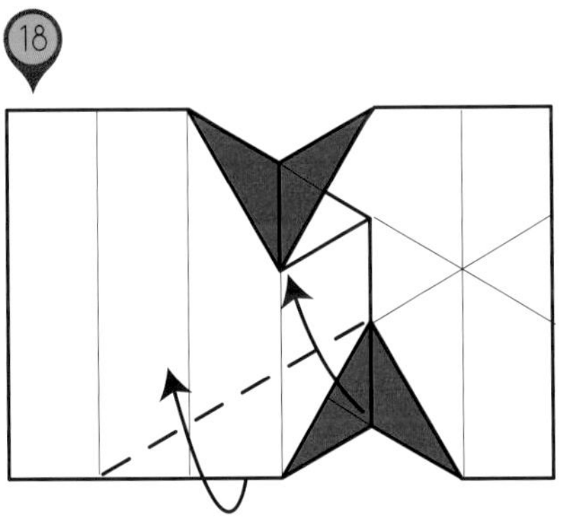

18) Fold this flap over as far as you can.

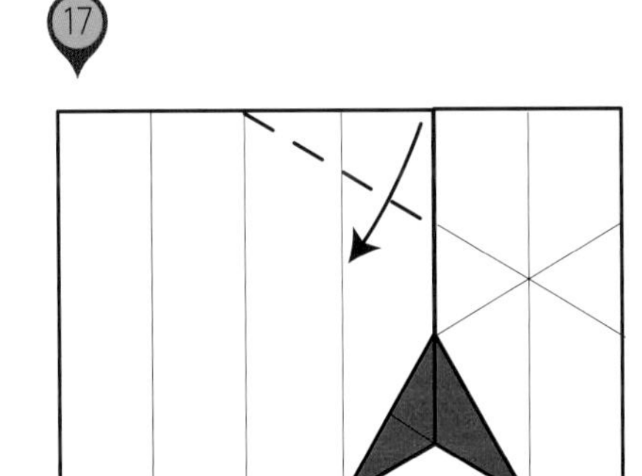

17) Fold this flap over as far as you can.

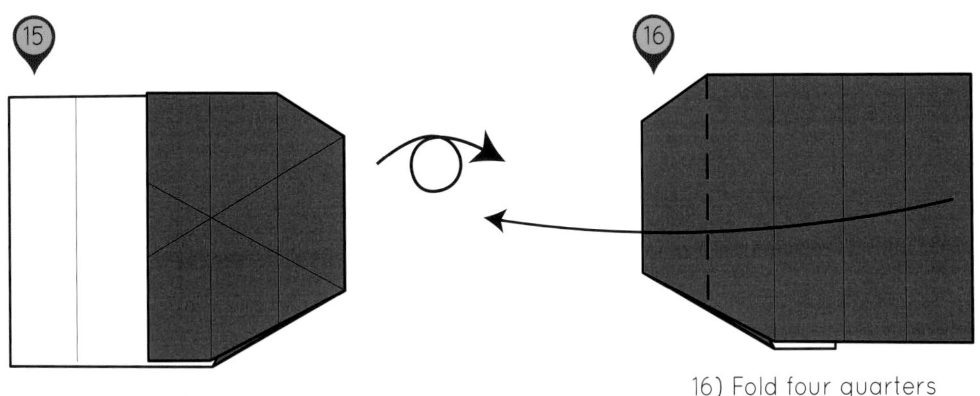

15) The result. Turn the paper over.

16) Fold four quarters to the left.

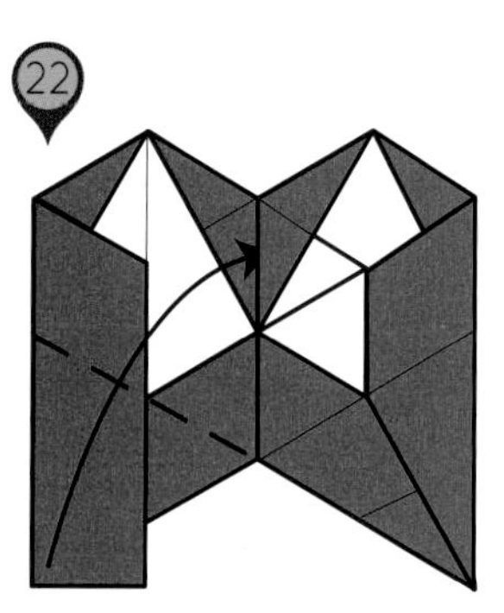

22) Fold the flap over and tuck it into the central pocket.

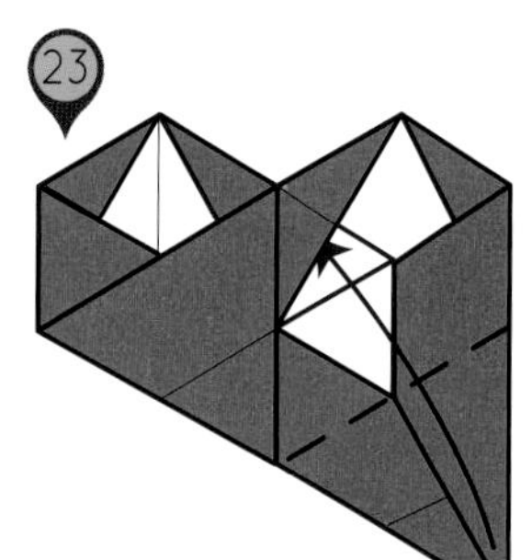

23) Fold the flap over and tuck it into the pocket.

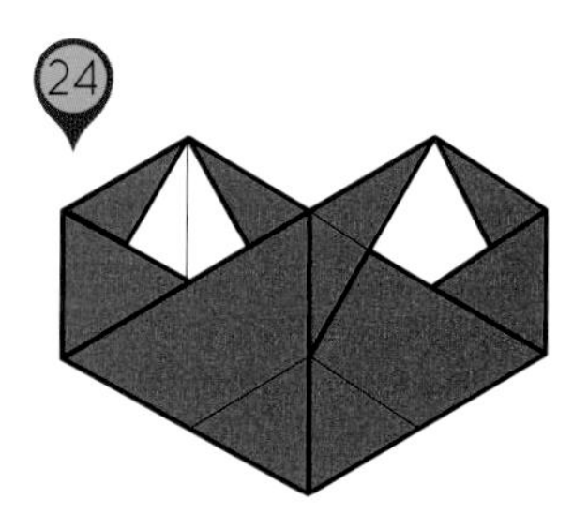

24) Turn the paper over.

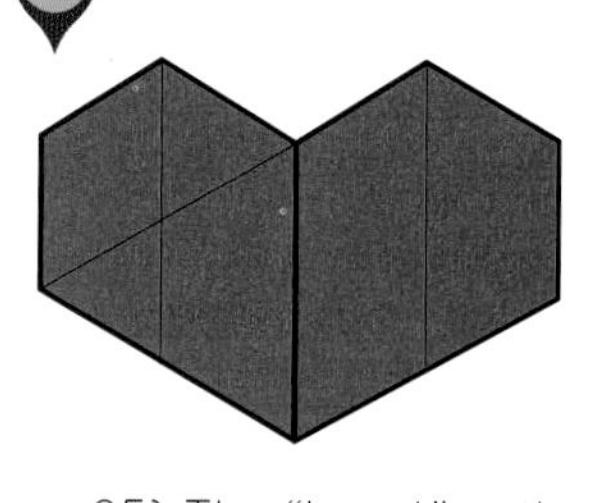

25) The "heart" unit is complete. Make a second in the same way.

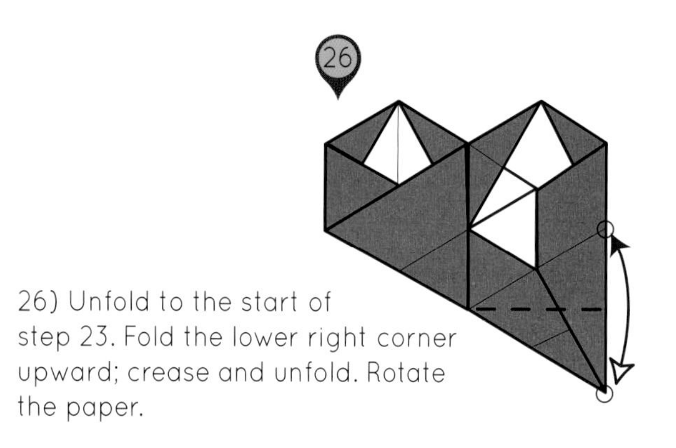

26) Unfold to the start of step 23. Fold the lower right corner upward; crease and unfold. Rotate the paper.

27) The first half of the butterfly is ready.

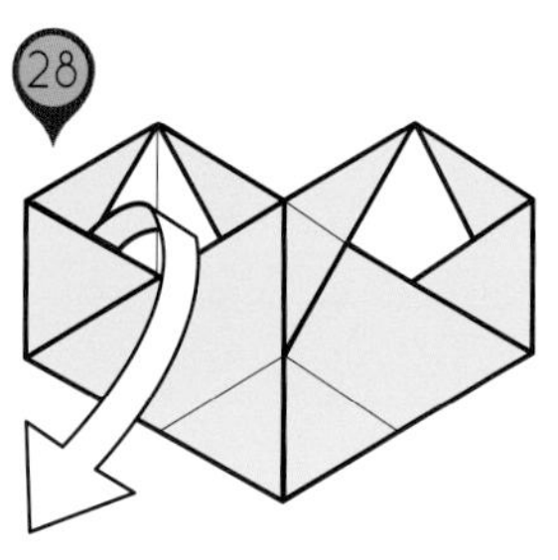

28) Start the other half at step 24 and unfold the layers on the left.

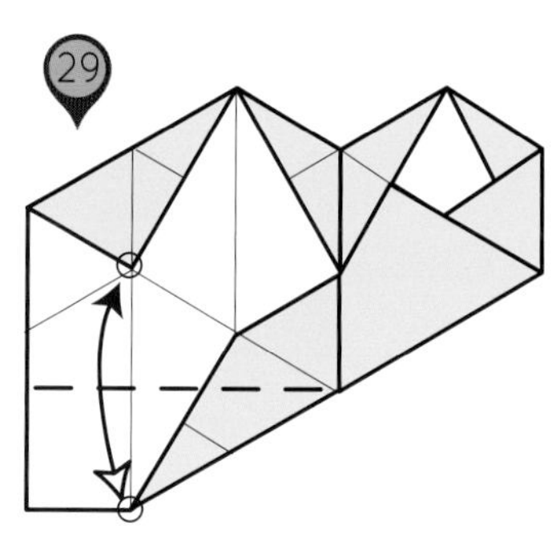

29) Crease and unfold.

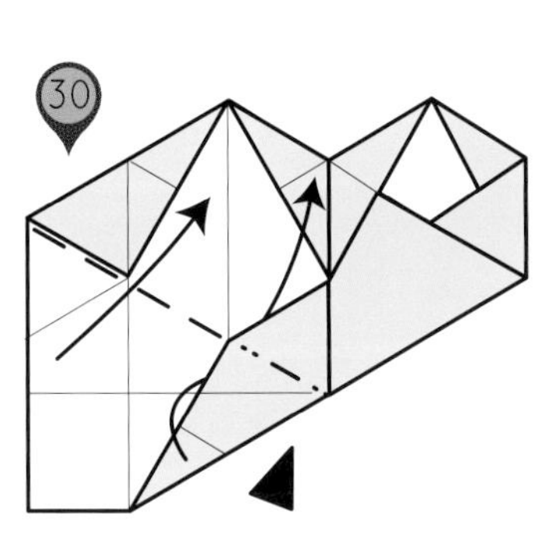

30) Fold the flap over, reversing the lower right corner.

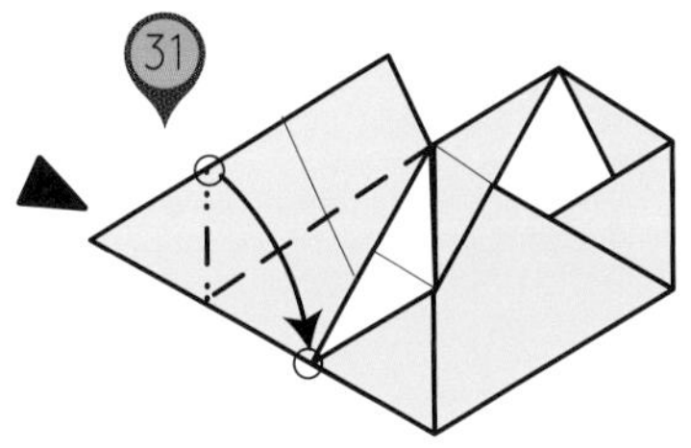

31) Fold the top left edge down, squashing the point.

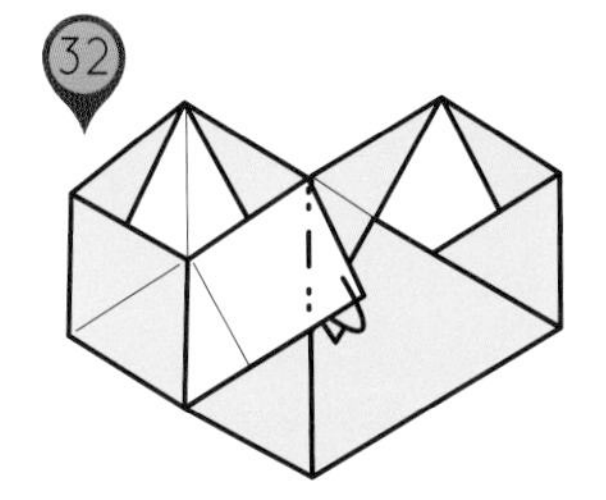

32) Wrap part of the white flap underneath along a hidden edge.

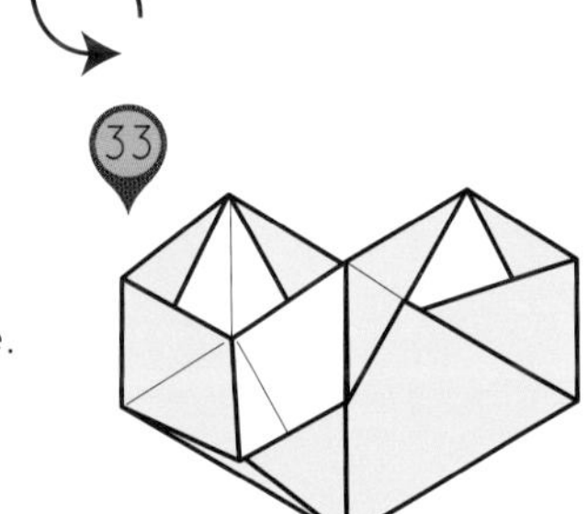

33) Rotate the model counter-clockwise.

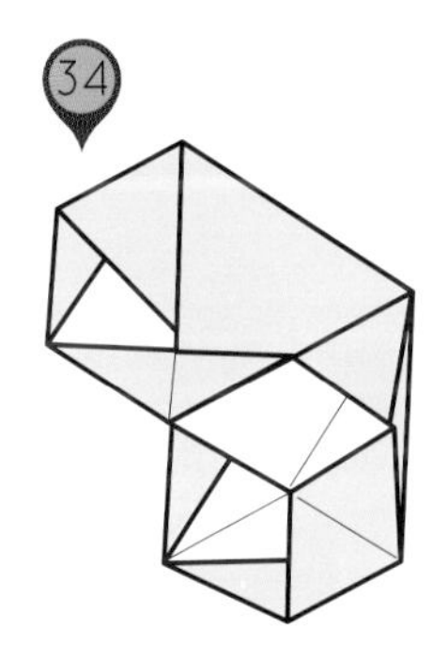

34) The second half of the butterfly is complete. Now we can join them.

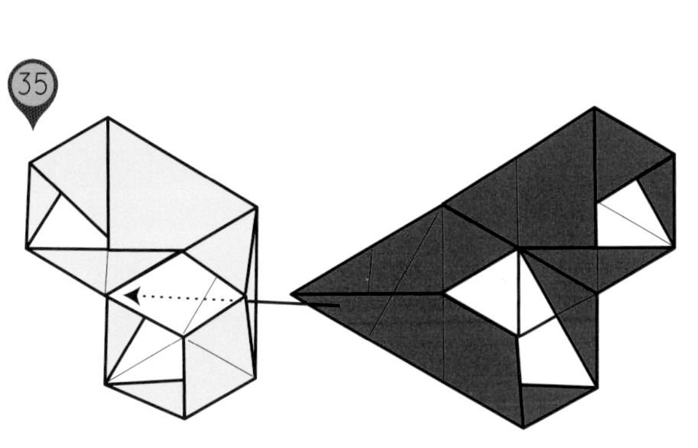

35) Arrange the two halves like this and slide the point into the pocket.

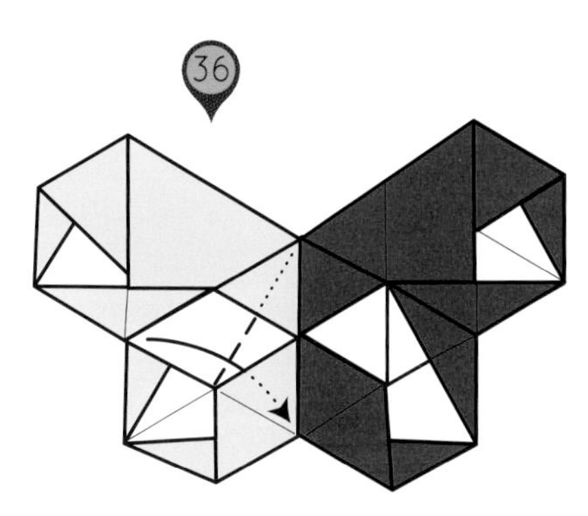

36) Fold the white flap over, tucking it under a layer.

37) Turn the model over (or leave it this way if you like the pattern!).

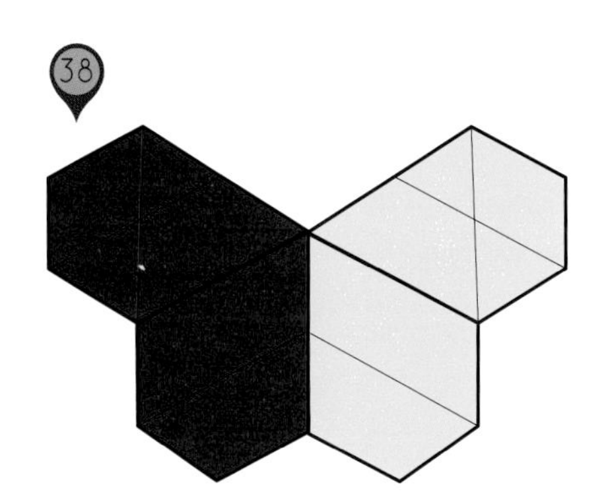

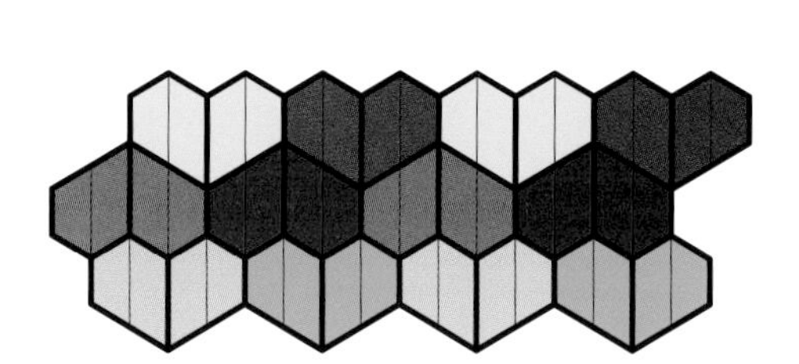

Here are some tessellations you can create using either complete or half butterflies!

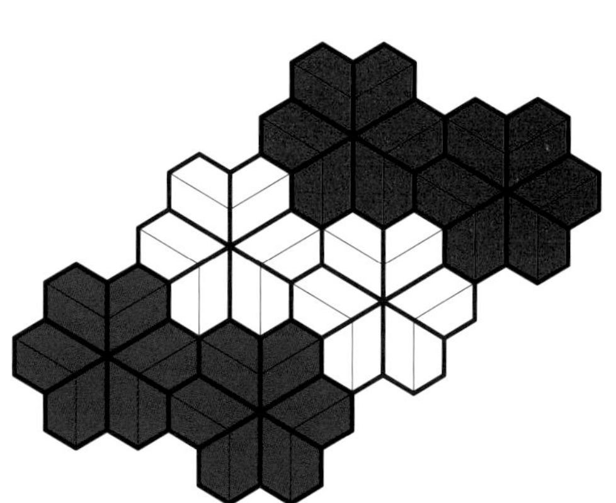

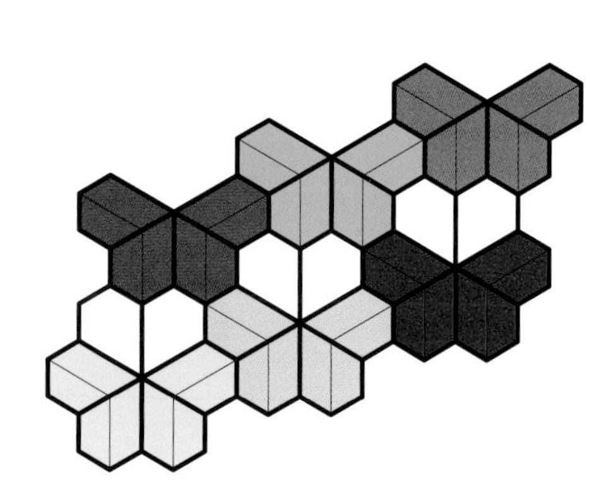

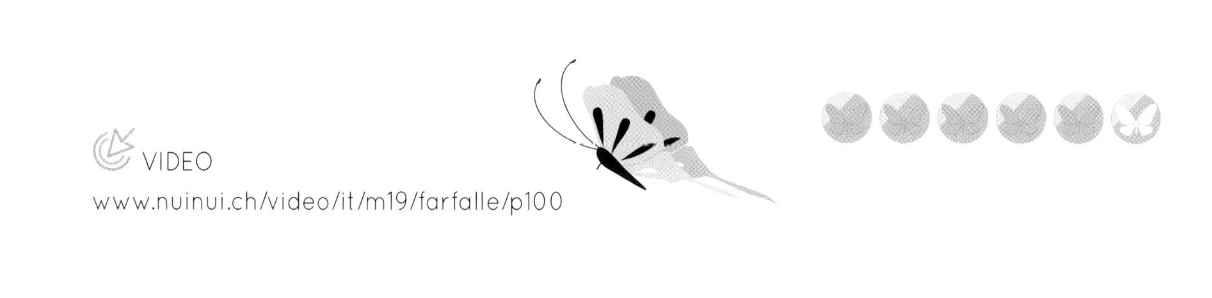

Donachie Butterfly

Rikki Donachie

You may need to fold this model a few times to really fold the wings neatly, but every time you refold it, it becomes more beautiful.

Size of the sheet: 7 x 7 in

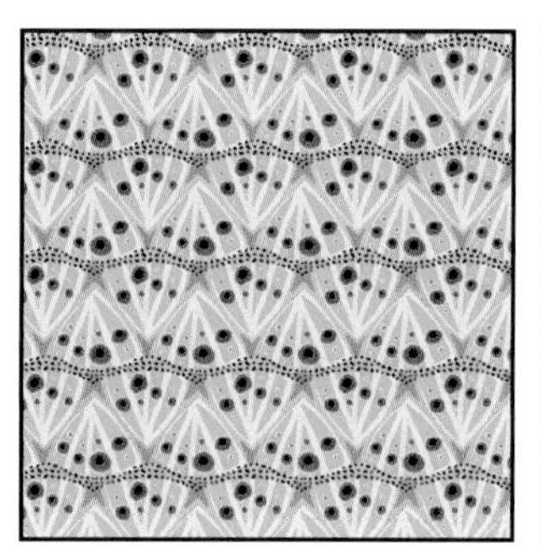

Paper

Relationship between the paper and the origami

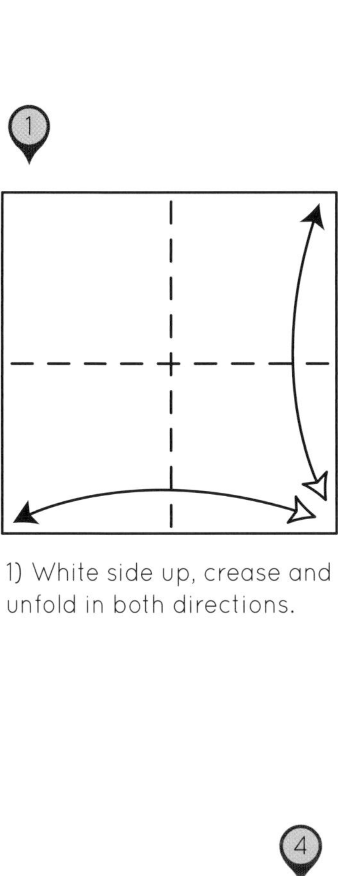

1) White side up, crease and unfold in both directions.

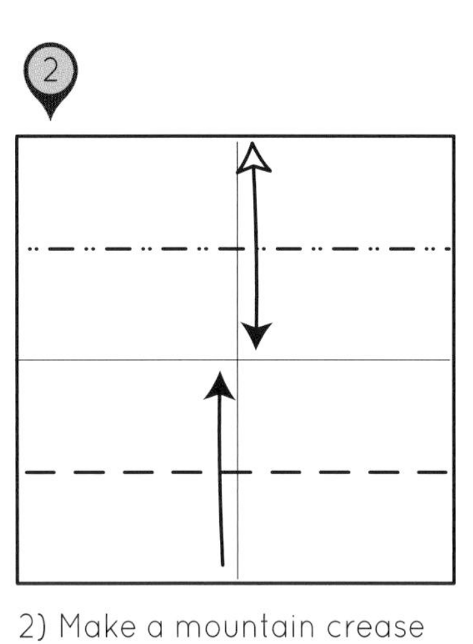

2) Make a mountain crease and unfold at the top; make a valley at the bottom.

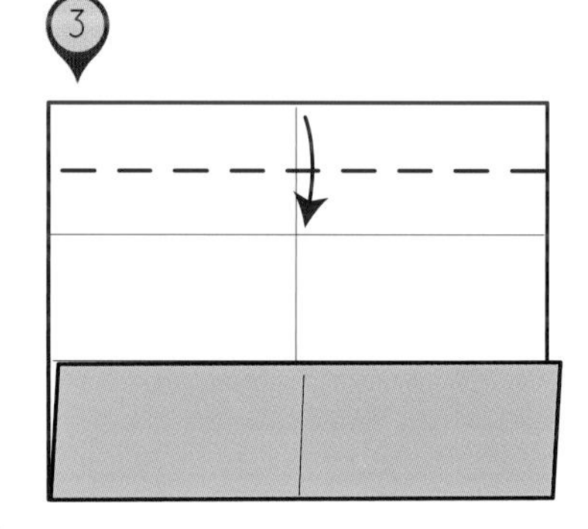

3) Fold the upper edge to lie on the recently made crease.

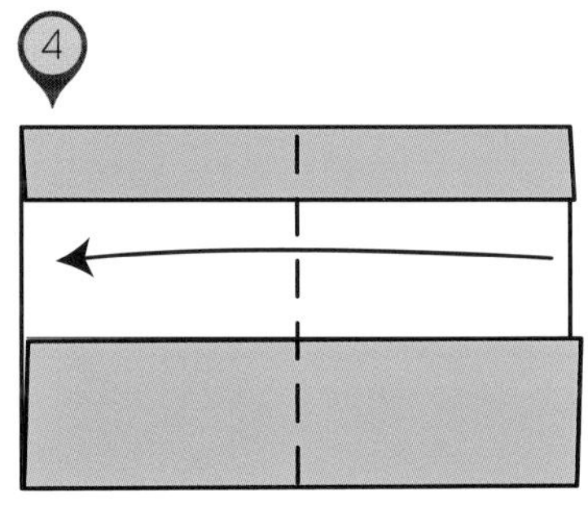

4) Fold in half from right to left.

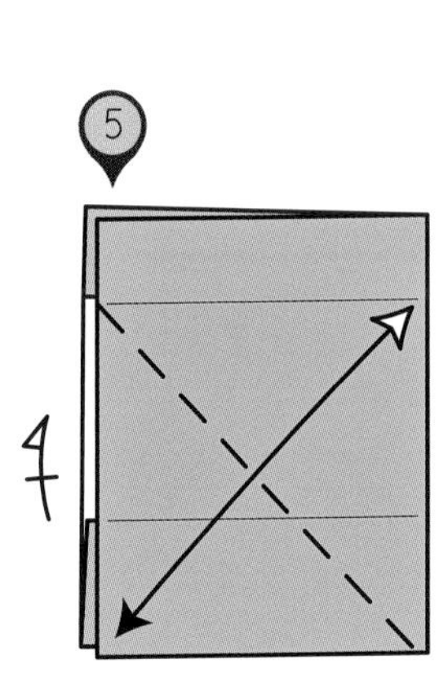

5) Crease and unfold. Repeat underneath.

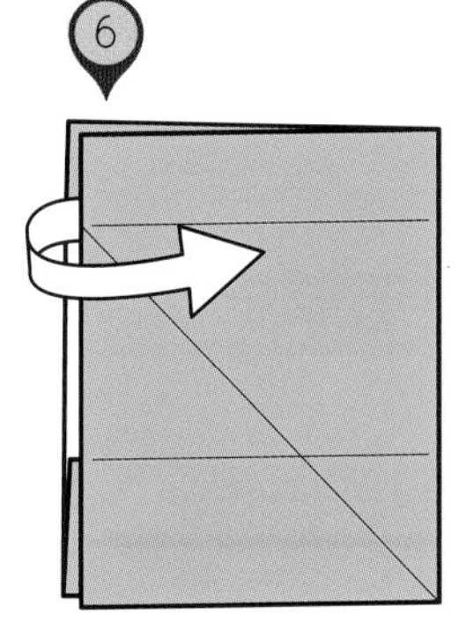

6) Unfold a flap.

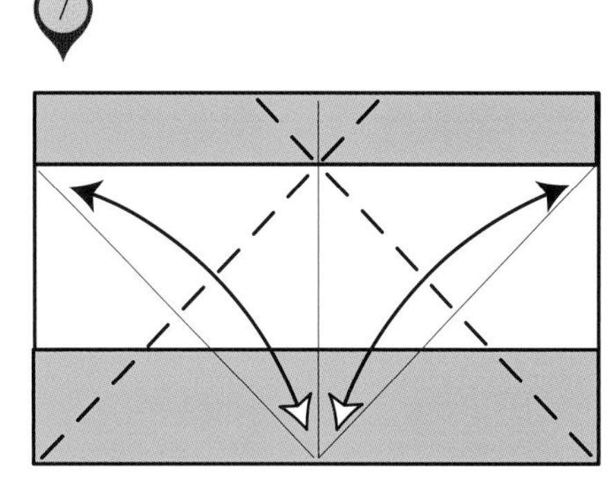

7) Crease and unfold on both sides.

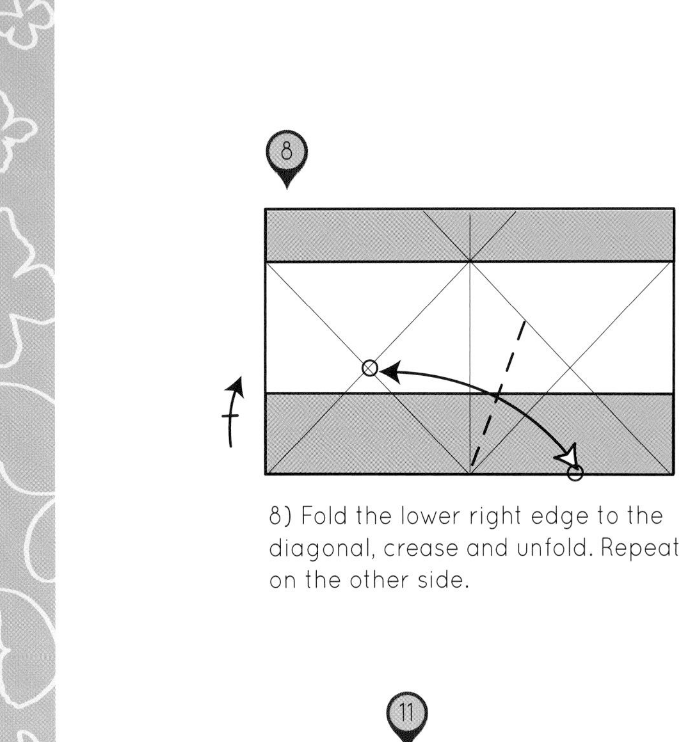

8) Fold the lower right edge to the diagonal, crease and unfold. Repeat on the other side.

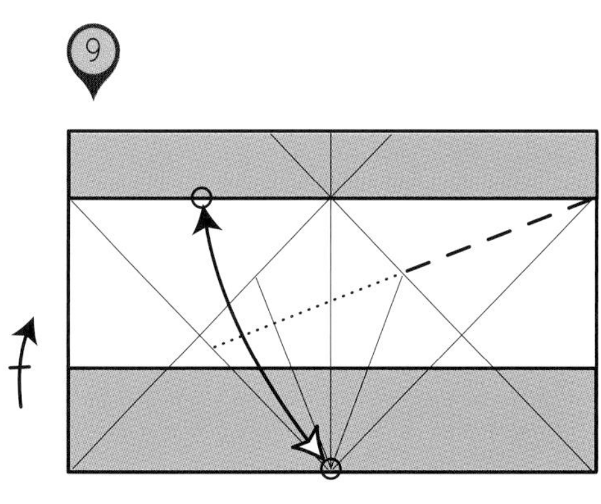

9) Again, crease and unfold on both sides.

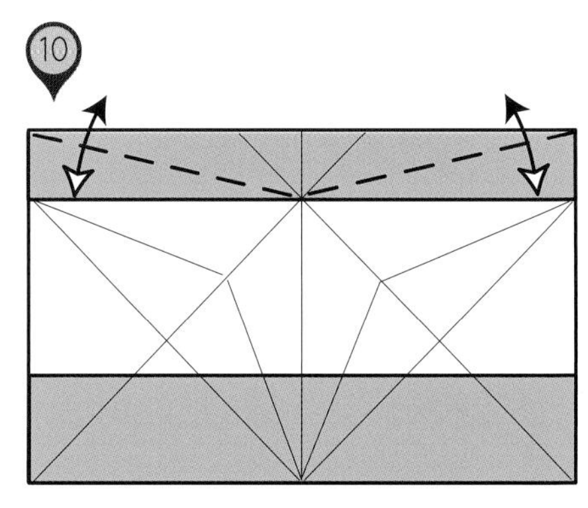

10) Carefully crease and unfold on both sides.

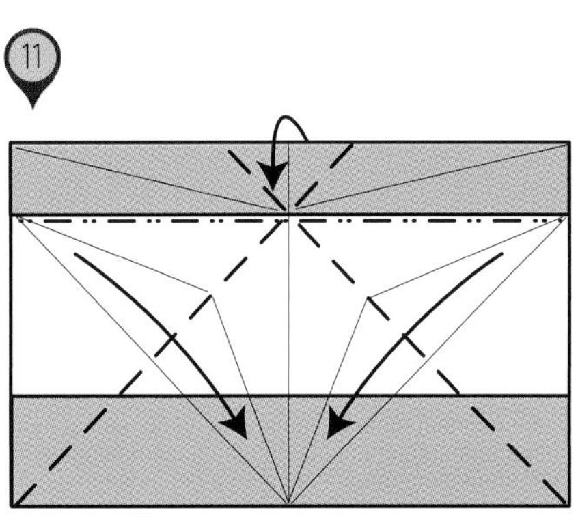

11) Fold each half of the mountain crease downward to meet in the center.

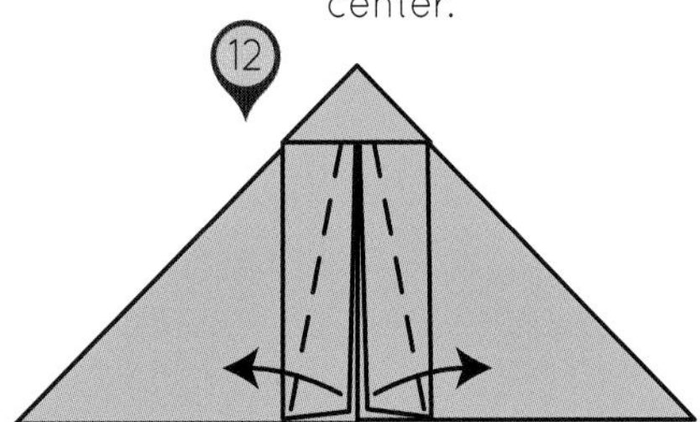

12) Fold out on existing creases.

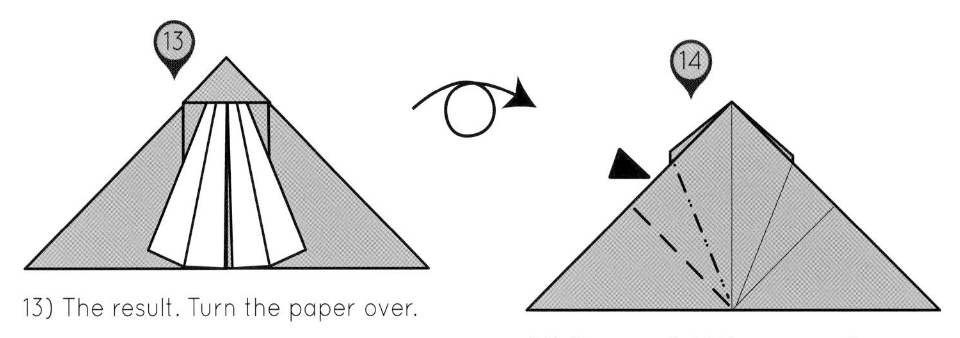

13) The result. Turn the paper over.

14) Reverse fold the corner in and out.

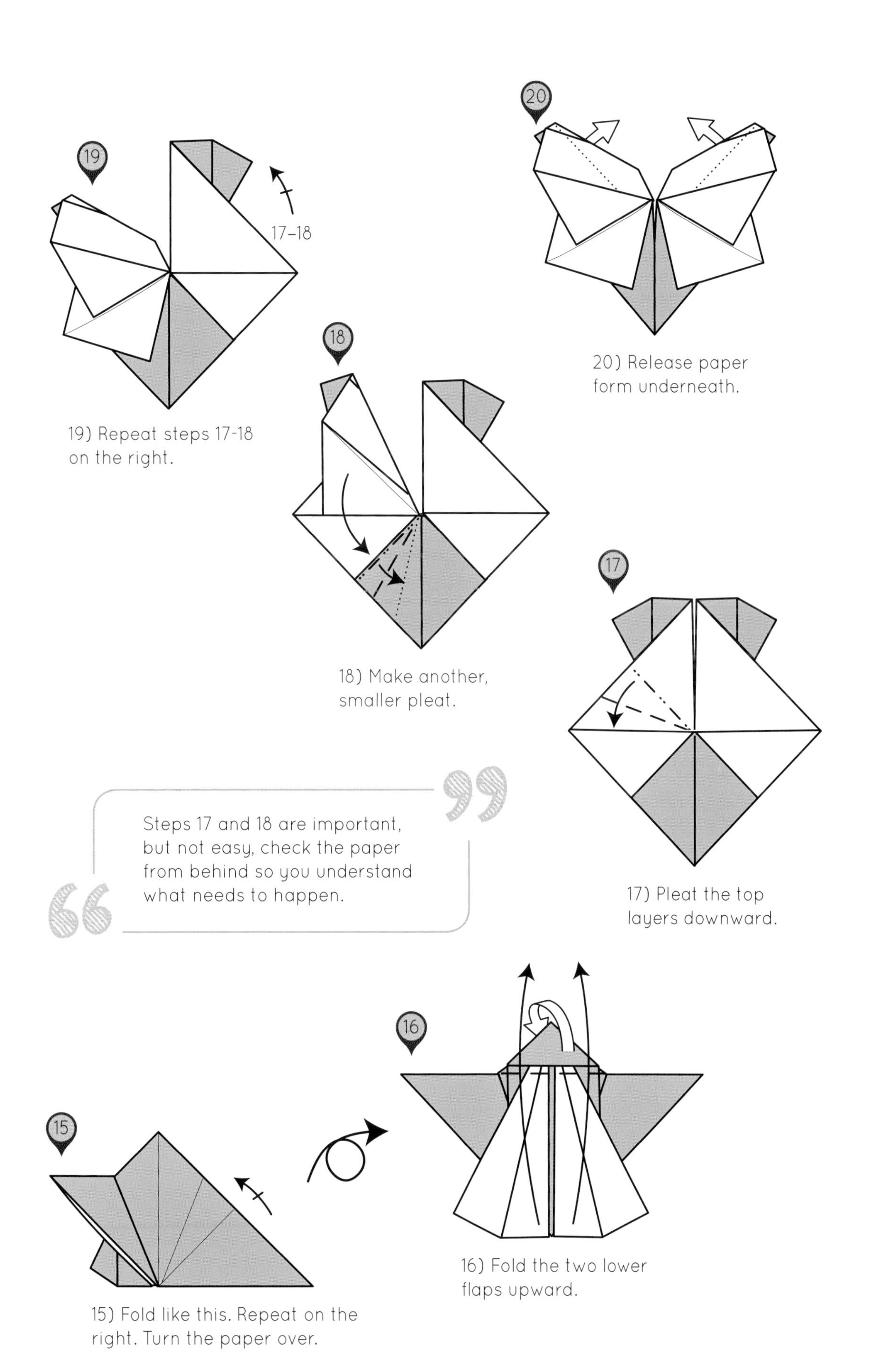

19) Repeat steps 17-18 on the right.

20) Release paper form underneath.

18) Make another, smaller pleat.

17) Pleat the top layers downward.

Steps 17 and 18 are important, but not easy, check the paper from behind so you understand what needs to happen.

15) Fold like this. Repeat on the right. Turn the paper over.

16) Fold the two lower flaps upward.

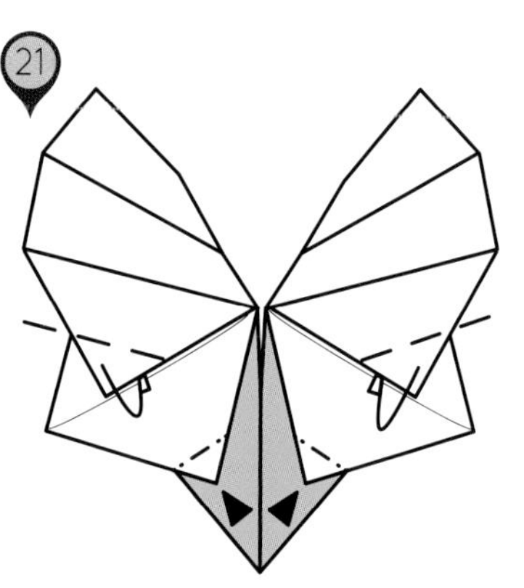

21) Fold two upper corners behind. Crease and reverse the lower corners inside. Turn the paper over.

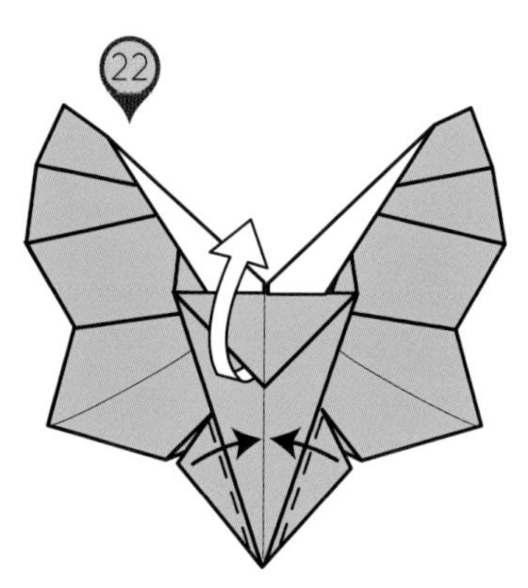

22) Fold the lower sides inward, flattening small corners. Lift the head upward and turn the model over.

23) The Donachie Butterfly is finished.

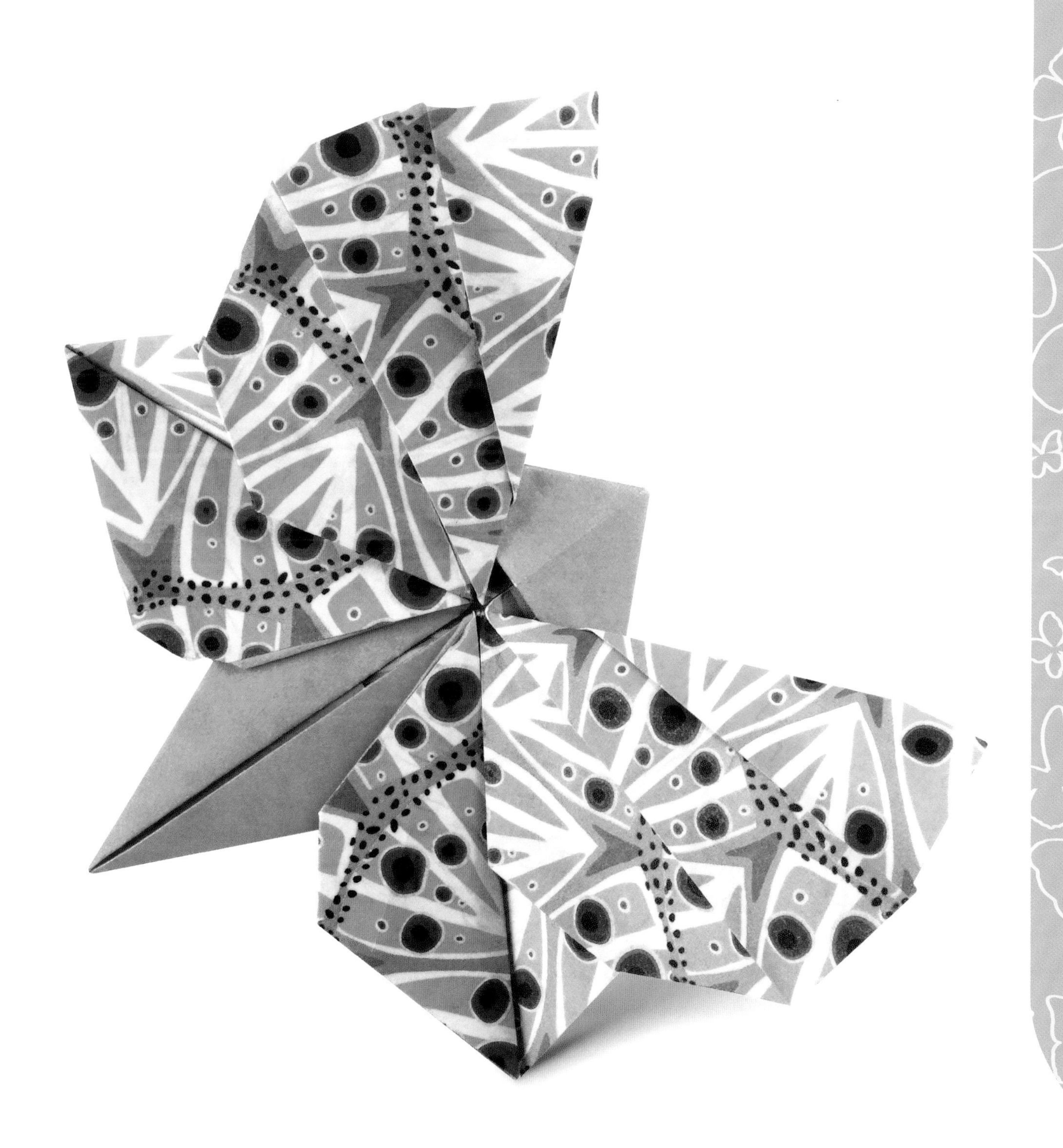

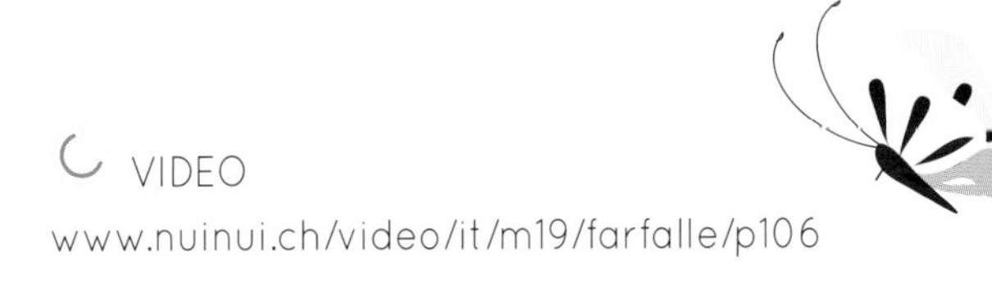

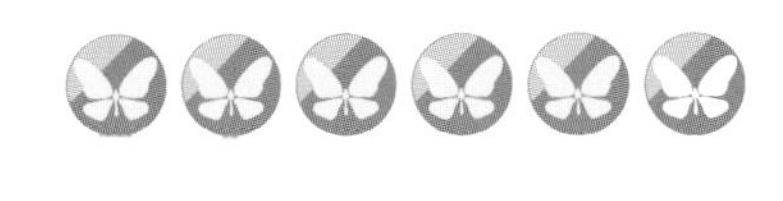

Caterpillar

Nick Robinson

The life cycle of a butterfly is one of nature's miracles.
Here, we try to capture the "squishy" nature of a caterpillar.
Try making more creases or using a longer rectangle of paper!

Size of the sheet: 7 x 7 in

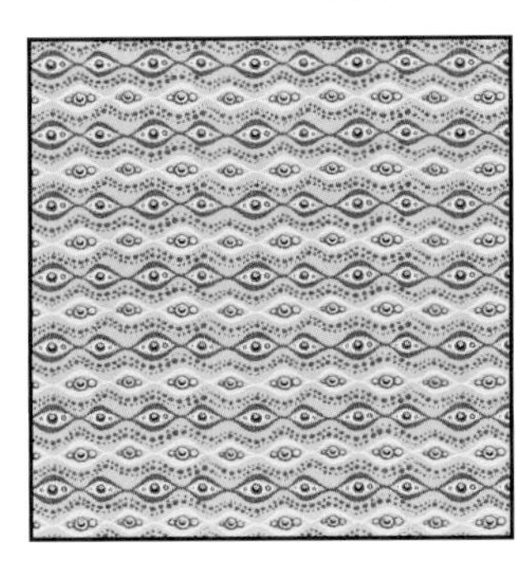

Paper

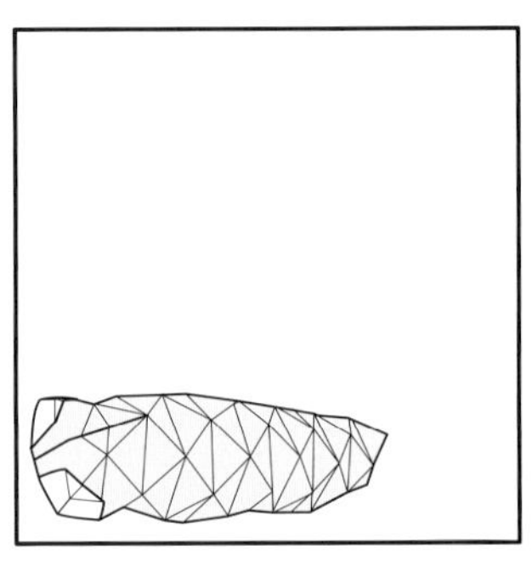

Relationship between the paper and the origami

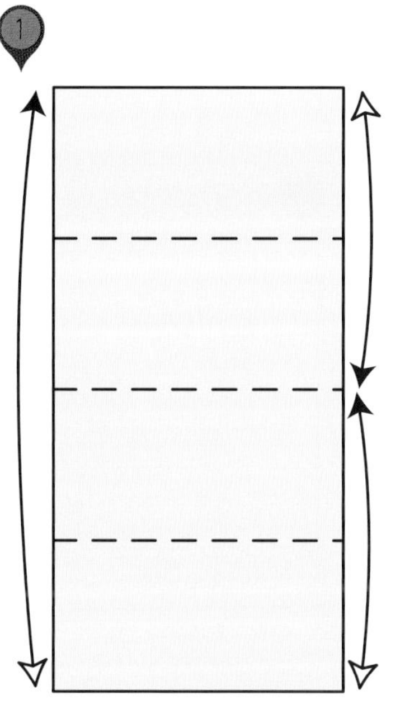

1) Colored side up, make a halfway crease, then add two quarter creases.

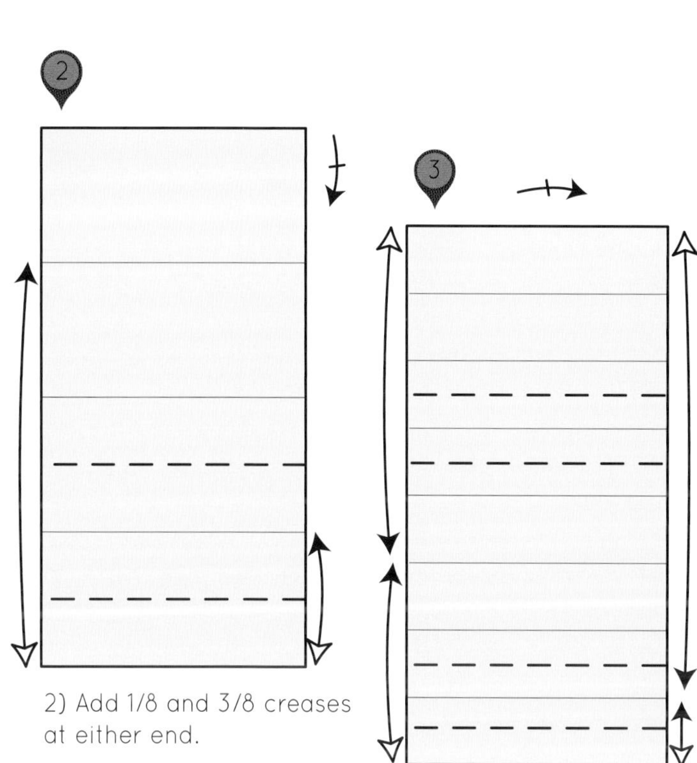

2) Add 1/8 and 3/8 creases at either end.

3) Add these creases at both ends.

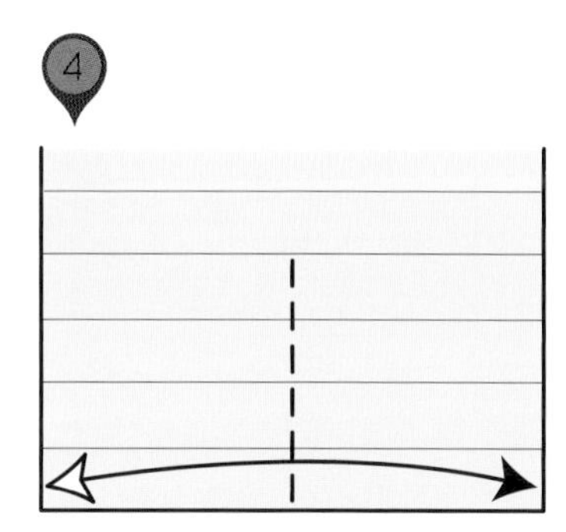

4) At the bottom, add a vertical center crease across 4/16.

5) At the top, add a vertical center crease across 2/16.

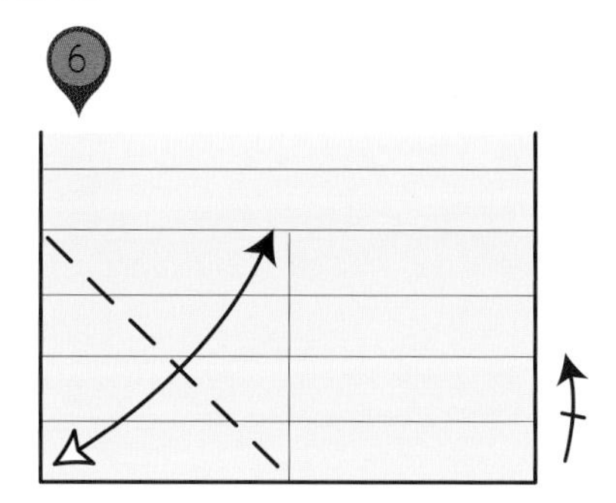

6) Add this crease on both sides.

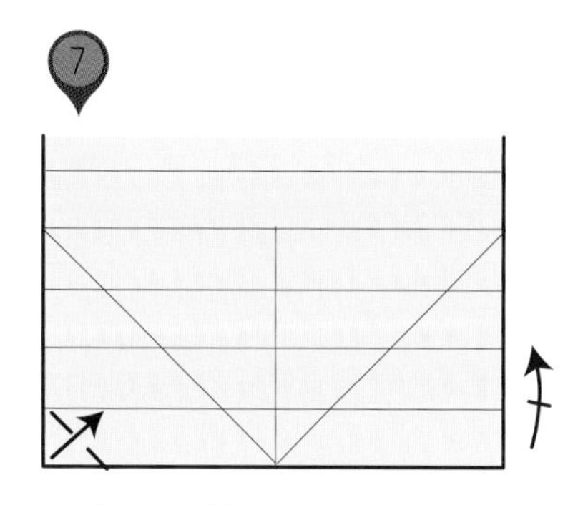

7) Fold to the nearest crease on both sides.

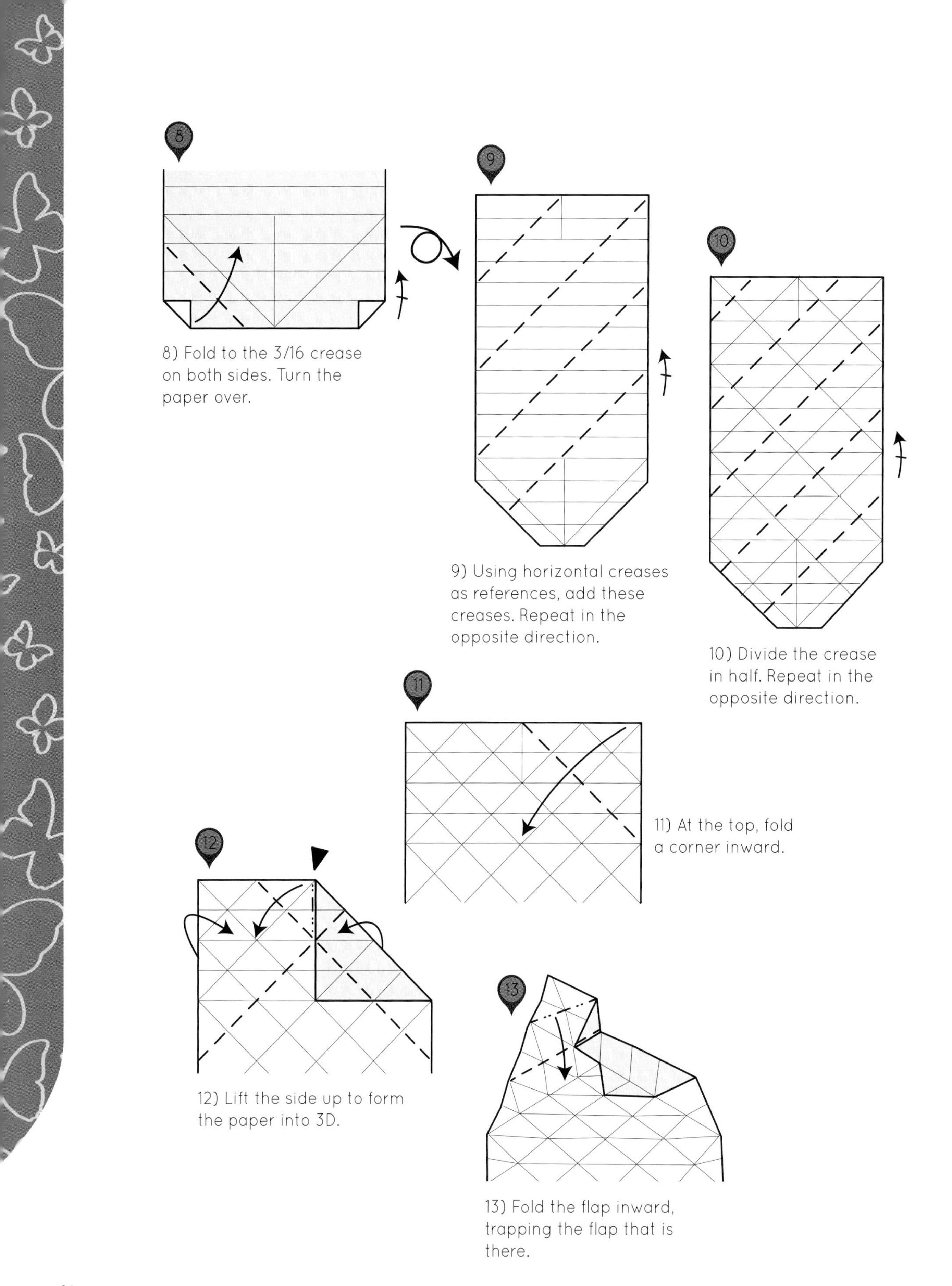

8) Fold to the 3/16 crease on both sides. Turn the paper over.

9) Using horizontal creases as references, add these creases. Repeat in the opposite direction.

10) Divide the crease in half. Repeat in the opposite direction.

11) At the top, fold a corner inward.

12) Lift the side up to form the paper into 3D.

13) Fold the flap inward, trapping the flap that is there.

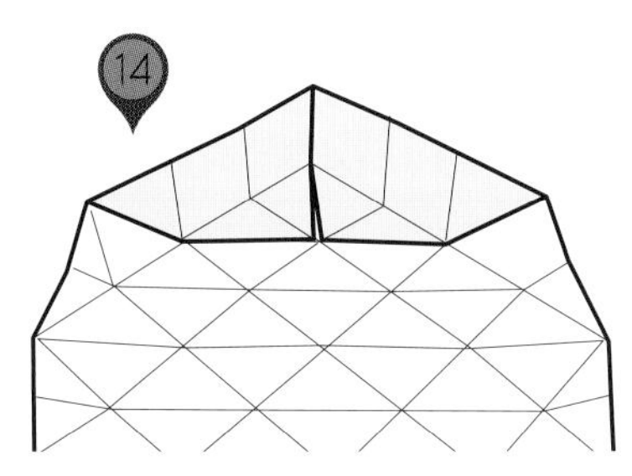

14) The result. Now we look at the other end.

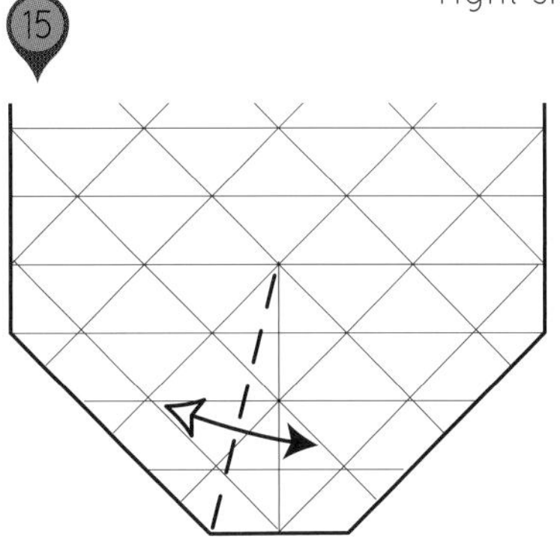

15) Make this crease, then unfold. Turn the paper over.

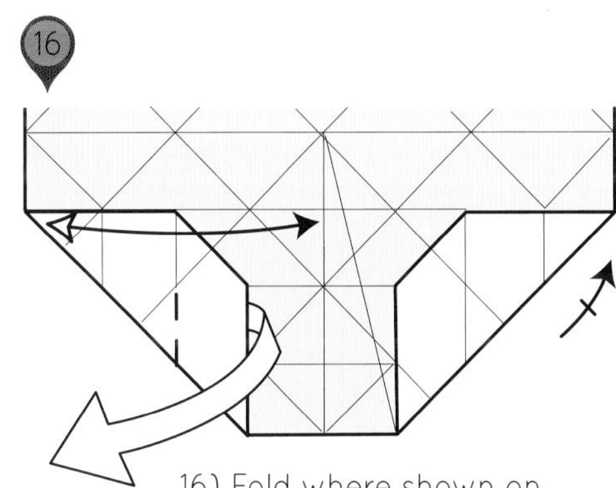

16) Fold where shown on the left, then unfold the white flap. Repeat on the right side.

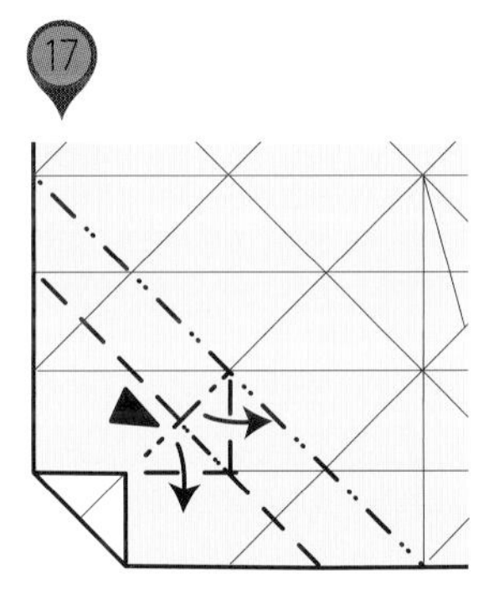

17) Carefully make these creases, forming the paper into 3D.

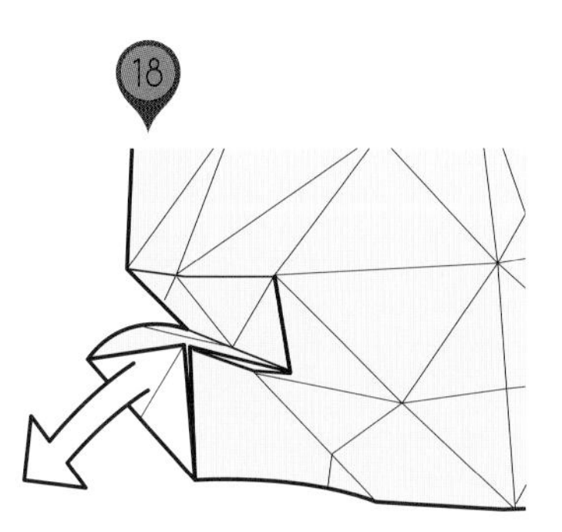

18) Flatten the creases firmly, then open out.

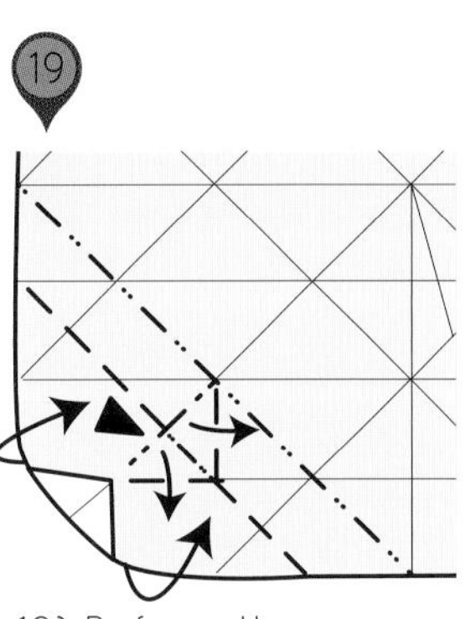

19) Reform the creases, but wrap the lower corner inward, so the folds in step 18 are hidden below a layer.

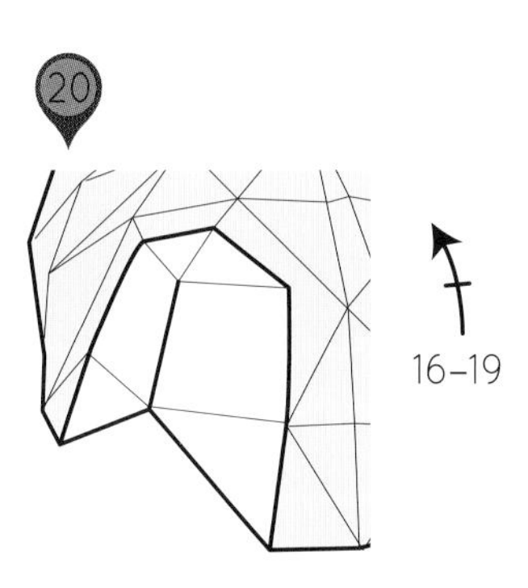

20) The paper is now 3D. Repeat steps 16-19 on the right side.

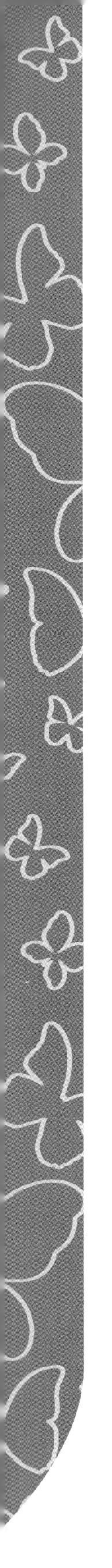

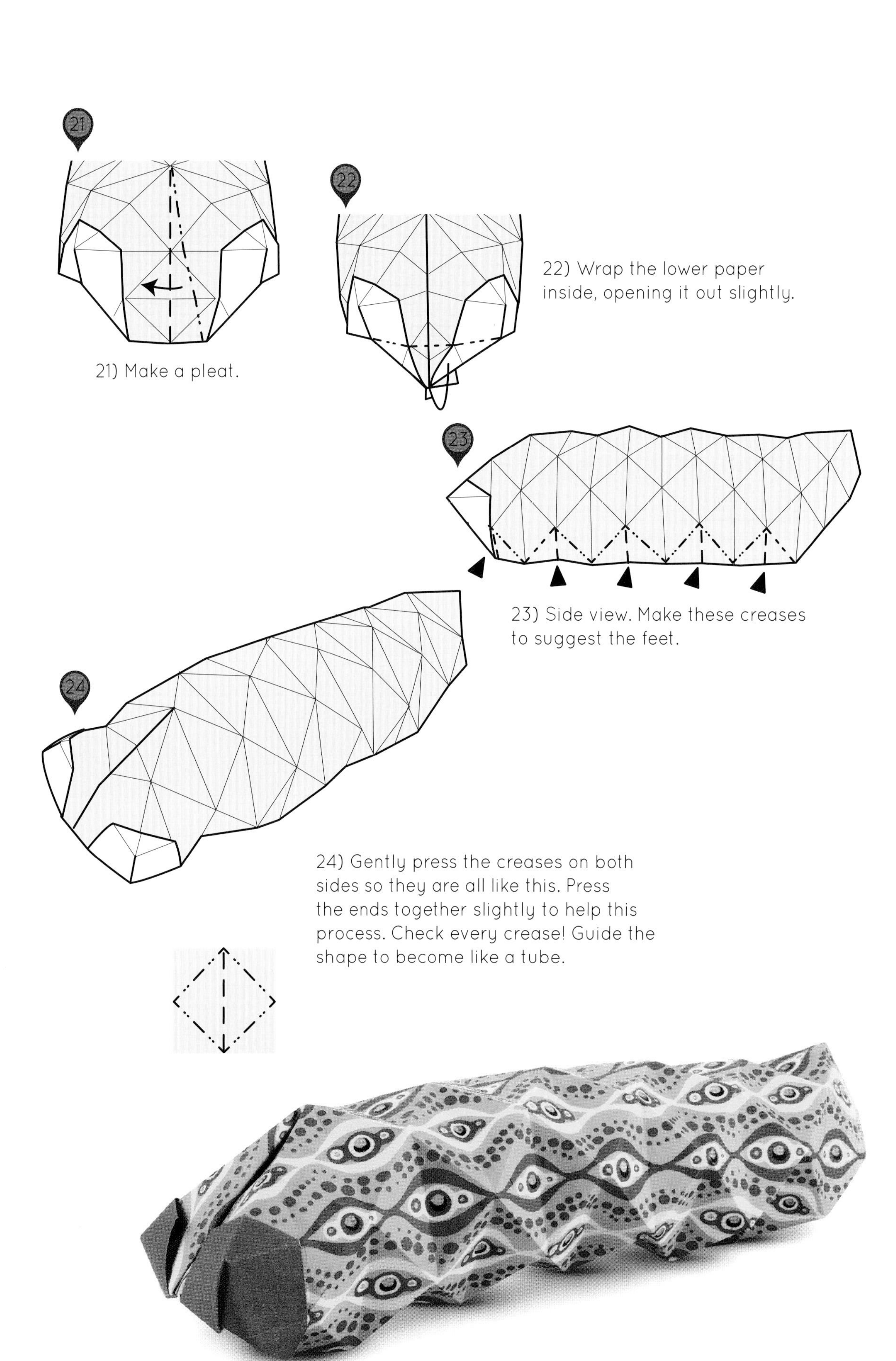

21) Make a pleat.

22) Wrap the lower paper inside, opening it out slightly.

23) Side view. Make these creases to suggest the feet.

24) Gently press the creases on both sides so they are all like this. Press the ends together slightly to help this process. Check every crease! Guide the shape to become like a tube.

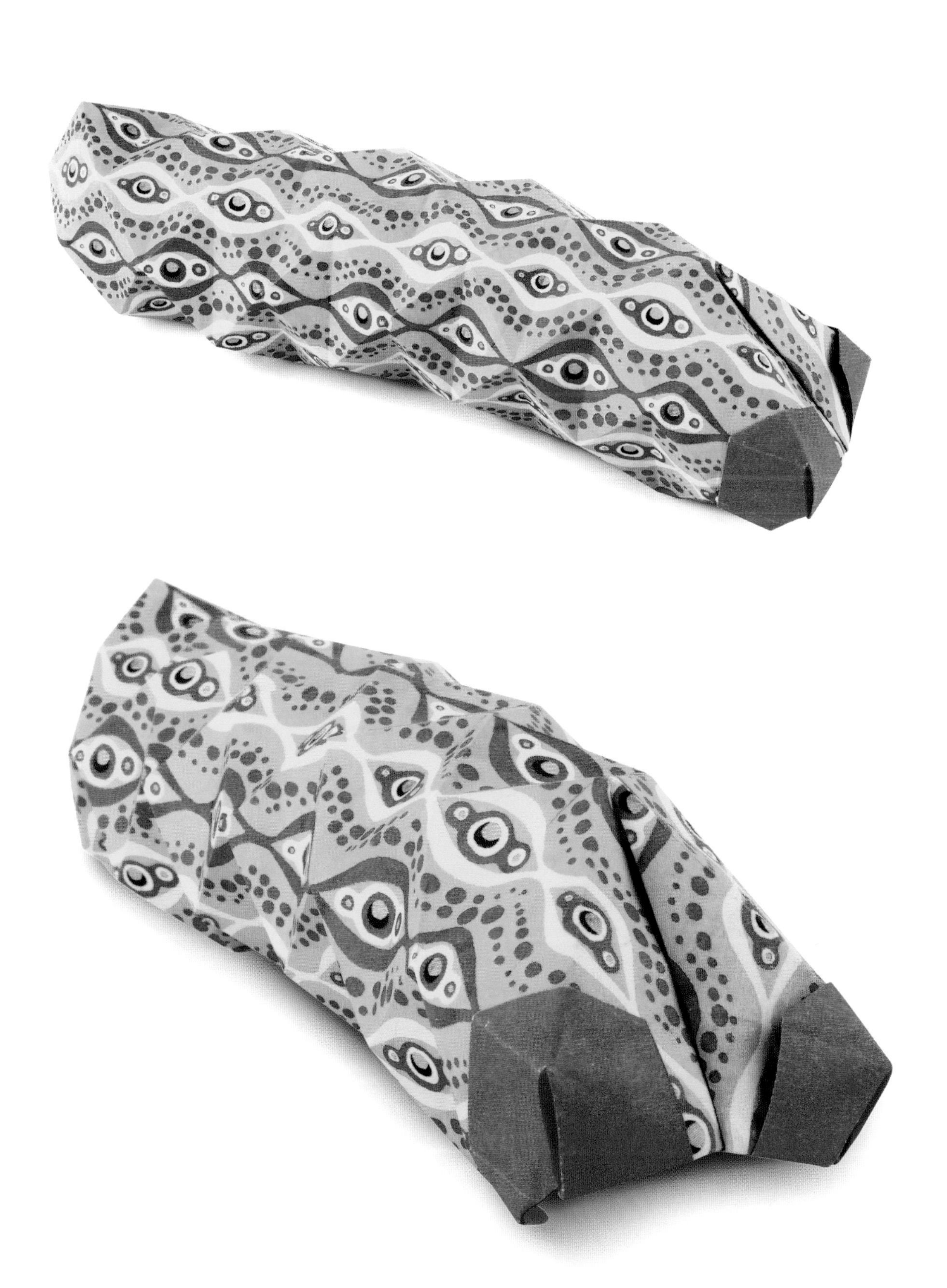

Butterfly for Nick Robinson

Michael LaFosse

One of a series of delightful butterflies created for people who Michael wished to thank. His system for folding butterflies has an almost infinite variety.

Size of the sheet: 7 x 7 in

Paper

Relationship between the paper and the origami

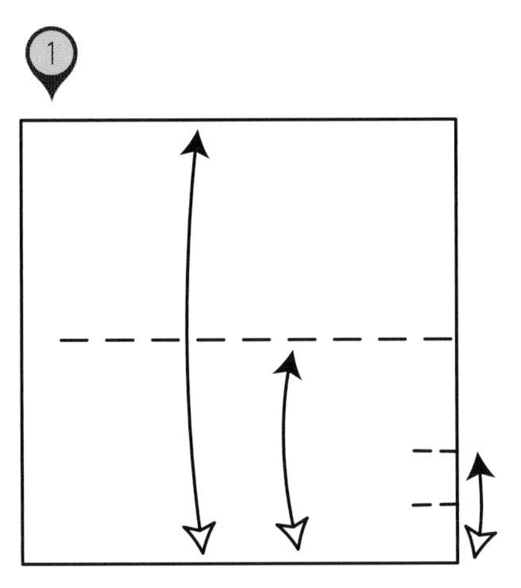

1) White side up, crease and unfold the center crease, then add two small pinch marks.

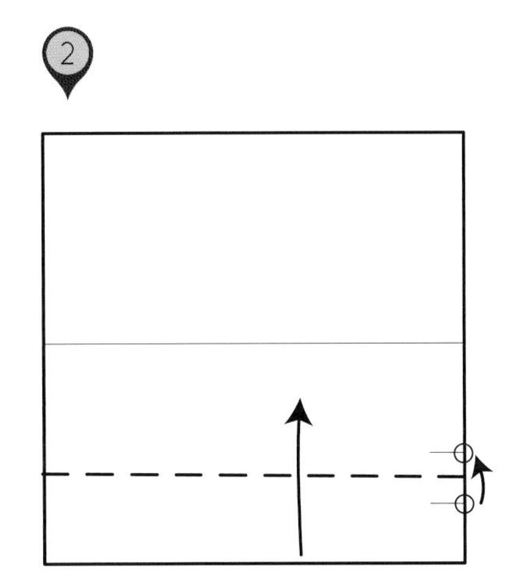

2) Fold so the pinches line up.

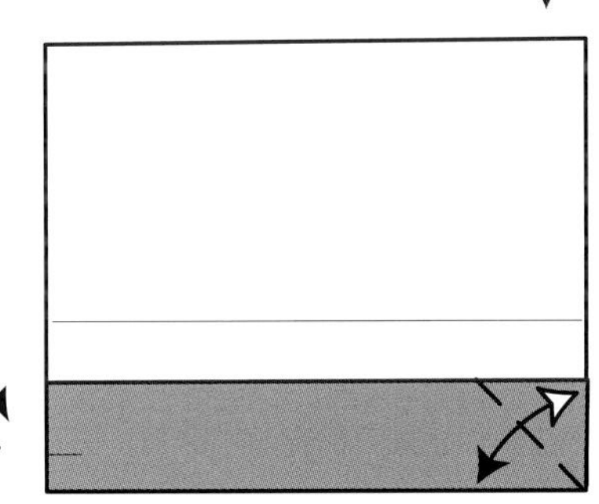

3) Fold a corner to the lower edge, then crease and unfold. Repeat on the left.

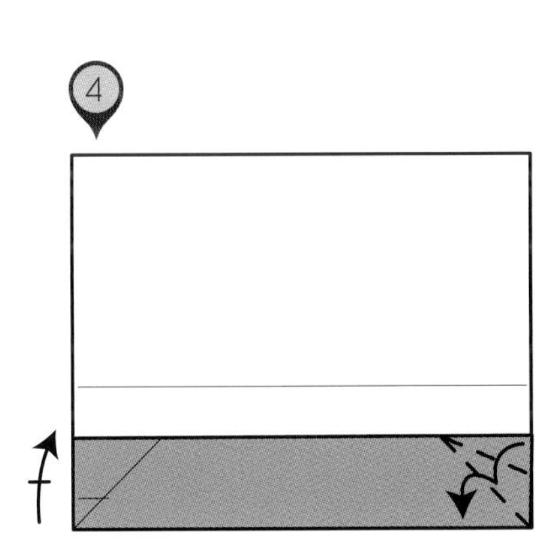

4) Fold to the recent crease, then fold over again. Repeat on the left.

I have known Nick for decades and have long been an admirer of his work and his dedication to the art of origami. Through his innovative original origami designs, his many publications, and his thoughtful ways of teaching, Nick has become one of the notables in spreading the joy of origami. Since the 1970s, when I began developing my origami butterfly design system, I have named my favourite versions in recognition of ambassadors of the art who have inspired me and so many other folders. In my estimation, Nick has "earned his wings."

Michael LaFosse

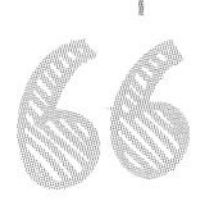

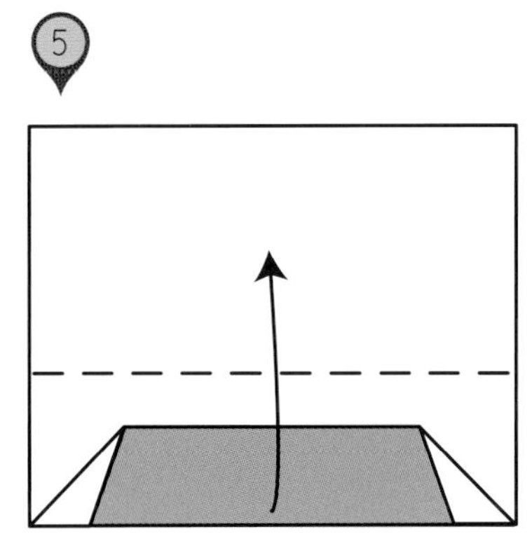

5) Fold up on an existing crease.

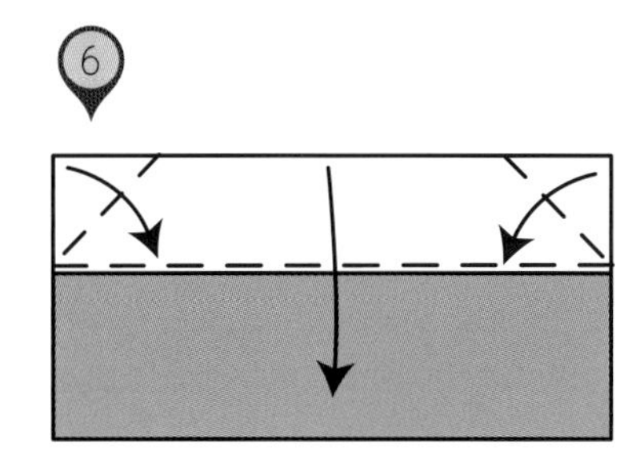

6) Fold the corners in, then fold the flap down.

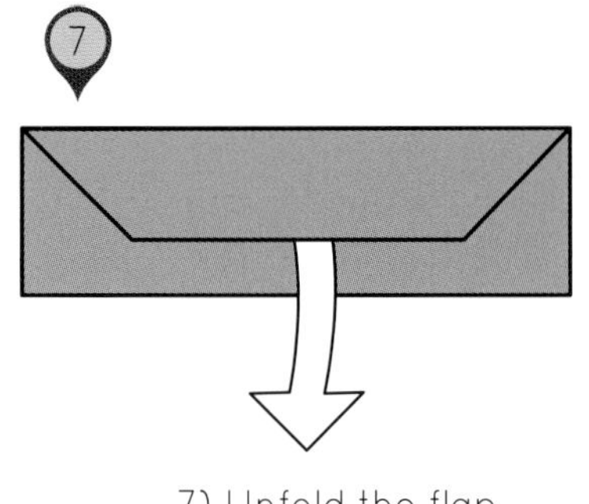

7) Unfold the flap from inside.

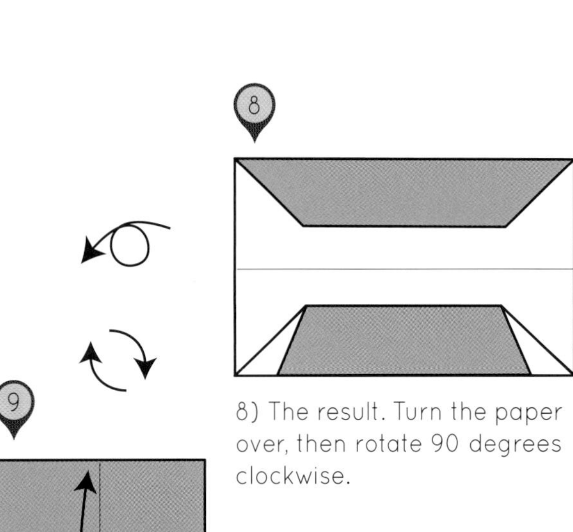

8) The result. Turn the paper over, then rotate 90 degrees clockwise.

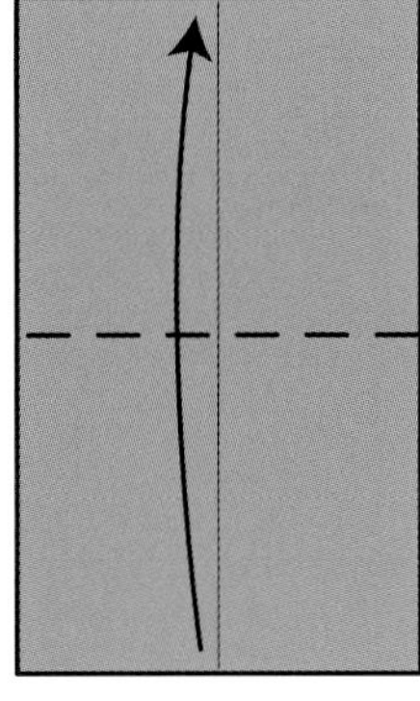

9) Fold in half upward.

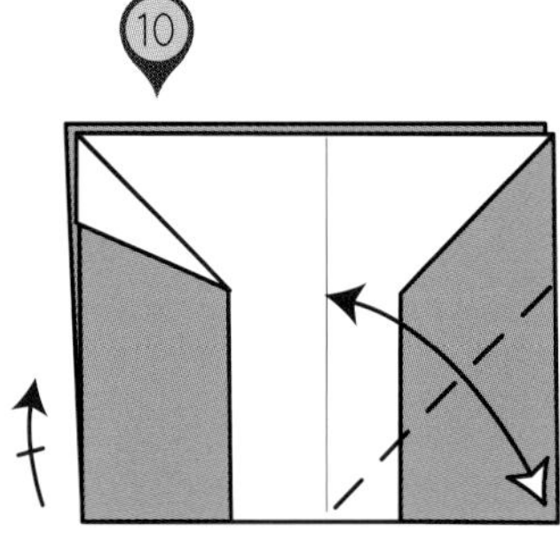

10) Fold the lower edge to the vertical center, crease and unfold. Repeat on the left.

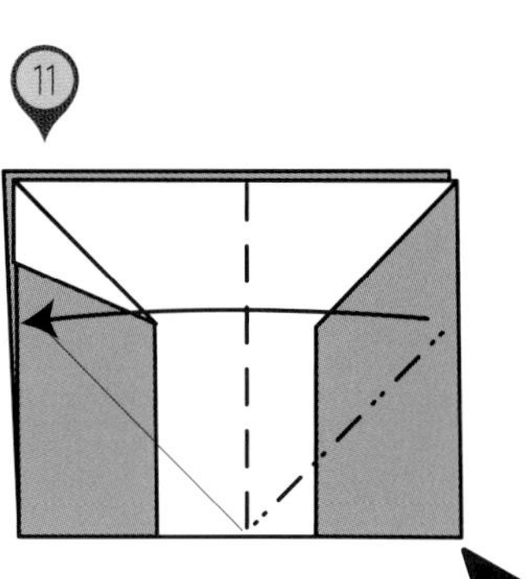

11) Squash the flap by folding to the left.

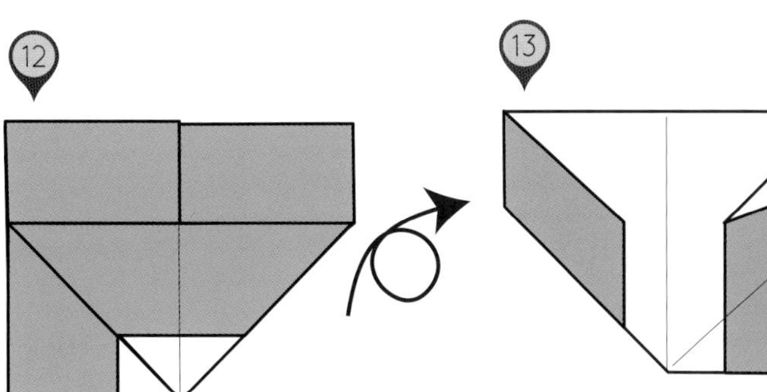

12) The result. Turn the paper over.

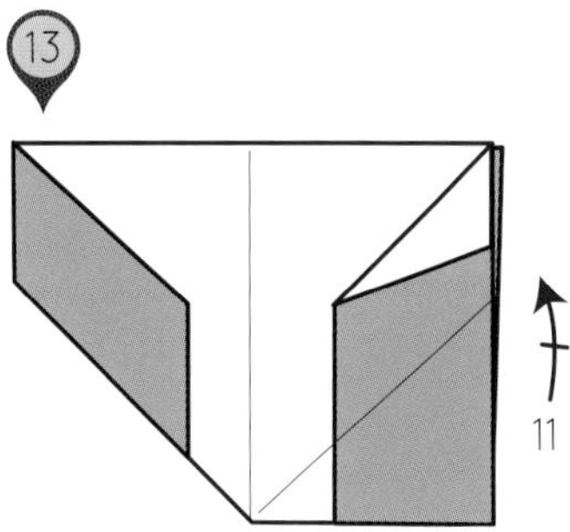

13) Repeat step 11.

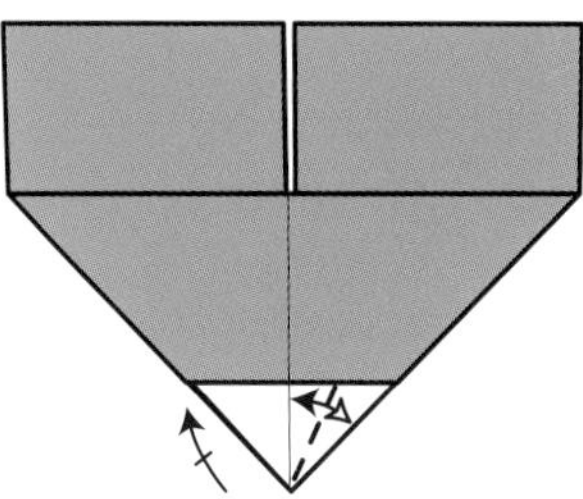

14) Fold the outer white edge to the vertical center, crease all layers and unfold. Repeat on the left.

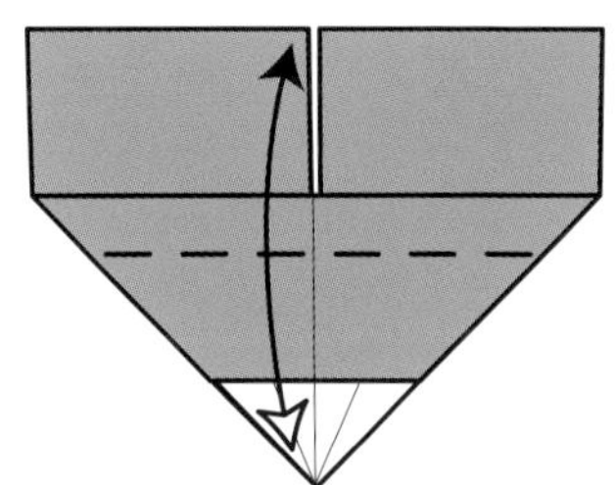

15) Fold in half vertically, then crease and unfold.

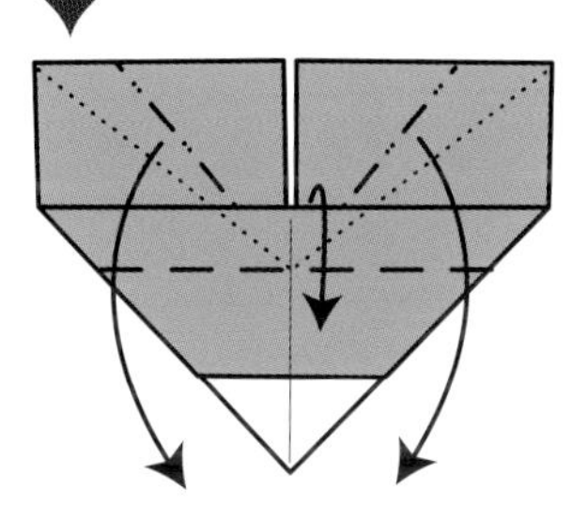

16) Fold the horizontal edge down; at the same time, squash open the upper layers. The dots show a hidden valley fold. Check the next drawing before flattening!

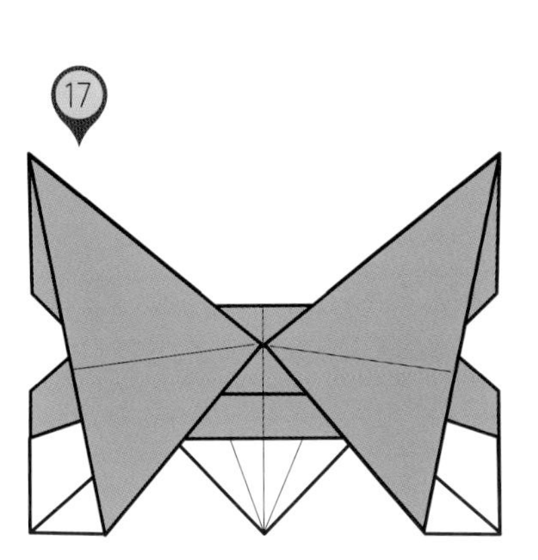

17) The result. Now we focus on the right wing.

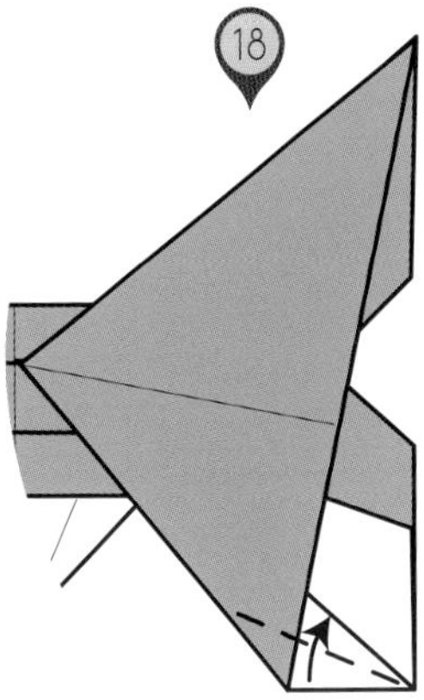

18) Fold the lower white edge to the colored edge.

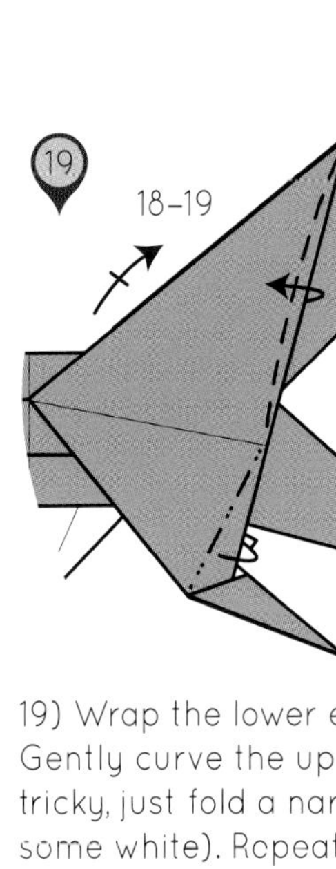

19) Wrap the lower edge of the flap inside. Gently curve the upper edge (if this is too tricky, just fold a narrow flap over to reveal some white). Repeat steps 17-18 on the left.

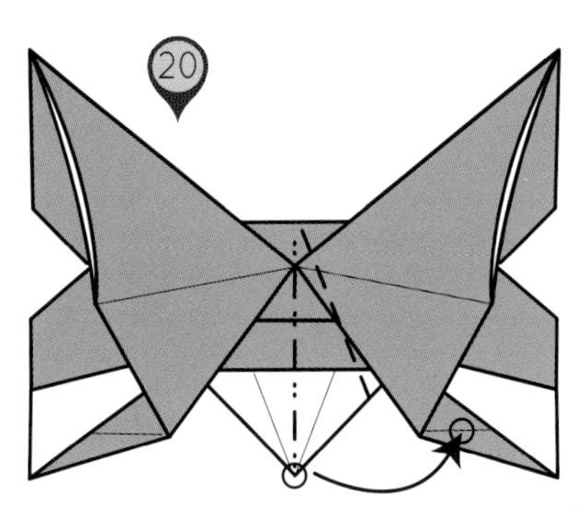

20) Make the mountain fold and swing it to meet the circled crease.

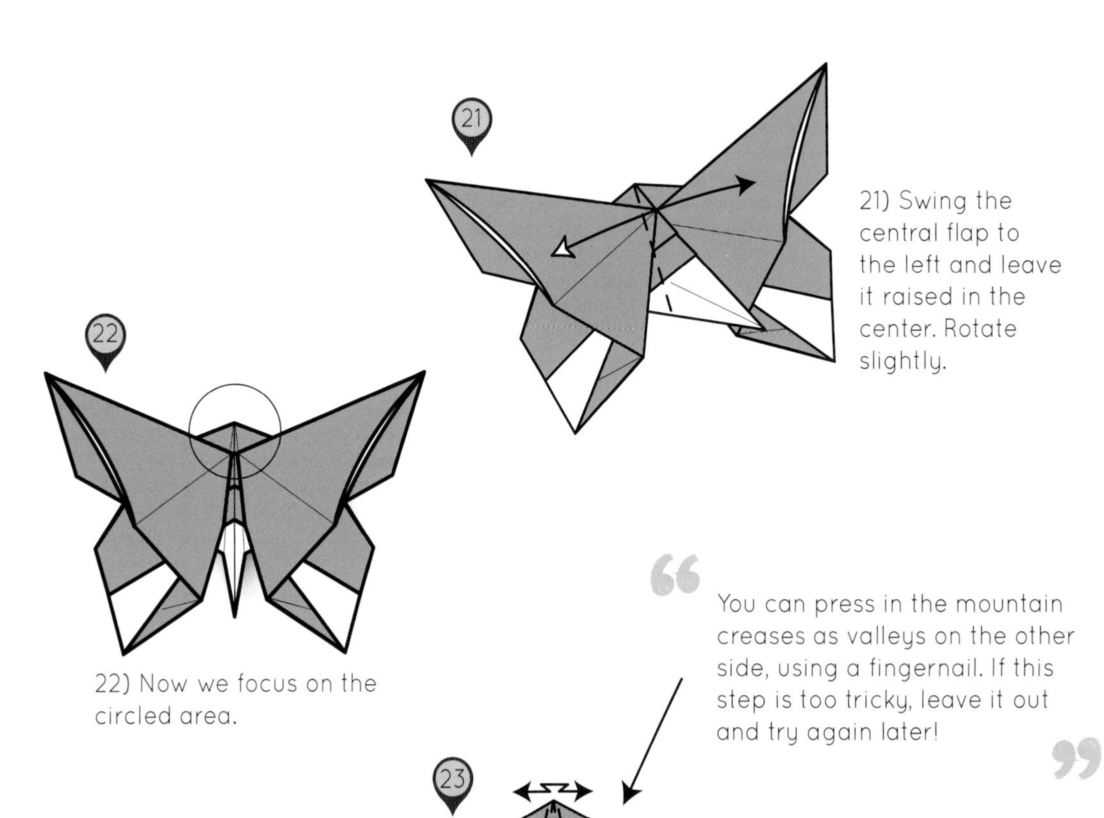

21) Swing the central flap to the left and leave it raised in the center. Rotate slightly.

22) Now we focus on the circled area.

“You can press in the mountain creases as valleys on the other side, using a fingernail. If this step is too tricky, leave it out and try again later!”

23) Carefully squash the raised central flap.

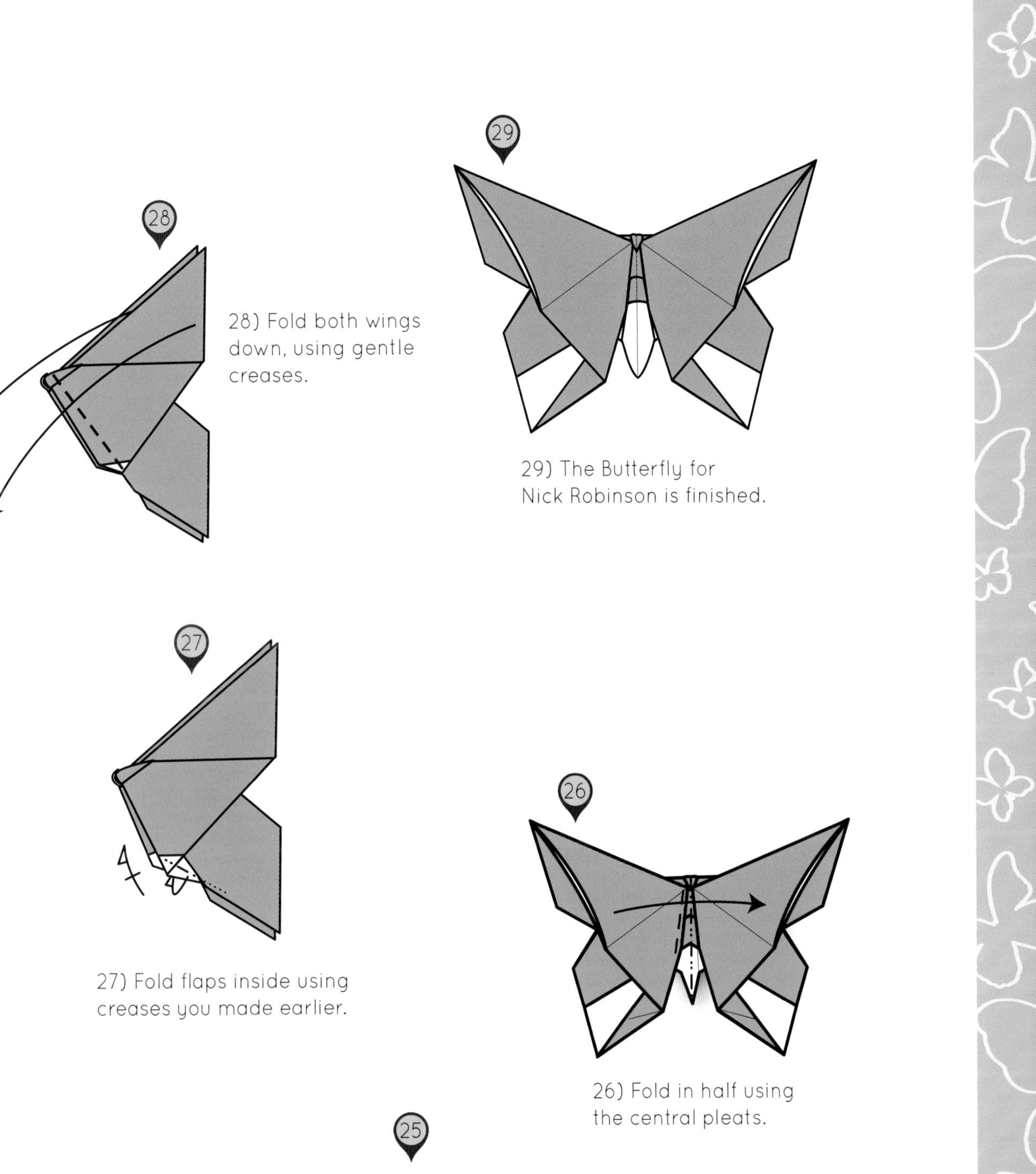

28) Fold both wings down, using gentle creases.

29) The Butterfly for Nick Robinson is finished.

27) Fold flaps inside using creases you made earlier.

26) Fold in half using the central pleats.

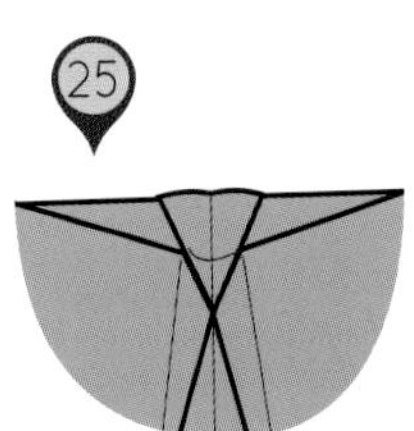

25) The head is complete.

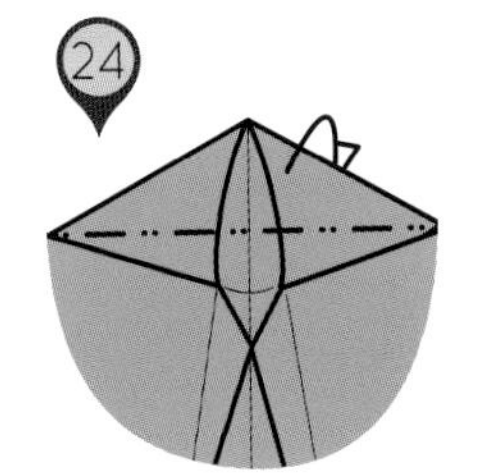

24) Fold the flap behind.

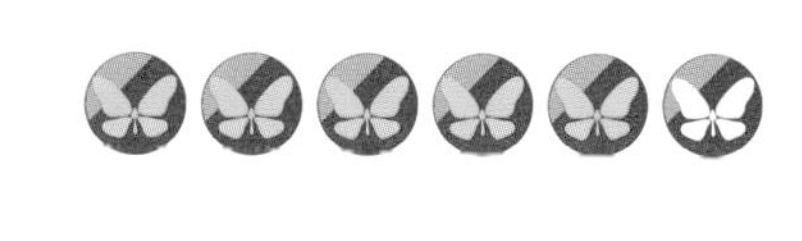

VIDEO
www.nuinui.ch/video/it/m19/farfalle/p120

Crowding Butterflies

Shuzo Fujimoto

An amazing design from the 1970s by the late Japanese master.
His influence on modern origami cannot be overstated.

Size of the sheet: 7 x 7 in

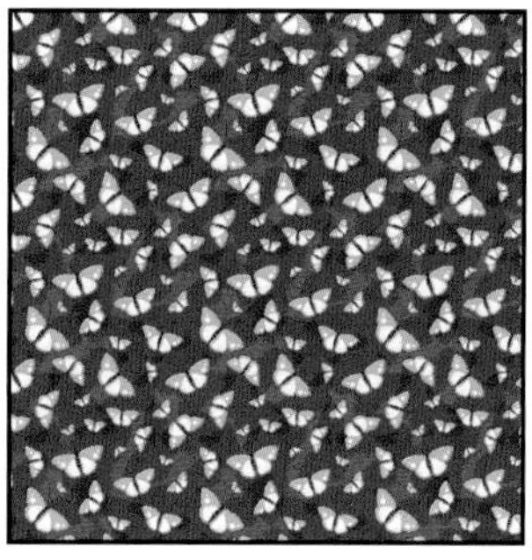

Paper

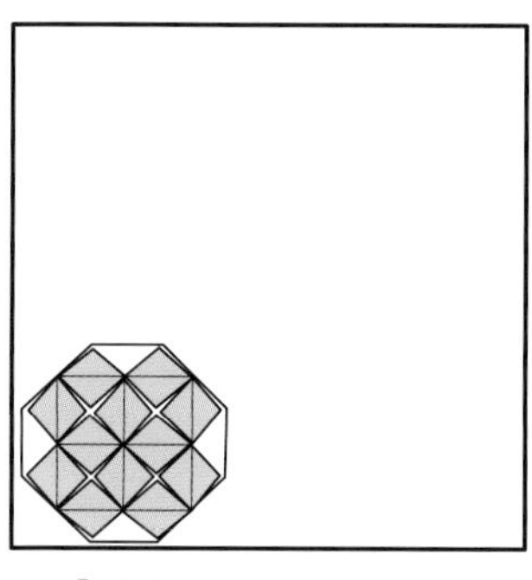

Relationship between the paper and the origami

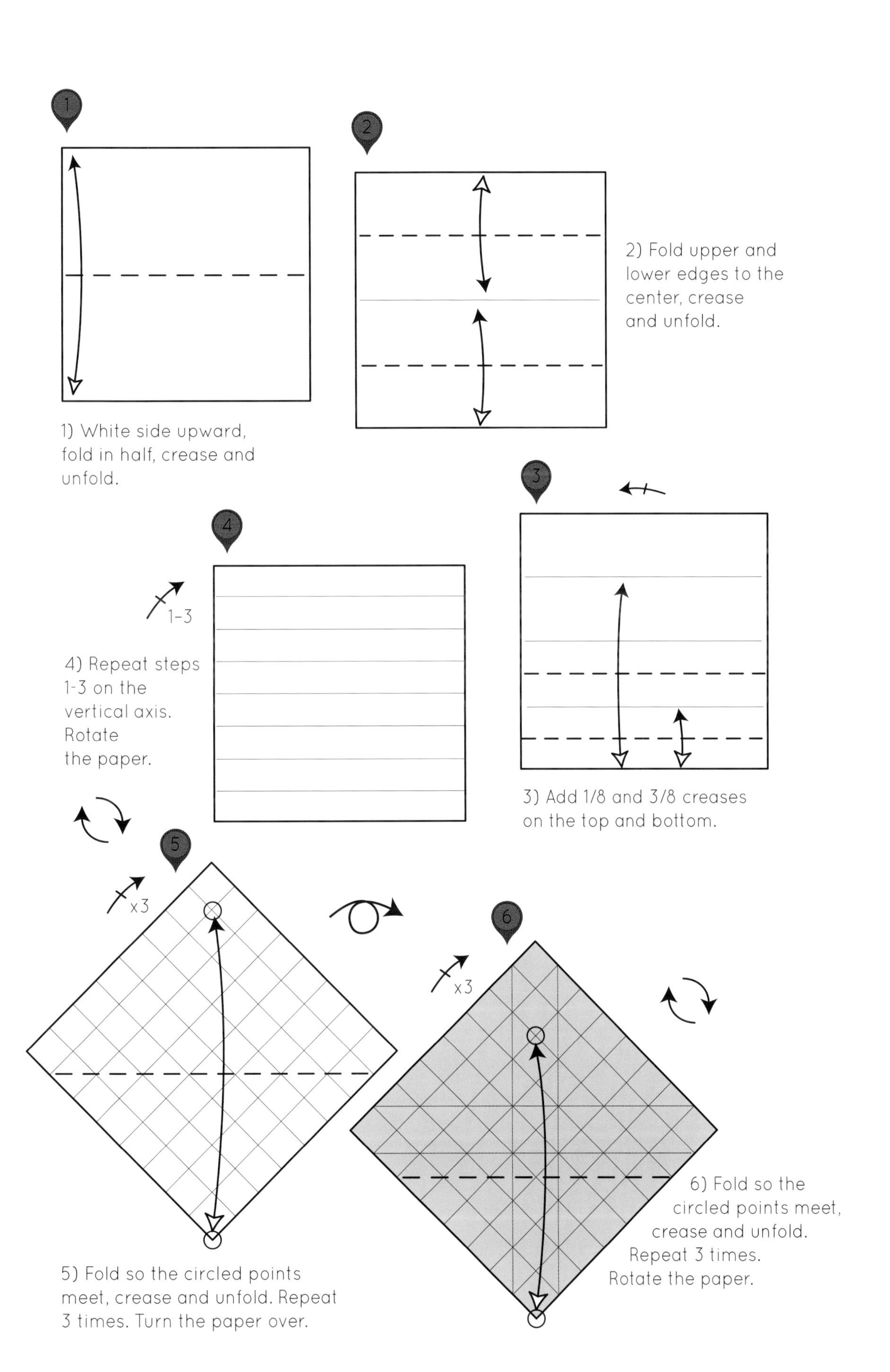

1) White side upward, fold in half, crease and unfold.

2) Fold upper and lower edges to the center, crease and unfold.

3) Add 1/8 and 3/8 creases on the top and bottom.

4) Repeat steps 1-3 on the vertical axis. Rotate the paper.

5) Fold so the circled points meet, crease and unfold. Repeat 3 times. Turn the paper over.

6) Fold so the circled points meet, crease and unfold. Repeat 3 times. Rotate the paper.

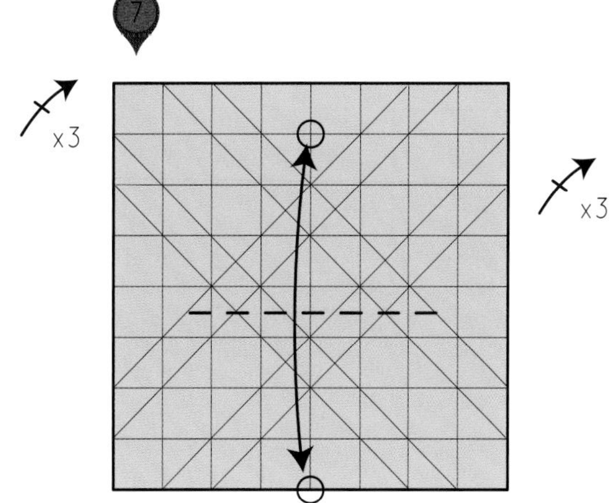

7) Fold so the circled points meet, crease where shown and unfold. Repeat 3 times.

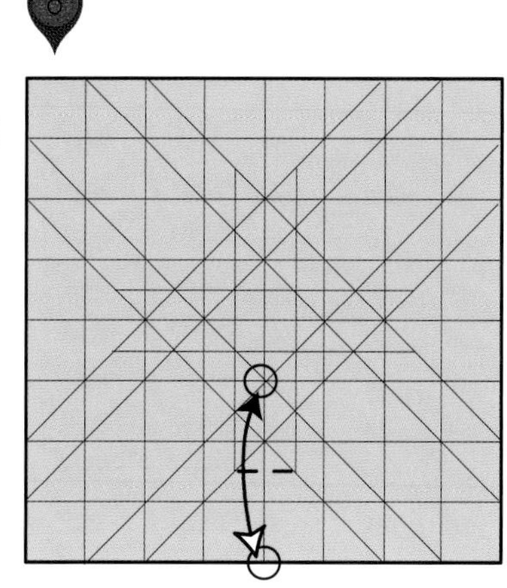

8) Again, fold so the circled points meet, crease where shown and unfold. Repeat 3 times.

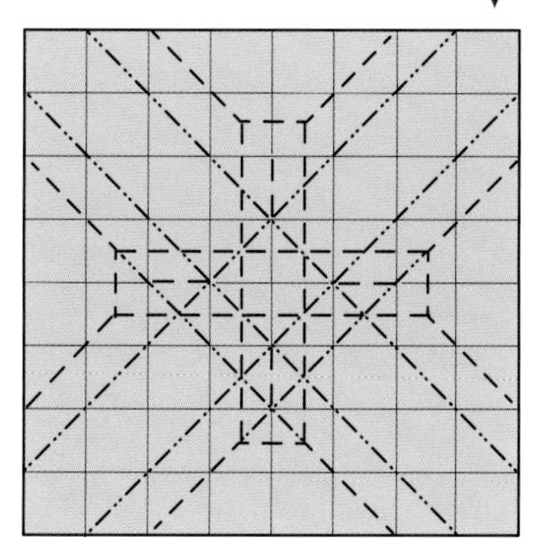

9a) Begin to form the paper into 3D with these creases.

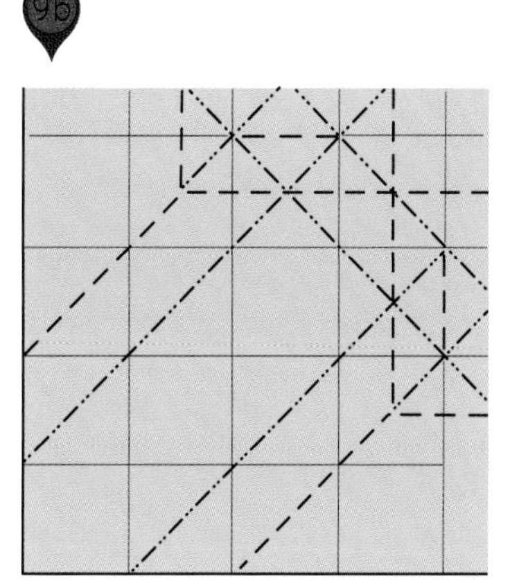

9b) Here are the creases for one quarter of the paper. Each quarter is identical.

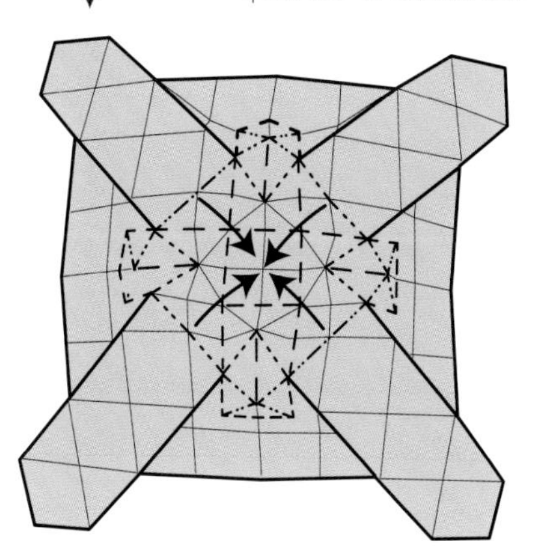

10) Keep emphasizing the creases and they will eventually meet towards the center.

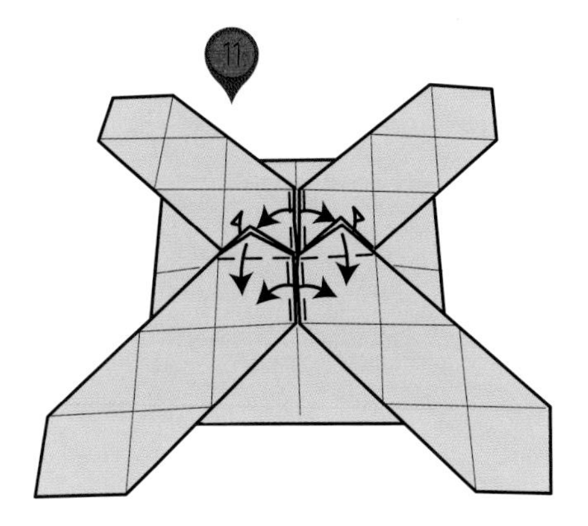

11) Open out the four flaps at the center of the paper.

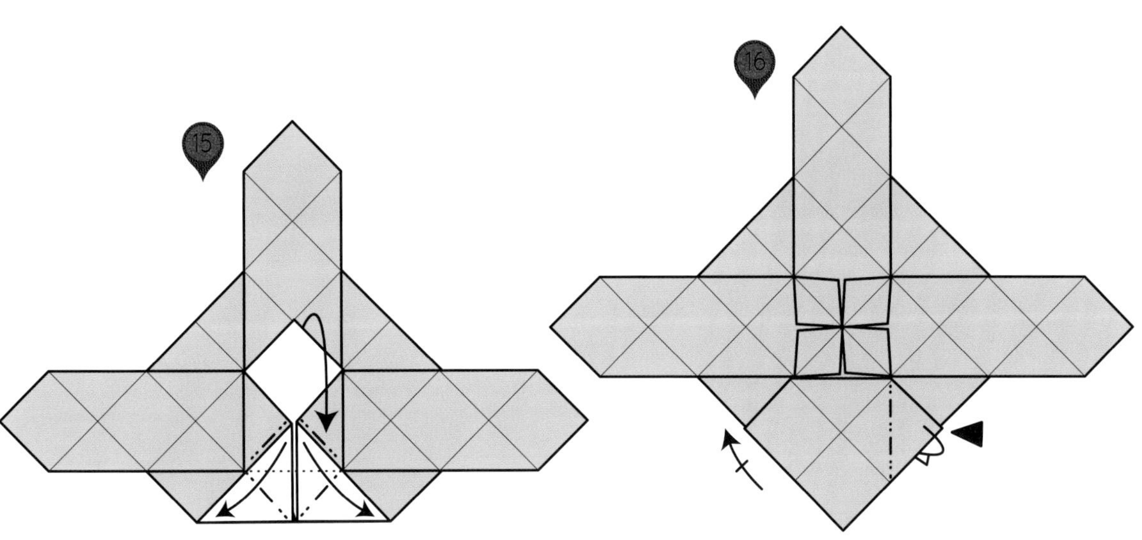

15) Open and fold the point down using these creases. The dotted line is a hidden valley fold.

16) Reverse the corner inside. Repeat on the left.

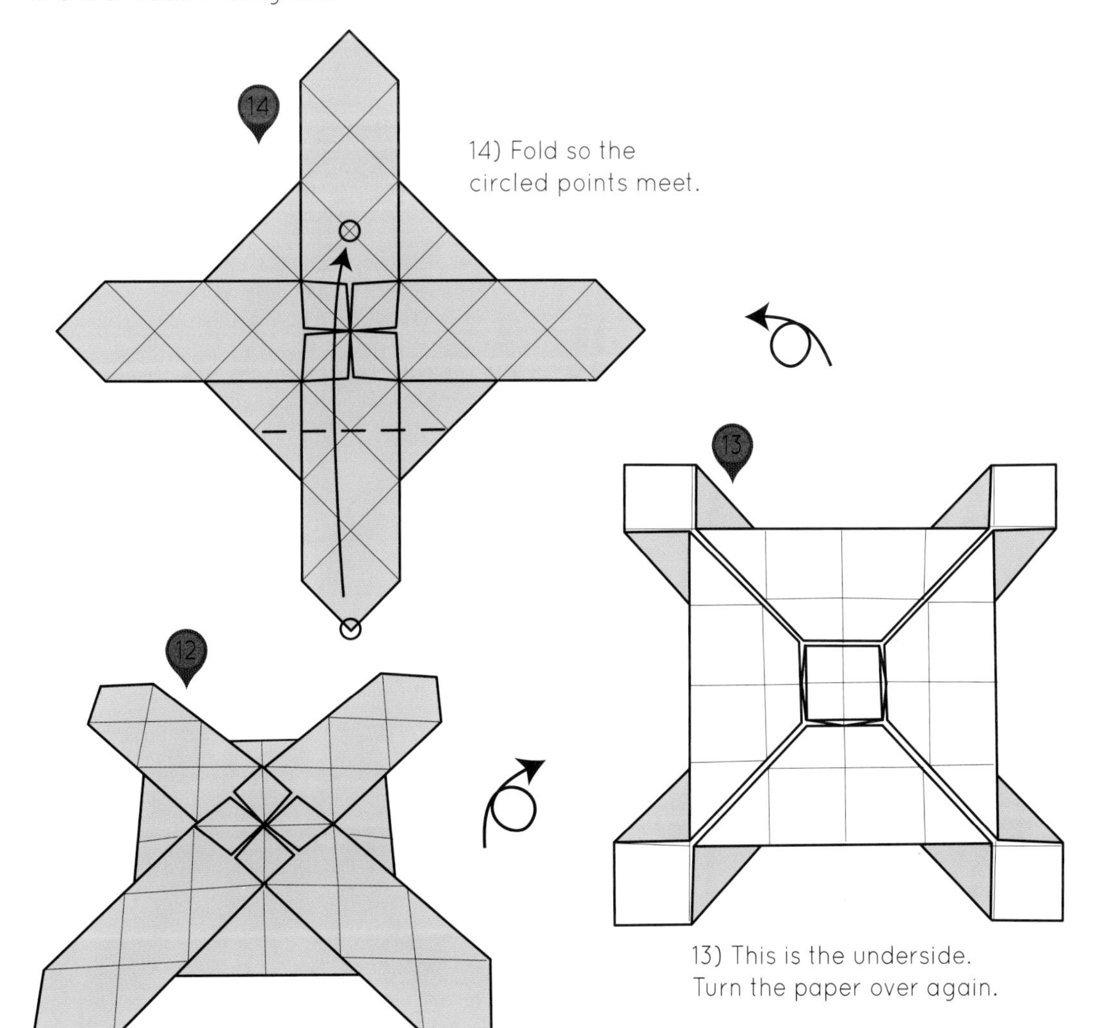

14) Fold so the circled points meet.

13) This is the underside. Turn the paper over again.

12) The result so far. Turn the paper over.

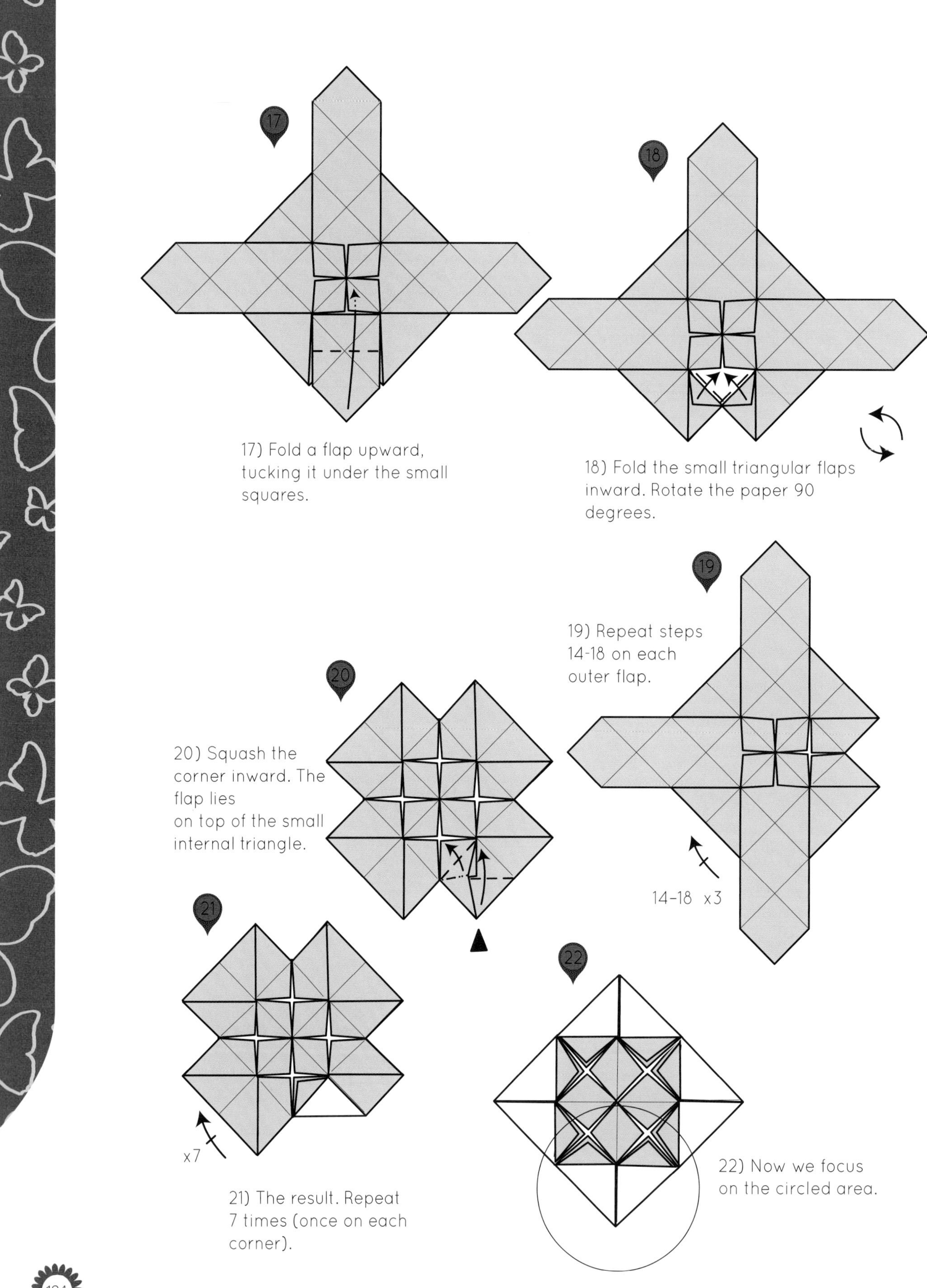

17) Fold a flap upward, tucking it under the small squares.

18) Fold the small triangular flaps inward. Rotate the paper 90 degrees.

19) Repeat steps 14-18 on each outer flap.

20) Squash the corner inward. The flap lies on top of the small internal triangle.

21) The result. Repeat 7 times (once on each corner).

22) Now we focus on the circled area.

26) The corner is complete. Repeat steps 24-26 on the other three corners.

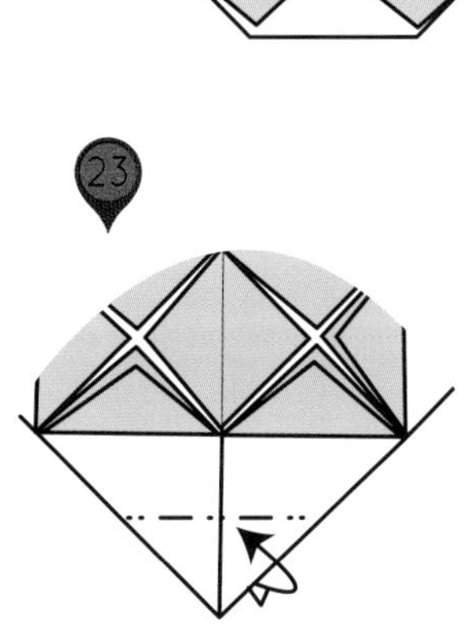

23) Fold the corner behind, then unfold.

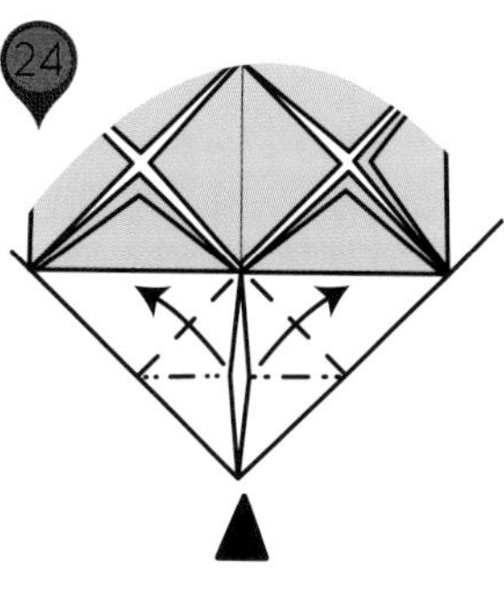

24) Squash the lower corner inward.

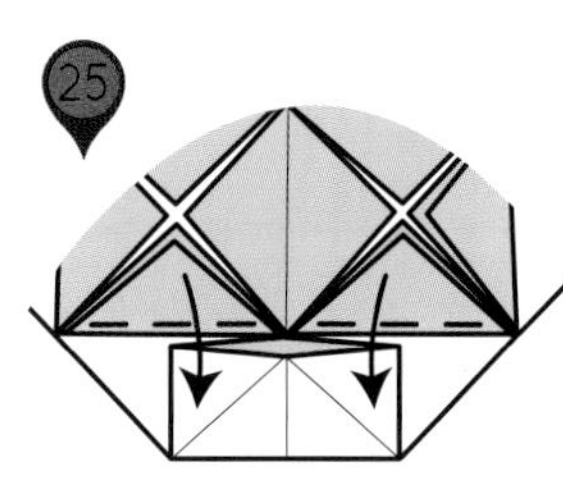

25) Fold the triangular flaps downward.

NICK ROBINSON

Nick Robinson has been folding paper since the early '80s, and for over 30 years has been a member of the British Origami Society, of which he is an honorary member as well as running their website. In 2004 he was awarded the "Sidney French medal"—the highest award the society can bestow, in recognition of his outstanding contribution to origami.

Nick has been a professional origami teacher for nearly 30 years. He has taught and lectured on origami all over the world, including America, France, Germany, Austria, Switzerland, Spain, Italy, the United Arab Emirates, and Japan. He has fulfilled numerous commissions for magazines, television and internet advertising campaigns. Over 300 of his original origami creations have been exhibited around the world. He has written and illustrated over 60 origami books and is the most-published European origami author. A former professional musician, he still performs occasional solo improvised guitar concerts.

As well as this book, he has published *Origami intriganti, British Origami, Pesci in Origami, Dinosauri in origami, Gatti in Origami* and three volumes of the Kit Origami series.

If you enjoyed this book, why not think of joining an origami group?

France
Mouvement Français des Pliers de Papier (MFPP) - www.mfpp-origami.fr

Germany
Origami Deutschland - www.papierfalten.de

Great Britain
British Origami Society - www.britishorigami.info

Italy
Centro Diffusione Origami - www.origami-cdo.it

Netherlands
Origami Sociëteit Nederland - www.origami-osn.nl

Spain
Asociación Española de Papiroflexia - www.pajarita.org

United States
OrigamiUSA - https://origamiusa.org

Thanks: to my wife Alison, children Daisy and Nick plus cats Rhubarb and Pickle for their love and support. To Lee Armstrong for proofreading the diagrams. To Joan Sallas and Xiăoxián Huárnng for their love and friendship. To Marcello Bertinetti and Federica Romagnoli from NuiNui for their ceaseless desire to produce the best origami books possible. To all the amazing staff at the Northern General Hospital, Sheffield, who helped me through a serious illness during the final stages of producing this book. Finally, to the British Origami Society (www.britishorigami.info) for all their support and inspiration.

My folding website is
www.origami.me.uk
and my music site is
www.looping.me.uk

CREDITS

- Caterpillar, Daisy Butterfly, Emerging Butterfly, Spotted Butterfly, Sunbathing Butterfly were created by the author.
- Pinwheel Butterfly: Traditional

Thanks to the following designers, who generously allowed me to share their creations:

- Yoshizawa's Butterfly: Akira Yoshizawa
- Donahue's Butterfly: David Donahue
- Butterfly Envelope: Evi Binzinger
- 9-Fold Butterfly: Lee Armstrong
- Butterfly for Nick Robinson: Michael LaFosse
- Butterfly Card: Michel Grand
- Loving Butterflies: Mick Guy
- Donachie Butterfly: Rikki Donachie
- Snyder Butterfly: Rob Snyder
- Australian Butterfly: Shoko Aoyagi
- Crowding Butterflies: Shuzo Fujimoto
- Gigandet Butterfly: Stéphane Gigandet
- Moth Silhouette: Thea Anning
- Meadow Brown: Wayne Brown

Origami has thousands of creative folders, and it is entirely possible that other people have created similar designs, and they are credited to the best of my knowledge. If this is not the case, please let me know.